# GUIDE TO
# CALIFORNIA
# PLANNING

# GUIDE TO CALIFORNIA PLANNING

## WILLIAM FULTON

POINT ARENA, CALIFORNIA

Published July 1991 by
SOLANO PRESS BOOKS
P.O. Box 773
Point Arena, California 95468
Second Printing, March 1992

Printed in the United States of America by
L. GRAFIX
Portland, Oregon

ISBN 0-923956-05-0

Library of Congress Catalogue Number 91-60454

Cover and book design by
TORF FULTON ASSOCIATES

# TABLE OF CONTENTS

# INTRODUCTION

# WHAT PLANNING IS SUPPOSED TO BE
# — AND WHAT IT IS

California today may be the most affluent fast-growing society on earth, and the dimensions of a place fueled by two such powerful forces as affluence and growth are staggering indeed. By the turn of the century, California will contain close to 35 million people. That's a Texas and a half, or New York doubled. It's more than Canada or Columbia, and more than the other 12 Western states combined. At the beginning of 1991, California also contained 10 million houses and apartments, almost 14 million jobs, and 22 million cars and trucks — twice as many vehicles as only 20 years ago. Despite its vast size, the California growth machine is still accelerating. More people arrived in California in the 1980s (6 million, including me) than ever before arrived in any one state in any one decade. In fact, if all the people added to California's population in the 1980s formed a separate state, it would be the 15th-largest state in the union, right behind Virginia.

And this growth is not an aberration. Global economic forces appear likely to push growth into California, especially Southern California, for another generation at least. Regional planners predict that the Greater Los Angeles region alone will add 600 new residents, 320 new jobs, and 280 new houses every single day for the next 20 years — by which time L.A. will rival New York as the nation's biggest metropolis.

All of these people and houses and jobs and cars take up land, and not surprisingly, in the category of land consumed, California is also a leader. The Greater Los Angeles metropolitan area (including Orange County and the Inland Empire) is more than 100 miles across and 100 miles deep, stretching from the coast well into the desert and oozing so far south that L.A. is beginning to congeal with San Diego. If Greater Los Angeles were located on the East Coast, it would stretch all the way from New York to Boston, and bulge as far to the northwest as Albany, taking in most of western Massachusetts and virtually all of Connecticut.

Similarly, the San Francisco Bay Area, though barely half the size of L.A., is bursting out of its traditional envelope, even though that envelope already contains nine counties. Thousands of commuters brave the winding and mountainous Highway 17 twice a day in order to get from secluded homes in the Santa Cruz Mountains to jobs in the Silicon Valley. Thousands more now race across the floor of the fertile San Joaquin Valley from their relatively inexpensive homes in Stockton and Modesto to jobs on the edge of the Bay Area in Livermore and Pleasanton.

And, just as L.A. is oozing southward toward San Diego, the Bay Area is oozing toward Sacramento, 90 miles to the northeast. Currently, about 3.5 million acres of California land is devoted to urban uses, and that figure is rising by more than 60,000 acres per year.

Given those numbers, it should be no surprise that planning has become one of the most contentious areas of public debate in the entire state. In virtually every community, large or small, local politics revolves around the question of "growth" — how to accommodate it, how to shape it, and, often, how to repel it. Deep-pockets developers bankroll local political campaigns and hire armies of consultants in hopes of getting their projects approved. Powerful citizen groups raise the banner of environmental protection, historic preservation, or "quality of life" in order to stop the developers or slow them down. Financially strapped city governments seek to extract from new development the funds they can no longer obtain from property taxes. On the community level in California, planning is a lever used by virtually every interest group on the local scene to get what it wants.

This is not quite the way things are supposed to be. In theory, planning is supposed to be a more sober and objective process — the process used to arrange buildings, roads, and other man-made structures on the ground so that society can function efficiently and effectively. But even this seemingly simple statement highlights the conflicts and contradictions inherent in California planning today.

The legal rationale for planning in California is straightforward and idealistic, and it carries a touch of the state's deeply rooted environmentalist ethic. Land, according to the California Zoning, Planning, and Development Law, is "an exhaustible resource." The purpose of planning is "to insure its preservation and use in ways which are economically and socially desirable in an attempt to improve the quality of life in California."* In this way, planning is supposed to serve the public interest.

But land is not only a resource requiring preservation. Under the American system of values, economics, and government — and, especially, in a fast-growing economy like California's — land is also a commodity to be owned, traded, and exploited for profit. Private property rights are respected by the courts and jealously guarded by civil libertarians. And private landowners' decisions about where to invest and what to build are dictated primarily by the demands of the private real estate market, not by the principles of good city planning.

Environmentalists, preservationists, and planners may want to preserve and protect scenic wonders, fragile eco-systems, and rare buildings. But developers want land uses arranged to maximize the marketability of their projects, and investors want to protect their investment by preserving the convenience, attractiveness, and future sales potential of the properties they own. (This last category, of course, includes California's 5 million or so homeowners, whose financial well-being, thanks to home prices that are double the national average, rests more than ever before in the value of their houses.)

* Government Code §65030.

This difference in attitude between the public goals of planning and the private goals of real estate investors is important, because most plans, however inspired, are not self-executing. They are only translated into reality when private landowners take the initiative and try to build something. Planners may shape the broad contours of growth and development according to public concerns. But the specific patterns that appear on the ground are created, ultimately, by private investors seeking to maximize financial gain. (Occasionally, of course, public entities such as redevelopment agencies and port districts are able to initiate projects themselves, but they too must rely on the response of private investors for success.)

These two world views — land as resource and land as commodity — come into conflict continuously in the planning process, and in so doing they shape its effectiveness. Each has some legal currency. Each has advocates skilled in manipulating the levers of power to their advantage. And each acts as a brake on the other.

In a way, of course, this adversarial relationship is good, because it helps to maintain a balance among the different interests at work in the planning process. At the same time, however, the conflict between these two attitudes often prevents planning from becoming the visionary and future-shaping exercise that idealistic planners believe it to be. Because of the friction between land as resource and land as commodity, planning is not always able to achieve the sober and objective goal of arranging the physical environment for maximum efficiency. Rather, planning usually operates as a classic regulatory system — a governmental mechanism designed to restrain private businesses in order to achieve a public good that the private market apparently can't provide.

But even this modest definition doesn't accurately describe how planning really works. The regulators are usually unable to take positive action in order to achieve their goals; rather, they spend most of their time reacting — telling people what they cannot do, or how to modify what they would like to do. Furthermore, citizen groups have gained tremendous leverage over the land-use process in recent years, and, if well organized, they can snag virtually any project they dislike in California's vast legal underbrush. And like all regulatory systems, planning is highly susceptible to manipulation by those it is supposedly regulating. Many of these "realities" serve to hold the system accountable to the public interest. Sometimes, however, they appear to pervert the process instead. In any event, these realities shape the way planning actually works in California as much as any law, any court case, or any principle of good city planning.

## WHAT PLANNING IS

Throughout this book, the word "planning" will be used to encompass the broad range of areas usually lumped together under the terms "urban planning" and "regional planning," including housing policy and environmental planning. In most instances, however, this term will refer specifically to land-use planning — that is, the process by which government agencies determine the intensity and geographical arrangement of various land uses in a community, such as residential projects, shopping centers, office and industrial employment centers, transportation facilities, agricultural land, and parks.

At various times in its history, planning has also sought to encompass a broad range of social policy and economic development issues. This book's definition of the word "planning" does not include social policy and economic development directly. These areas are dealt with only to the extent that the way land is used and distributed within a community affects people's social and economic circumstances.

Planning occurs in a variety of different settings — urban, suburban, rural, even regional.

There is the planning of mature cities, which has two aspects to it: the recycling of older neighborhoods and business districts into denser communities, which often raises questions of how to concentrate development in one area in order to protect another; and attempts to revive ailing inner-city neighborhoods, which often involves luring new development to areas perceived as risky.

There is the planning of fast-growing suburban areas developing for the first time — places such as Riverside County — which often raises questions of infrastructure finance, site planning, traffic flow, and protection of some open space. (This type of planning is often conducted by the smaller cities — those with populations up to 100,000 — that govern most suburban areas in California.) There is the planning of small towns and rural areas, which often focuses on preservation of farmland and historic buildings, as well as economic development. And there is planning at the regional level — assuring that each region has a good mixture of jobs, housing, and other land uses required for communities to function.

This book will focus, at one time or another, on all these different types of planning. But more than anything else, this book will deal with the planning of emerging suburban areas, simply because that is where most of the planning effort in the state is concentrated. Much of the material in the book will also be applicable to older urban and close-in suburban areas that are experiencing rapid growth, because planning laws and processes are often used to manage that growth. Though this book will cover the relationship between planning and local government finance, it will not deal extensively with economic development, or with redevelopment of inner-city areas (except to point out how the tool of redevelopment is not put to good use for this purpose). Ideally, the problems of inner-city residents would receive higher priority among planners. But the truth is that most planning in California deals with the growth and development of more prosperous areas, whether they are newly developing or being "recycled" by real estate developers.

## HOW PLANNING REALLY WORKS

On the surface, the most important change in California planning during the late '80s was the shifting balance of power between property owners and the government planners who regulate their activities. This shift came about largely because of two U.S. Supreme Court rulings, the so-called *First English* and *Nollan* cases.* In both cases, the U.S. Supreme Court upheld the constitutional rights of property owners against governmental agencies seeking to regulate the use of their land. Essentially, the court ruled in both cases that a zoning ordinance, a planning scheme, or a specific development approval, if its condi-

* *First English Evangelical Lutheran Church of Glendale v. County of Los Angeles*, 482 U.S. 304 (1987), and *Nollan v. Coastal California Coastal Commission*, 483 U.S. 825 (1987).

tions are too extreme, can sometimes constitute a "taking" of property. In such cases, the property owner is entitled to compensation from the government just as if the land had been purchased. Of course, all planning regulations limit a landowner's power in some fashion — if you own a lot zoned for single-family residences, that's all you can build — and the court did not say that all regulations constitute a taking. Rather, the Supreme Court said that a taking occurs if a landowner loses all economic use of his land. (Significantly, both *First English* and *Nollan*, which will be discussed in detail later in this book, came from California.) The *First English* and *Nollan* cases haven't exactly caused government planners to cower under their desks when a developer walks in the door, as some planners had feared (and most developers had hoped). But there is no question that these cases have changed the landscape of planning, especially here in California. From the '60s through the mid-'80s, the California courts gave governmental agencies a free hand in restricting construction and regulating land. Now the hand is no longer quite so free. Cities, counties, and state agencies can be held accountable by property owners who feel wronged by regulation. At the very least, the two cases opened the door of the county courthouse to such landowners and their lawyers.

Underneath this shift in legal attitude, however, lies a curious irony that reveals a great deal about how planning actually works. The *First English* and *Nollan* cases are meant to protect property owners from overly restrictive land-use regulations. But land-use regulations, as originally conceived and used early in this century, were actually meant to protect private property owners — or, at least, certain groups of private property owners. The first important zoning ordinance in this country, the New York City ordinance of 1916, was designed mostly to halt the march of tenements up Fifth Avenue toward the mansions of the bourgeoisie. Thus, some 75 years ago, well-to-do New Yorkers had learned one of the basic facts of land-use regulations: that even though they may be grounded legally in lofty statements about the public welfare, they are most powerful as a tool of manipulation by narrow interest groups. This fact remains at the root of many planning controversies today — and, unfortunately, the manipulation of the land-use system by a variety of interest groups (ranging from developers to environmentalists) often prevents planning from serving as a tool to help shape a vision for a community's future. Because most land-use power lies in the hands of elected local government officials, turning it to one's own advantage requires political power, and this leads us to yet another undeniable reality. No matter how idealistic a field it may

seem, planning is inseparable from politics. The well-to-do New Yorkers who wanted to protect their homes from the encroaching slums down Fifth Avenue back in 1916 were simply exercising their political clout. Similarly, when slow-growthers in Thousand Oaks passed an initiative 64 years later that re-

stricted the city to only 500 building permits per year, they weren't simply enacting a land-use regulation; they were establishing a base of political power. (In fact, in Thousand Oaks — and in dozens of other California cities since then — the passage of a growth-control initiative has been accompanied by the election of growth-control advocates to the city council.)

And because land-use regulations are highly susceptible to political pressure, they can be exploited by anyone able to gain leverage over a city council or county board of supervisors — not just homeowners or slow-growthers, but also big-time developers who need a zone change or some other governmental approval in order to build a project. The history of zoning in America is filled with colorful examples of municipal corruption. During the first half of this century, it was not uncommon for elected and appointed officials in the "machine politics" cities of the Northeast and Midwest to "sell" zone changes for personal gain.

California has been surprisingly free of out-and-out corruption over the years. But large landowners still manage to influence the process in subtle ways. Chief among these is the use of campaign contributions. Developers bankroll many local political campaigns in California. The reason is simple: There is no other group of potential contributors with so much to gain from a local government's decisions. A local council member's vote can literally turn a pauper into a millionaire if he owns the right piece of property (or vice versa if he owns the wrong piece).

In return for campaign contributions, these developers expect, at the very least, a sympathetic ear from local council members or supervisors. In small cities, the financial power of developers is often overcome by sheer grassroots power: precinct-walking and telephone campaigning by dedicated volunteers. In larger cities — and in counties, which often have large areas of unpopulated territory — it is much harder to assemble a corps of campaign volunteers capable of counteracting developers' money.

Perhaps even more insidious is the revolving door between local government and the real estate industry, especially in Southern California. Once they know the system, talented planners commonly leave the public sector for higher-paying jobs with consulting firms that work for developers. And top public officials who are friendly with developers are often assured of lucrative long-term careers in the real estate industry after they leave office — largely because of their perceived ability to manipulate the land-use system.

Landowners large and small are also able to use legal pressure as well. California's state requirements for local planning are largely procedural in nature, and these procedural requirements are so numerous, and so detailed, that virtually any plan or development project can be held up in court at least for awhile.

Such legal challenges often try to stand planning or environmental laws on their head just for the benefit of an angry property owner. For example, when the City of San Francisco wanted to condemn a mortuary in crowded Chinatown, in order to tear it down and create a park, the mortuary sued — under the California Environmental Quality Act! Ignoring the benefits of creating a park in a crowded section of the city, the mortuary's lawyers claimed it served as an important piece of the cultural environment because it was the only establishment in Chinatown that still performed traditional Chinese funerals. This ridiculous argument got all the way to the Court of Appeal before being slapped down for the sham it really was.

## THE GROWING ROLE OF CITIZENS

In a peculiar way, the fact that the mortuary's owners were able to get so far with their argument was a tribute to the inclusionary nature of California's planning process. Once the exclusive (and somewhat private) domain of developers and political dealmakers, this process has opened up remarkably over the last 20 years to include ordinary citizens and the groups they have formed. Most state planning laws, buttressed by expansive court rulings, now require considerable public participation in the planning process. Other laws, such as the California Environmental Quality Act, or CEQA, require the release of vast amounts of information about proposed development projects, and establish intricate procedures that must be followed, so that local officials cannot shut the public out.

If the process is more open now, it is because citizen groups of all kinds pushed their way into the process. They have certainly had few champions among elected officials. For example, the passage of the Coastal Act in 1972 — a seminal law that established the Coastal Commission to protect the coast from overdevelopment — occurred only because environmental groups placed it on the ballot as an initiative. The law had been unable to pass the state legislature.

Citizen groups have also made effective use of California's long-standing tradition of "citizen enforcement" of laws in the planning field. Few state planning laws are enforced by the state government itself — that is to say, state bureaucrats do not stand over the shoulder of local planners and developers, threatening to punish them if laws are not followed. In most cases, the only way to hold developers and local governments accountable is by suing them. Occasionally the state Attorney General will file such suits, but more often it is the citizen groups themselves who initiate such litigation. In many areas, these lawsuits have been extremely effective. The breadth of CEQA, for example, has been greatly expanded through "citizen enforcement" suits.

There is no question that the inclusion of the public has been the most profound and heartening change in planning that California has witnessed over the past 20 years. This "empowerment" of all citizens, rich and poor, has created a grassroots constituency for planning on a scale that never existed before. All sorts of citizen groups have become fixtures in the plan-

ning process: homeowner groups, neighborhood groups, preservationists, environmentalists, and so on. And the results are evident throughout California. Many fragile neighborhoods have been saved from destruction by a freeway or some other potentially destabilizing construction project. Many historic buildings have been reused rather than razed. Many wetlands, wildlife habitats, and areas of scenic beauty have been preserved. Perhaps most important, consideration of all these interests has become a permanent part of planning in California — as have the interest groups that have sprung up to protect them. At the same time, the heightened participation of all these groups has made community consensus and a shared sense of vision more difficult to achieve.

*   *   *

## CURRENT ISSUES IN CALIFORNIA PLANNING

Planning issues would not seem so urgent in California if the state were not growing so fast. But the growth juggernaut is still churning forward and still gaining speed. This massive growth has brought planning in California to a flashpoint. The rapid change that growth engenders comes into conflict with a creaky and often outmoded planning system. This conflict has, in turn, helped to create several significant political and financial issues that pervade all planning efforts in California. We will lay these issues out now, and return to them again and again throughout this book, because they underly many of the difficulties California planning faces today. They include the following:

### INCREASING POLITICIZATION OF PLANNING

To begin with, the whole planning process has become far more political than ever before. Developers have always been political players, of course, but during the development boom of the '80s, land prices soared, and therefore developers began playing for much higher stakes.

At the same time, California's citizen groups learned — quite suddenly — how to transform their new-found legal leverage over planning into political power, at least on the local level. The most dramatic illustration of this rise to political power was the number of slow-growth initiatives appearing on local ballots. Through 1985, no more than 20 land-use measures had ever appeared on the state's local ballots in any one year. Suddenly, in 1986, the number of measures soared to 50 — and by 1988 there were was more than 100.

Over time, these citizen groups moved into electoral politics and began to elect political leaders, at least at the municipal level, who reflected their views. After 1988, the number of initiatives levelled off — largely because, in many communities, the old political guard had been replaced by a new crew dedicated to slowing or managing growth. The speed with which this transformation occurred was remarkable, especially in traditionally conservative areas of Southern California. In 1985, virtually all the old-line pro-development politicians in Southern California appeared unchallenged. But by decade's end, in even the most conservative areas of California, politicians who advocated unrestrained growth did so at their political peril.

This political transformation did not put an end to growth and development as a controversial issue, however. Rather, in community after community, the transformation simply heightened the battle between developers and slow-growthers. The more that the development community tried to exert its influence over local politics, the better organized and more politically astute slow-growthers became. The more powerful the slow-growthers became, the more money developers shoveled into supporting pro-growth candidates and opposing local initiatives. Both sides honed their political skills, but in most communities they were not able to overcome the pro-growth/slow-growth confrontation.

## INTEREST-GROUP POLITICS

The rise of citizen groups and the increased politicization of the planning process have brought with them many characteristics of the interest-group politics common in Congress and the state legislature. And this has caused problems. To operate successfully, a regulatory system must rest on a common understanding of what seems to be the public interest. But planning in California does not have a strong, unified sense of the public interest any more. Instead, each group claims to represent the public interest — while, in fact, most groups represent a more narrow interest (the environment, the neighborhood, the real estate industry) and mistrust the other groups. For this reason, interest groups often refuse to accept the outcome of the political process — causing endless uncertainty and instability on planning issues.

California's intricate planning and environmental procedures, while opening the process up, have probably given these groups too many opportunities to reject the political outcome. Frequently, procedural attacks are used when a political battle over a project's merits has been lost. And the procedural attack need not be a bald perversion of the law, as the Chinese mortuary's lawsuit was, in order for it to work against the defined public interest. Often, a group of environmentalists or homeowners will make some sort of technical or procedural challenge — the adequacy of an environmental impact report, for example, or consistency with the local general plan — simply because it is the only avenue left open to them. Their goal is not really to produce a better EIR, or a project more consistent with the general plan, but to kill the project altogether by making life miserable for the developer.

Because the threat of a procedural attack is always present, all those involved in the land-use process are forced to focus on meeting procedural requirements, rather than truly examining the environmental or planning implications of a particular development project. For this reason, many well-intentioned planning laws merely produce pieces of paper, rather than change in the real world, and planners, bureaucrats, and lawyers often feel that they have done their jobs so long as the pieces of paper are produced.

Perhaps the most vivid example of planning by procedure is the California Environmental Quality Act. For 20 years, citizen groups have used CEQA to challenge the adequacy of "environmental impact reports" on all sorts of projects, and they have usually won in court. (Environmental impact reports, or EIRs, are research documents designed to identify the likely environmental effects of a development project. They are discussed in more detail in Chapter 9.) The result is an ever-expanding set of issues that must be considered in an EIR: cumulative impacts, alternative sites, mitigation monitoring, and so on. Properly used, this environmental information can aid the planning process. But too often it is sought merely as a means of shutting down a particular development project.

Another good example is the state requirement that each local government prepare a five-year housing element subject to state approval. (Under state planning law, a local government's "general plan" must contain seven different sections or "elements," including one element dealing with housing.) The goal of the law is to force local governments to assure that enough housing is constructed to meet the state's needs. But because the state's review is mostly procedural, the debate among planners and bureaucrats almost always focuses on whether the legal requirements of the housing element law are met. Meanwhile, the question of whether enough housing is actually being built — perhaps the key public-policy question in the entire state — is rarely addressed.

*   *   *

THE RED HEAD IS THE ONE DEMANDING A DAY CARE CENTER, THE LOUD MOUTH WANTS A PARK, EVERYONE IS AGAINST CONDOS EXCEPT THE DEVELOPER ... HE'S THE ONE TURNING GREEN.

## THE 'FISCALIZATION' OF LAND USE

At the same time that planning in California has become "politicized," it has also become "fiscalized." The fiscal elements of planning have also made it much more difficult to discern the public interest in which planning is supposed to be grounded.

The passage of Proposition 13 in 1978 hit local governments hard. The initiative cut property-tax rates by about two-thirds, and then made it virtually impossible for local governments to increase those rates. Routine municipal services were curtailed, of course, but perhaps the biggest long-term problem created by Proposition 13 was a lack of capital funds for infrastructure. Unable to raise property taxes to support bond issues (a two-thirds vote is required), and reeling from a sudden drop-off in state and federal grants, local governments found themselves without the means to build new roads, sewers, schools, and the other essential building blocks of their communities. So they turned to the only source of funds they had any leverage over: developers.

The fiscalization of planning took two forms. First, cities and counties started encouraging some types of development and discouraging others based on financial considerations. In particular, big sources of sales-tax revenue, such as auto dealerships, hotels, and shopping malls, became prize acquisitions, because Proposition 13 did not restrict sales tax. (Often, a powerful governmental tool called "redevelopment" — a successor to "urban renewal" programs — was used to finance and facilitate these lucrative projects.) By contrast, housing tracts, which produced only a dribble of property-tax revenue and cost a lot to serve, quickly became unfashionable.

Second, local officials, seeing the typical developer as a goose that lays golden eggs in their town, began leaning on those developers to set aside a few eggs for public purposes in order to make up for the lost capital funds. Typically, developers now must build the infrastructure to serve their projects and set aside land for schools, parks, and libraries. In a growing number of jurisdictions, they also pay substantial development fees to assist in the construction of freeway interchanges, transit lines, low-income housing, and even child-care centers. During the extreme drought that began in 1987, some cities even required developers to pay fees to "offset" increased water use; the fees were used to pay for replacement of antiquated plumbing in other buildings.

The fiscalization trend fed into the politicization trend in several important ways. Perhaps most important was the fact that a city or county government's interests in the planning process gradually became uncoupled from the interests of its citizens. The government as a whole needed funds and wanted to lure big tax producers. But citizens more often identified themselves with the narrower interests that had emerged from the "empowerment process," such as the homeowner group that fears more traffic or the environmental group fighting to protect open space.

The availability of the developers' golden eggs obscured the public interest even more. Frustrated by local governments' lack of financial resources, citizen groups quickly realized they might be able to get a developer to finance their pet programs in exchange for their support of a big real estate project — whether that project was a child-care center, an arts project, or the construction of low-income housing. No longer did underfunded civic organizations need to lobby the local government for a piece of the budget; no longer did they need to compete with other interests for public resources. All they had to do was gain leverage over a developer trying to get a project approved.

## LACK OF COORDINATION

Fiscalization and politicization have led to an "every city for itself" attitude which is damaging planning and quality of life at a regional level. In manipulating the land-use system to their own financial

advantage — using redevelopment and zoning to bring certain developments in and keep others out — cities and counties acting independently have created vast regional imbalances throughout California.

In both the Bay Area and Los Angeles, job centers tend to be located in areas where housing is expensive, while starter-home tracts are being built 40 to 70 miles away, where land is cheap. This peculiar pattern is the result of two factors: slow-growth sentiment and the financial squeeze. Older communities with established neighborhoods often foster a slow-growth attitude, which cuts down on the amount of new housing constructed in the inner ring of suburbs, such as the San Fernando Valley in Los Angeles and the Peninsula in the Bay Area. At the same time, many of these same communities — in need of tax money to support their older, low-density land-use patterns — target shopping center and auto malls at the expense of housing.

At the same time, new business and cultural centers — new "downtowns" — have emerged in the suburbs, partly because suburban city governments have encouraged their creation. The decade of the 1980s saw the emergence of hundreds of these centers in California — from the office towers that rose from lima bean fields in Orange County to the industrial parks on the outskirts of Sacramento. These suburban centers also have changed commuting patterns, making people more dependent on the automobile.

Sometimes, perversely enough, redevelopment powers were used to encourage this sort of suburban development for tax purposes. At the same time, while specialized business (office-based businesses, high-end retail) thrived in some downtowns, inner-city areas have received little investment in recent years. Thus, while the planning process has aided the suburbanization of jobs and houses, it has largely ignored urban areas in need of help. And because the concept of local planning is so strongly rooted in California's planning laws, no structure exists to address the regional imbalances that have resulted.

## CONCLUSION

This, then, is the world of planning in California today. It is a world far more open and inclusive than it was 20 or 30 years ago. In a way, it is a wonderfully messy democratic process, with interest groups forming and creating coalitions, citizens assuming political power, and the future of each community being debated far more publicly and thoroughly than ever before.

Yet, at the same time, it is a world disturbingly open to manipulation by special interests. It is a world where developers use heavy-duty political firepower to try to get their projects approved. It is a world where cities and counties use their land-use powers to maximize their own financial gain. It is a world where homeowners use both political and legal tactics to protect their investments. It is a world where civic organizations use their leverage over new development to finance their pet projects. It is a world, in other words, where so many narrow claims are made to the public interest that the term has lost much of its meaning.

This is not to say that planning does not "work" in California today. There are planners out there with vision, and developers who want to build good projects, and politicians and citizens who want to make their communities better. These people often work together well, and no doubt the public interest sometimes emerges from their joint effort, as it often does in legislative forums.

Nevertheless, for anyone who hopes to operate in the world of planning in California, it is important to understand from the outset that the system works to the advantage of the manipulators and as a result the ideal is rarely achieved. In the chapters ahead, I will discuss in great detail the processes and laws that must be observed in California planning, and how they are supposed to be used to create better communities. But I also hope to show how those processes and laws are used — for better or worse — by the people who play the game.

# CHAPTER 1

# THE PLAYERS AND THEIR POWER

Whether you want to put up a building or stop somebody else from doing so, your first stop will probably be city hall or the county courthouse. That's because the most basic elements of planning power rest with local governments. Zoning ordinances and general plans are drawn up at the local level. Building permits and other development approvals are issued at the local level. Environmental review is usually conducted under the guidance of local planning departments. Virtually everyone engaged in planning and property development winds up standing in front of a local planning commission or city council sooner or later.

That does not mean, however, that local government is the only entity with power over land-use planning and real estate development. True, local government is the linchpin of the land-use regulatory system; it deals with most of the day-to-day decisions and takes most of the political heat. But virtually all the players in the vast array of our political/governmental system have a role in determining how planning works at the local level in California. The local planning commission or city council may have power over the zone change or the building permit, but the nature of that power is shaped by other forces, usually involving higher levels of government. Judges, the state legislature, various governmental agencies, even Congress and the U.S. Supreme Court all play a role in determining how your local planning commission or city council is permitted to regulate the use of land. And in the long run, this ability to shape local government's land-use power may be more important than the power itself.

## The Legal Authority for Planning

It doesn't take long, in investigating the legal underpinnings of planning, to realize that they are far removed indeed from city hall. Like all governmental power in this country, the power to regulate the use of land stems ultimately from the U.S. Constitution. The Tenth Amendment to the Constitution — the so-called "reserved powers doctrine" — states that any powers not specifically granted to the federal government in the Constitution are reserved by the states. Chief among these is the so-called "police power." No legal term is more important to planning.

The police power is the power of a governmental entity to restrict private activity in order to achieve a broad public benefit. In California, police power is used to protect the health, safety, morals, and welfare of the public. Throughout legal history, the police power has been used as the basis for a broad range of governmental activities from the court system to general relief. For more than a century, it has also been the legal vehicle used to justify governmental regulation over the use of land.

But police power does not rest inherently at city hall. Local governments in California exercise police power over land uses only because the state government has delegated that power to them. Article XI, Section 7, of the California Constitution states: "A county or city may make and enforce within its limits all local, police, sanitary, and other ordinances and regulations not in conflict with general laws."

The courts have interpreted this clause liberally, and the term most often used to describe the police power in dealing with land use is "elastic." California land-use law scholar James Longtin has called the police power "capable of expansion to meet existing conditions of modern life and thereby keep pace with the social, economic, moral, and intellectual evolution of the human race."* Thus, interpretations of the police power that would have seemed outrageous a generation ago — requiring dedication of land for a child-care center, for example — have become commonplace today.

Nevertheless, the local exercise of police power is far from absolute. Local actions must be "reasonably related" to the public values of health, safety, morals, and welfare. They must not contradict constitutional principles, especially the concepts of due process, equal protection, and the unlawful taking of property without compensation. And they must be subordinate to state laws.

So even though local governments think they have a lot of land-use power, they are really very much at the mercy of the state and federal governments, who shape their land-use power through both legislation and litigation. This means that legislators, judges, bureaucrats, and others become "players" in the land-use game just as much as planning commissioners or city council members.

## THE LEGAL STRUCTURE OF CALIFORNIA PLANNING

Planning procedures in California derive from a broad array of state laws. The ones most directly applicable to conventional land-use planning appear in the Government Code, which is the section of the state's laws dealing with governmental actions. Many others are scattered throughout other sections of state law, including the Public Resources Code and the Health and Safety Code. Together they form the basis for California's planning system. The most important pieces of this legal structure include the following:

*Planning, Zoning, and Development Laws* (Government Code §65000 *et seq.*). This set of laws lays out the legal basis for the state's interest in planning and establishes the requirement that all local governments create "planning agencies."

*General Plan Law* (Government Code §65300 *et seq.*). These code sections require that all local governments prepare a "general plan" for the future development of the city, and lay out all the state's requirements governing what a general plan should contain. The general plan

---

* *Longtin's California Land Use*, page 43.

is the same as the document that most planners outside California refer to as the "comprehensive plan" or the "master plan" — that is, a comprehensive document that establishes the city's land-use policies and also details the likely future development patterns of the city.

*The Subdivision Map Act* (Government Code §66410 *et. seq.*). This law governs all subdivision of land. It requires that local governments establish regulations to guide subdivisions, and grants powers to local governments to ensure that the subdivision occurs in an orderly and responsible manner.

*The California Environmental Quality Act* (Public Resources Code §21000 *et seq.*). This law requires local governments to conduct some form of environmental review on virtually all public and private development projects. CEQA's requirements, which are mostly procedural, sometimes cause local governments to prepare "environmental impact reports" on specific development projects, detailing the likely environmental damage the projects would cause.

*The Coastal Act* (Public Resources Code §30000 *et seq.*). This law, originally passed as a ballot initiative in 1972, establishes special planning requirements for coastal areas and creates a powerful state agency, the Coastal Commission, to oversee coastal planning.

*The Community Redevelopment Law* (Health & Safety Code §33000 *et seq.*). This law gives cities and counties great power to redevelop blighted areas. It is perhaps the most powerful single tool local governments possess, other than the basic laws permitting them to engage in planning at all.

*The Cortese-Knox Local Government Reorganization Act* (Government Code §56000 *et seq.*). This law is not strictly speaking a planning law. However, its provisions play an important role in local planning because it governs procedures by which local government boundaries may be changed. Under the Cortese-Knox Act, all annexations, incorporations, and other boundary changes must be processed through a special countywide agency called the Local Agency Formation Commission.

Many other laws come into play at one time or another, and these will be dealt with in the chapters to come. However, these seven sets of laws form the core of California's planning system.

# THE PERMIT PROCESS

Developer brings application to Planning Department, which examines project and conducts environmental review.

Developer then presents project to Planning Commission.

Citizens comment ... and, under Permit Streamlining Act, Planning Commission must act within one year of original application. Decision may be appealed to City Council or Board of Supervisors.

## THE PLAYERS

### THE LEGISLATIVE BRANCH:
### THE U.S. CONGRESS AND THE CALIFORNIA LEGISLATURE

These are the legislative bodies of the federal and state government, respectively. Therefore, they are charged with making all laws, and in so doing they are pretty much free to make whatever laws they like, so long as they don't contradict their respective constitutions.

Congress is important because of the ubiquitous nature of the federal government. But its role in planning is indirect. The concept of a "national land-use policy" was kicked around on Capitol Hill in the '70s, but Congress has never interfered directly in the land-use area, preferring to leave those matters up to the states. Nevertheless, Congress has passed a vast array of laws — mostly environmental in nature — that do affect the land-use process at the local level.

Laws designed to protect endangered species and wetlands, for example, give federal agencies the power to block development, even if local officials disagree. Federal air and water quality laws often affect the size, location, and nature of industrial plants by requiring a reduction in pollutants. Also, federal projects are not subject to local land-use controls, though, in practice, some federal-local negotiation usually takes place. The U.S. Forest Service and the Bureau of Land Management own large tracts of land in California, over which they exert essentially unchallenged control. In addition, the National Environmental Policy Act, or NEPA, requires environmental review of all federal projects, which sometimes gives local governments or local citizens leverage.*

The California Legislature plays a far more direct part in establishing the roles of local planning. Over the past 80 years, the Legislature has created the entire framework for local planning in California. The Legislature passed the first Subdivision Map Act in 1907 and the first general plan law in 1927. Specific elements were first required in a city's General Plan in the 1950s, and the requirement that a zoning ordinance and general plan must be consistent with each other passed

---

* 42 United States Code 4321 *et seq.*

the Legislature in 1971. The Legislature has also passed a slew of other laws that affect land use, including the Community Redevelopment Law, which dates from the early 1950s, and the California Environmental Quality Act, which dates from 1970.

Furthermore, these laws do not simply go on the books and stay there. The Legislature tinkers with them every year. The exact process by which the California Assembly and Senate pass a bill is complicated and does not merit much discussion here. (The process is virtually the same as the process in Congress — committee hearings, votes in both Houses, conference committee, and review by the governor, who has veto power.) But thousands of bills are introduced each year and hundreds pass, most of them amending laws that are already on the books.

Sometimes these amendments create marginal, almost imperceptible changes, but over a period of time they can create a significant change in the thrust of a law. Amendments to the state's redevelopment law are a good example. As a successor to urban renewal, redevelopment is designed to give local governments the tools (land acquisition, infrastructure finance) to make depressed areas more attractive to developers and investors. After Proposition 13, cities began using the redevelopment law as a way of producing new taxes, mostly by subsidizing development of big tax producers like shopping malls and auto dealerships. When legislators saw that the production of housing was suffering, they began to enact amendments forcing the cities to set aside redevelopment funds for housing. No single amendment, by itself, created significant change — partly because cities lobbied against them. Gradually, however, the housing amendments began to impose requirements on more and more redevelopment projects, and they made the housing requirements tougher and tougher. Finally, by the beginning of the '90s, redevelopment experts predicted that the focus of their entire business would soon shift from commercial to residential development.

Many laws are passed simply because the legislature has reached a consensus that they are in the public interest. But such purity of motive is not always the rule. The legislative arena is highly susceptible to politics and other external forces. Typically, bills are proposed — or even written — by a lobbying organization with something to gain. Many of the bills cracking down on redevelopment, for example, have been proposed by California's counties, which lose considerable tax revenue when redevelopment projects are created. And occasionally, a developer will ask a friendly legislator to carry a so-called "juice" bill — a bill that looks general on its face, but actually carries some specific provision designed to help that developer push his project through back home.

Once a bill is introduced, many different interest groups lobby the legislators (and the governor), encouraging them to pass the bill, defeat it, or amend it to make it more favorable to their interests. On land-use bills, leading lobbyists will typically include the League of California Cities, the County Supervisors Association of California, the California Building Industry Association, perhaps the California Association of Realtors, and sometimes environmental groups such as the Sierra Club. The opposition of any one of these groups is often enough to kill a bill. These groups sometimes neutralize each other's lobbying impact, meaning that a successful bill is likely to be a cautious one. This is why, as with redevelopment law, a needed shift in state policy evolves incrementally. Over time, evidence mounts that change is needed, but a powerful group that feels threatened by the proposed change will give up only a little ground each year.

Individual organizations, such as a developer or a company, may lobby on a particular bill if they believe they have a lot to gain or lose by its passage. In 1987, for example, the legislature considered a controversial bill that would have permitted the city of Indian Wells, near Palm Springs, to spend its redevelopment money on low-income housing outside its city limits. It was the most heavily lobbied bill in the legislature that year, but the reasons were only partly related to redevelopment and low-income housing. The housing project was connected with a large resort project being proposed inside Indian Wells, and the stakes involved in that project were enormous. The Marriott Corporation, which had recently opened a resort in neighboring Palm Desert, opposed the Indian Wells resort; so the company brought its considerable lobbying power to bear against the redevelopment bill, hoping that would help kill the resort project. In the end, Marriott's lobbying paid off because Governor George Deukmejian vetoed the bill. (Partly as a result, the project was never built, though other factors were also involved.)

Other external forces can sometimes play a role in the fate of a bill as well. In 1988, for example, the California Building Industry Association appeared likely to succeed in pushing through a small but important bill without attracting much attention. The bill would have granted many developers vested rights to build, even if a local growth-control ordinance passed. When the Assembly overwhelmingly approved the bill late in the legislative session, however, the *Los Angeles Times* ran the story on page 1 — not because it was especially important, but because growth control was a leading public issue in the state at the time. As a result, just a few days later this same bill — the one that had breezed through the Assembly — died in the Senate for lack of support. The media spotlight had changed the political climate for that particular bill.

The legislature is not the only statewide forum for resolving public policy issues in California. Any issue may also appear on the statewide ballot as an initiative or a referendum if enough signatures are gathered. As we shall see, initiatives and referenda have played a much more direct role in planning on the local level; but statewide ballot measures can be just as influential as the legislature in shaping the local planning environment. Perhaps the leading example in this area was Proposition 20, the 1972 coastal initiative, which established the Coastal Commission and gave it direct jurisdiction over development permits and planning in all coastal areas of California. An initiative with an indirect but perhaps more pervasive impact on local planning was Proposition 13, the 1978 measure that cut property taxes dramatically. By weakening local governments' general tax base, Proposition 13 ushered in an era of intense competition among cities and counties for tax-producing development — a competition often reflected in local land-use plans and development strategies.

\* \* \*

## THE EXECUTIVE BRANCH:
## THE PRESIDENT AND THE GOVERNOR,
## FEDERAL AND STATE BUREAUCRATS

Congress and the state legislature are responsible for making the laws, but they are not responsible for carrying them out. That responsibility falls to the executive branch of each government — specifically, to the president of the United States and the governor of California, and the executive departments they administer.

The power of state and federal bureaucrats depends on two things: first, the amount of authority and discretion that Congress or the legislature has granted them; and second, the zeal with which the president or governor wishes to enforce the laws. Individual situations vary widely, but it is fair to say that federal bureaucrats usually wield far more power than their state counterparts.

As mentioned above, federal environmental laws, such as the Endangered Species Act* and the wetlands provisions of the Clean Water Act,** have the power to virtually stop local development if the environment is threatened. The most vivid recent example of this power came when the grasslands of western Riverside County, perhaps the fastest-growing residential area in the country, was found to be a habitat for the Stephens' kangaroo rat, an endangered species. The U.S. Fish & Wildlife Service, a branch of the Interior Department, stepped in and threatened to stop all development unless a habitat for the rat was created. After a long negotiation, developers in the area agreed to pay a fee of close to $2,000 per acre to purchase a habitat for the rat, and development was permitted to continue.

But these processes do not occur automatically. They only occur if federal bureaucrats set them into motion. Under Section 404 of the Clean Water Act, for example, the federal government can intervene if new development threatens an existing wetland. But that does not mean the federal government does intervene every time a wetland is threatened; rather, if a wetland is involved, the Army Corps of Engineers must first assert jurisdiction. The Corps may or may not decide to assert jurisdiction, depending on the environmental sensitivi-

* 16 U.S.C. 1531 *et seq.*
** 33 U.S.C. 1251 *et. seq.*

ty — and the pending workload — of the Corps' regional officials. And, of course, the Corps' own attitude — like that of any other federal agency — is likely to depend on the president's commitment to a specific law. Because President George Bush has made many ringing statements about the need to preserve wetlands, federal bureaucrats are now far more likely to intervene in sensitive situations involving wetlands.

Federal bureaucrats can also play an indirect role in local planning if they choose to enforce other environmental laws aggressively. In recent years, for example, the Los Angeles area has been under intense pressure from the federal Environmental Protection Agency, or EPA, to draw up tougher air-quality plans. Partly as a result of this pressure, the South Coast Air Quality Management District's plan, passed in 1989, called for local governments to institute traffic-reduction programs and other measures that are sure to require changes in planning. Again, the president's attitude in such a situation is crucial. On the air-quality front, the truth is that the pressure on EPA has come more from environmentalist lawsuits than from any presidential directive. Other federal agencies, such as the Bureau of Land Management, also play an indirect role in local planning because they manage property owned by the federal government.

California state bureaucrats generally have less influence over planning, because state laws are more deferential to the power of local government. A good example is the state Department of Housing and Community Development, usually known simply as HCD. By law, all cities and counties must submit a draft of their general plan housing "elements" to HCD for review and comment. (An "element" is a section of a community's general plan.) But HCD has no legal authority to require improvements in the housing elements. In fact, local governments are not even required to give HCD a copy of the final version of their housing element (though most do). Furthermore, there is no administrative procedure to penalize the local governments if their housing plans do not measure up. However, with the Attorney General's assistance, HCD can file lawsuits against local governments in hopes of making them comply with the intent of the law.

Similarly, the Governor's Office of Planning and Research (OPR) serves as the leading state agency on most planning matters, but has little legal power. OPR has several statutory duties, including the preparation of the CEQA Guidelines, which despite their name are binding on local governments, and the General Plan Guidelines, which really are mere guidelines. The office also provides assistance to local governments on planning issues and administers certain other procedural requirements, such as the collection of all environmental impact reports around the state. State agencies often comment on local planning documents, especially the EIRs prepared for General Plans. Certain other documents must be submitted to certain other agencies; safety elements, for example, must go to the Division of Mines and Geology. Even though state agencies may comment on local documents, however, they usually do not have the ability to force local governments to act on those comments.

Occasionally, a state law will require local governments to prepare planning documents subject to a state agency's review. For example, the state hazardous-waste siting law (the so-called "Tanner law," named after the legislator who sponsored the bill) requires all counties to prepare hazardous-waste siting plans, which then must be approved by the state Department of Health Services. This power is a rare exception, however. The general rule remains that state agencies have little recourse in dealing with local plans.

Because these laws give more discretion to local governments to begin with, it is harder for any governor to exert more influence over the planning process. Nevertheless, a committed governor could place great emphasis on the law regarding housing elements, for example, if he sought to show his commitment to affordable housing. No recent governor has taken such steps, however.

Where the governor can have an influence, however, is in transportation planning, and in the few special state agencies that do have significant land-use power. For example, the state Department of Transportation, often known simply as Caltrans, has played a crucial role in establishing the state's patterns of growth. The unwavering commitment of postwar-era governors to the state's freeway system opened up many outlying areas for development, while the stingy road-building attitude of Governor Jerry Brown in the '70s constrained the opportunities for new development in the '80s. As state transportation funds have dwindled, however, so has the ability of Caltrans to establish growth patterns. More often than not, new highways in the '90s are constructed by local taxes and/or funds provided by individual developers.

Over the past 30 years, the state has established three regional agencies with direct power over land-use planning: the San Francisco Bay Conservation and Development Commission, the Coastal Commission, and the Tahoe Regional Planning Agency (a bistate agency with Nevada). Through his appointments and budgeting power, the governor can influence the direction these agencies take. In the '70s, Jerry Brown appointed many environmentalists to the Coastal Commission. (As with many commissions, the governor shares appointment powers for the Coastal Commission with key legislative leaders.) In the '80s, George Deukmejian appointed development-oriented members to the Coastal Commission and drastically reduced the commission's budget.

## THE JUDICIAL BRANCH: FEDERAL AND STATE COURTS

Typically, if you're miffed at your local city council over the way a development project was handled, your next step is to sue. Litigation is rife in land-use disputes, and there's little wonder as to why. Planning presents such a broad array of juicy legal issues that virtually anybody who threatens to sue can usually come up with a decent case.

Land-use cases usually fall into one of two categories. First is the constitutional case, in which the plaintiff argues that the local planning process has violated his or her constitutional rights. Often developers will feel, for example, that because their project was turned down, they were not accorded "equal protection" under the law, since, under the same circumstances, another developer's project might have been approved. Or landowners might feel that if their property is downzoned, some of its value has been "taken" from them by the government without just compensation.

The second category is the statutory case, in which the plaintiff argues that some state or federal law (sometimes called a "statute") has been violated. For example, a homeowner group might argue that the local zoning ordinance is not consistent with the local general plan, or that an environmental impact report should have been prepared on a project, as required by state law.

Statutory cases are fertile ground for disgruntled homeowners or developers because California planning statutes are so procedural in nature. A minor glitch can create an "inconsistency" between a general plan and a zoning ordinance; similarly, environmental review under the California Environmental Quality Act contains so many procedural requirements that it's hard to imagine any EIR that isn't legally vulnerable in some way.

Statutory cases can be productive because many planning laws rely not on the state but on citizen enforcement lawsuits. For example, while the Department of Housing and Community Development cannot penalize a city administratively if it does not have an adequate housing element, the state Attorney General can prosecute the city in court on HCD's behalf. (In fact, during John Van de Kamp's tenure as Attorney General, many housing advocates criticized him for not doing so more aggressively.) And for 20 years, environmental lawyers in California have expanded the scope of the California Environmental Quality Act by using aggressive legal arguments. When CEQA was passed in 1970, at first its provisions were applied only to public projects. But two years later, at the behest of some local citizens and environmental lawyers, the California Supreme Court ruled, in the landmark *Friends of Mammoth** case, that CEQA does apply to private real estate projects. And the law has been a burr in the side of California developers ever since.

Both state and federal courts play an extremely important role in shaping local land-use powers. Because most laws affecting local planning are state laws, most statutory cases wind up being heard in state courts. Similarly, because most of the constitutional questions in land use involve the U.S. Constitution, many constitutional cases wind up in federal courts. This division is not always stark. State courts often hear "takings" or due process cases. (In fact, the federal judiciary encourages this, in order to clear out their logjam of cases.) And landowners can occasionally sue under federal statutes, such as the Civil Rights

* *Friends of Mammoth v. Board of Supervisors,* 8 Cal.3d 247 (1972).

Act,* which permits them to claim that their civil rights were violated by a local government that refused to permit them to build their project. Because some state and federal laws are similar, many land-use lawyers are able to go "forum shopping" by filing a case in either state or federal court, depending on where they think they'll get a more sympathetic hearing of their case.

Both court systems are set up in a similar, three-tier fashion. Cases begin before local, trial-level judges (Superior Court judges in the state system and District Court judges in the federal system). Cases can then be appealed to an "intermediate" appellate court (the Courts of Appeal on the state side and the Ninth U.S. Circuit Court of Appeals in San Francisco on the federal side). Important matters of legal dispute may then be appealed to either the California Supreme Court or the U.S. Supreme Court (and a matter from the California Supreme Court can be appealed to the U.S. Supreme Court if a federal constitutional issue is involved). Cases usually have no value as a precedent until they have been ruled on by an appellate court.

To a surprising degree, the success or failure of any particular case depends not only on the legal arguments, but also on which judges are hearing the case. Trial-level judges, especially at the state level, often side with the landowners who come before them feeling wronged. On the other hand, California appellate judges, who frequently are more detached from the human emotions involved in a legal case, are often highly deferential to the actions of local governments. This fact is not necessarily related to the question of whether judges are "liberal" or "conservative." Liberal judges may be deferential to local governments because their philosophy gives them a preference for strong governmental intervention in land-use matters. On the other hand, the deference of conservative judges may come from a reluctance to appear as "judicial activists" by overturning local government actions.

This deference to governmental action is not quite as strong as it once was, especially given George Deukmejian's many Republican appointments to the bench and the U.S. Supreme Court's rulings in the

---

* 42 United States Code 1983. Because of the code section, suits under the Civil Rights Act are sometimes known as "1983 actions."

*First English* and *Nollan* cases in 1987, both of which were very favorable to private landowners. Nevertheless, such deference is deeply rooted in the important cases handed down over the past 20 to 30 years in California, and a radical change in judicial attitude is not necessarily likely.

### REGIONAL AGENCIES

A variety of regional agencies play an important role in California planning. As mentioned above, three state agencies have direct land-use regulation power over specific areas of the state: the Bay Conservation and Development Commission, the Coastal Commission, and the Tahoe Regional Planning Agency. Local governments in these areas have little choice but to abide by the wishes of these powerful organizations.

The nominal "regional government" in most parts of the state is the "council of governments" (COG) — the Southern California Association of Governments (SCAG) in Los Angeles, the Association of Bay Area Governments (ABAG), the San Diego Association of Governments (SANDAG), and so on. These agencies were formed in the '60s, when state and federal officials thought powerful regional governments would serve a useful purpose. Their only real power, however, came from administering federal and state grants; when those grants waned, so did the power of the COGs.

But since the COGs were usually run by a group of local officials, rather than officials with a regional constituency, they rarely proved effective as regional governments anyway. (The one exception has been SANDAG, which reflects the cohesive attitude of local officials in San Diego County.) Because they draw up regional transportation plans and administer some transportation grants, they still have some power in this area. Generally, however, the COGs serve mostly as information sources and "think tanks" for regional problems.

As on the state level, the agencies that build infrastructure on a regional level are among the most powerful entities in the whole planning and development process. Like Caltrans, the Metropolitan Water District of Southern California, or MWD, has played a crucial role in establishing the state's development patterns. Essentially a consortium of local governments, MWD operates the Colorado River Aqueduct and doles out water to cities and counties. Many other regional and local water agencies have also played an important role in establishing development patterns by deciding which areas would receive water and which would not. As with Caltrans, these agencies historically did not make an effort to link their actions with the planning actions of local governments, nor has there ever been anything that might be called a statewide comprehensive plan for such agencies to adhere to. Like Caltrans, they simply responded to perceived demand.

Several other regional agencies established by the state also play an important role in land-use planning. Perhaps the most important are air-pollution-control districts and local agency formation commissions (LAFCOs).

Under the U.S. Clean Air Act, the air-pollution districts were established by the state in each county (and on a regional basis in Los Angeles and the Bay Area). Traditionally, they have regulated only "stationary" sources of air pollution, such as factories and oil refineries. Under pressure from both the federal government and environmentalists, they are now moving into aggressive efforts to cut down vehicle trips — an effort that may lead them directly into planning.

LAFCOs are established in each county by state law, and are made up of a combination of local officials. Though they have no direct power over land use, they rule on all incorporations, annexations, and other boundary changes. These boundary changes play an important role in establishing local development patterns because neighboring jurisdictions often have differing attitudes about growth. LAFCO boundary decisions also regulate the conversion of rural and agricultural land into urban development within cities. (Counties may allow new, urban-scale unincorporated communities without LAFCO approval.)

## LOCAL CITY COUNCILS, BOARDS OF SUPERVISORS, AND PLANNING COMMISSIONS

Once Congress, the legislature, and the courts have made the rules, local governments work within those rules to shape local land-use policies in the form of general plans, zoning ordinances, and decisions on individual projects. This work constitutes the guts of planning in California, and will be treated in great detail in later chapters. Nevertheless, a few introductory words about local governments and their role are necessary here.

California has only two types of "general purpose" local government: counties and cities. There are also many "special districts," formed to supply a specific service, such as water and sewer service or police and fire protection. These special districts do not have land-use regulation power, and usually they simply respond to the demand for water, police protection, etc., rather than plan and manage the growth of the community. Some unincorporated areas form "community service districts" — sometimes called "junior cities" — which do not have planning and zoning power but can regulate growth by controlling water, sewer, roads, and other services required by new development.

The legal purpose of cities and counties is different. Counties are creatures of the state government. They are subdivisions of the state (every square inch of California falls within one of its 58 counties); they were created by the state and their primary purpose is to implement state policy. Unlike many other states, California has not politically subdivided the counties into smaller entities such as townships.

Unlike counties, California's cities (of which there are about 450) are not creatures of the state. Rather, they are created by local citizens to serve their own purposes, especially to provide "urban" services (such as water and sewer service and a police force). Most counties are geographically large, while cities range from 1 square mile (Lawndale) to more than 400 (Los Angeles). Both cities and counties range in population from just a few hundred to several million.

Both counties and cities exercise power over land-use matters. Land-use power within city boundaries rests with those cities; land-use power outside city boundaries — in "unincorporated" areas — rests with counties. Thus, cities have a certain strategic territorial advantage. Any time a city incorporates or annexes more land, it wrests land-use power (as well as tax revenue) away from the county. At the same time, however, counties have important land-use powers as well. Counties are responsible for rural areas and therefore often determine the future of agricultural land. And counties also retain the opportunity to shape some communities, since new developments are often located in unincorporated areas. Many of these communities eventually incorporate or annex to cities, but many others do not; virtually all counties are responsible for some communities that are essentially urban or suburban in character.

Not all cities are created equal in California. Larger cities — as well as many smaller, older ones — are "charter" cities, meaning their city charters give them more discretion to establish land-use processes. (Such changes are subject to a vote of the city's residents.) Most smaller cities are "general law cities," meaning they do not have a city charter and must adhere more closely to state law. Thus, charter cities are more clearly separate entities from the state government, while general-law cities are more dependent.

Under state law, every county and every city has a legislative body and a planning "agency." A county's legislative body is called the board of supervisors, while a city's is called the city council. Almost all boards of supervisors, as well as most city councils, have five members. But there are some exceptions. The board of supervisors of the combined city and county of San Francisco (the only combined city and county in the state) has 11 members, while the Los Angeles City Council has 15. Most other large cities have seven-member city councils. But the board of supervisors in Los Angeles County, the largest local government in the country (with 8 million residents), has only five members.

Most local governments have separate planning commissions, though in a few tiny cities, the city council assumes the planning commission's duties. Most planning commissions consist of five or seven members appointed by the legislative body (though in Los Angeles and San Francisco the commissioners are appointed by the mayor as a check against the legislative body's power). Most local governments have a slew of other boards and commissions, but the planning commission is one of the few local bodies, other than the city council or board of supervisors, with the power to make legally binding decisions. (Most, if not all, such decisions are appealable to the local legislative body.)

Not all decisions made by local governments hold the same legal status. That's because local governments play more than one role. On the local level, the city or county can act, in a way, as legislature, court, and bureaucracy. That's why local decisions are divided into three categories: legislative, quasi-judicial, and ministerial. These categories are extremely important, because they define the duties of the legislative body and the planning commission; they determine which decisions are subject to initiative and referendum, and to CEQA; and they often determine the type of review a local decision will receive in court.

*Legislative* acts are general policy decisions, such as general plan revisions and zoning ordinances. These acts, which usually take the form of local ordinances, are no different than laws passed by the legislature or by Congress: They are policy statements that establish the rules by which everyone must play. For this reason, legislative acts are binding only when they are approved by a city council or board of supervisors. A planning commission may recommend a general plan amendment or zoning ordinance, but only the legislative body can approve and adopt it. Under California law (liberally construed by the courts), any legislative act is subject to initiative and referendum — meaning that virtually any general plan amendment or rezoning can be placed on the ballot.

*Quasi-judicial* acts are decisions that apply legislative policy to individual development projects, much as a court might apply legal precedents to a particular case. Like legislative acts, quasi-judicial acts involve some discretion on the part of the local government, meaning that a conditional use permit or a zoning variance could be turned down based on the judgment of the local officials. However, because quasi-judicial actions merely interpret policies, rather than set them, the planning commission's ruling is legally binding, though these decisions can be appealed to the city council or board of supervisors. For this same reason, quasi-judicial decisions cannot be placed on the ballot through the initiative and referendum process. (However, local citizens might force a reconsideration of the matter by the local council or board if they file a lawsuit with merit.)

*Ministerial* acts are actions in which the local government has no discretion. Usually a ministerial act involves the mandatory issuance of a permit if certain conditions are met. For example, if a development

**Types of local government decisions**

project has already been approved by a planning commission or a city council, then most likely the issuance of the building permit is a ministerial act, meaning the permit must be issued if the conditions of the development approval are met. Because they involve no discretion, ministerial decisions can sometimes be delegated to the staff level. Significantly, ministerial acts are not subject to initiative and referendum — and, unlike legislative and quasi-judicial acts, they are also exempt from environmental review under CEQA.

## LOCAL PLANNING STAFFS

Although they merely recommend actions to planning commissions, city councils, and boards of supervisors, local planning staffs wield tremendous influence over planning in California.

The planning department is typically headed by a planning director, who is in charge of all cases that come before the planning commission. In many cities, the planning department is part of a larger community development department, which encompasses related city activities such as housing, transportation, and building code enforcement. A city or county community development director will often interact with both planning commission and city council, especially on matters of policy, such as general plan amendments and zoning ordinances. A city manager or county administrative officer — though responsible for all day-to-day operations of the jurisdiction's departments — may also become personally involved in land-use issues when they are significant. Thus, these staff members hold primary responsibility for research and recommendations on virtually all actions in local government.

Staff members at the local level exert considerable influence for one particularly important reason: While state legislators, members of Congress, and judges work essentially full-time at their jobs, most members of city councils and planning commissions serve only part-time, with virtually no pay. (Large cities such as Los Angeles and San Diego have full-time council members, and county supervisors receive a full-time salary as well.) Of course, officials at higher levels of government must rely on their staff members as well, especially since they have such a broad range of responsibility. But because most local council members and planning commissioners have full-time jobs outside city government, they rarely have the opportunity to investigate an issue or a case independently. They have no choice but to rely on the information they receive from their staff. A planning commissioner may drive by a parcel of land before a meeting and look at it, but it is the staff planner who will research the history of the property in question and the codes that govern its use, and examine a proposal in detail for its merits..

Not all city council members or planning commissioners follow staff recommendations; in fact, some are hostile to the staff's ideas because they want to appear independent of the staff (or sometimes for ideological reasons). And, of course, local officials are not entirely dependent on the staff, because public hearings give them a chance to hear the views of the proponents and citizens directly. The truth is, however, that staff members control most of the information that goes to a local city council or planning commission, and they always have the last word in a debate at a public hearing.

Also, in many communities, staff members can assume some of the planning commission's functions by conducting public hearings and approving conditional use permits, or their equivalents, by sitting as "zoning administrators." The government code allows such quasi-judicial authority to be delegated to the staff by ordinance.

This does not mean that staff members always wield great power. In many cities they are mere functionaries who carry out the demands of elected officials, whether those elected officials have a slow-growth bent or close ties to developers. But because of their training and experience, top staff members are often regarded by their employers as experts in the field whose views must be given great weight. Their influence is far greater than their job descriptions might suggest.

## OTHERS

The organs of government are not the only important players in the planning process. Two groups outside the government also play an important role. Neither holds legal power — at least not technically — but both have legal rights that can be exercised aggressively. Both groups often initiate action that forces the organs of government to begin operating. And the two groups often (though not always) find themselves in opposition to each other.

The first group is usually referred to, in shorthand, as "developers," though this group really consists of a variety of people: farmers and other landowners; real estate developers and speculators; and individual homeowners and business people who seek the permission of local governments to build new structures or expand old ones. The second group can be called "citizen groups," though it really includes an amalgamation of all sorts of people who seek to influence the land-use process in order to pursue goals that are personal or principled in nature, as opposed to business goals. These include homeowner and neighborhood groups, who seek to protect and improve their neighborhoods as they see fit; as well as environmentalists, preservationists, and others who hope to protect a value they hold dear in the face of new real estate development.

In truth, these two groups drive the planning process as much as any legislator, judge, or bureaucrat. When a law is proposed in Congress or in the legislature, usually it is proposed at the request of one or more of these groups. On the legislative front, this might mean a coalition of environmental groups in Washington seeking tougher federal wetlands laws, or a group of homebuilders in Sacramento asking for more protection against slow-growth initiatives. In court, it could mean a local builder suing to prove a city's general plan inadequate, or a slow-growth group suing to force an environmental impact report on a big project. With local governments, of course, developers virtually always initiate specific projects; citizen groups frequently oppose the projects or, at least, suggest changes. Both groups are usually intimately involved in the creation of local general plans and zoning ordinances — with many developers and citizen-group representatives, for example, serving on advisory commissions.

The balance of power between these two groups is not always equal, though it is much closer to parity than ever before in California. Developers frequently have far more money to apply to a particular project or lobbying effort than their citizen counterparts do. This situation stems from the simple fact that developers are in business, and their actions, if successful, will lead to profit; while citizen groups — even if they are well-organized national institutions like the Sierra Club — must rely on memberships, donations, and grants for their funds. Thus, a developer trying to gain approval for a project can probably afford to hire lawyers, economists, site planners, and other consultants to bolster his case, while local homeowners must plot out their response in somebody's living room, often without any professional help. Similarly, a local slow-growth group campaigning for a growth-control initiative must rely on volunteers to run a successful campaign, while developers who oppose the initiative can probably pay campaign workers.

Over the past 20 years, however, state and federal laws designed to encourage citizen participation have narrowed the gap between developers and citizens. Environmental impact reports, required of all "significant" projects under CEQA, have provided citizens with a tremendous amount of information on the impact a proposed development is likely to have. The procedural requirements of CEQA and state planning law have given many citizen groups leverage over developers, and "citizen enforcement" powers give them the right to sue local governments if procedures are not followed. The political transformation of many small suburban cities from pro-growth to slow-growth has given many citizen groups a voice as well. Thus, on many projects, city governments require an extensive public review process, with lots of citizen participation. If negotiations take place between developer and city, citizen groups have a seat at the table as well. And occasionally, if the project is controversial enough and the citizens have enough leverage, developers will give citizen groups money to hire their own expert consultants.

## CHAPTER 2

# THE EMERGENCE OF REGULATORY TOOLS IN PLANNING

Governments may regulate the use of land because they hold "police" power — the power that permits them to restrict private activities in order to protect the public health, safety, and welfare. The legal basis for this power is strong. As the last chapter explained, this power is well established in common law; it is granted explicitly to local governments in the California Constitution; and the courts have expanded the definition of police power over the years.

Nevertheless, the true breadth and depth of the police power always seems to be in flux. The balance of power between the private property owner and the land-use regulator often changes, depending on the prevailing political and legal winds. The leeway that states allow their local governments in regulating land varies. And planning, a process which deliberately grants centralized regulatory power to government agencies, sometimes comes into conflict with the goals of a democratic society. In many ways, these three conflicts shape the regulatory tools used in planning.

The battle between land-use regulators and private property owners has been going on before the U.S. Supreme Court for more than 60 years now, from *Euclid v. Ambler* in 1926, which first upheld the constitutionality of zoning, to *First English Church v. Los Angeles County* in 1987, which established that an overly restrictive land-use regulation can constitute a "taking" of property. Regulators and property owners are always engaged in legal skirmishes on the frontier of land-use planning, moving the boundary of acceptable regulation back and forth.

During two periods in recent American history, states have reached out and grabbed considerable power from local governments over the regulation of land. The first period was in the early '70s, when environmental consciousness was at its zenith; it was during this period, for example, that the California Coastal Commission was established. The second period began in approximately 1985, when concerns about traffic congestion and suburban sprawl led to state-level "growth management" movements in states such as Florida and New Jersey. This current era of interest in state growth management has continued into the '90s — but largely without the participation of California, where local governments clung jealously to their land-use power and the state showed no interest in intervening.

Part of the reason California has resisted this recent movement — indeed, part of the reason that land-use regulation has remained largely in the hands of local governments everywhere — is the citizenry's understandable skepticism about centralized control of land. But some of the original impulses for land-use planning can be fairly described as elitist, and much of the recent history of the field has been a struggle to democratize a field not easily adapted to democratic processes.

Planning commissions and planning processes were originally designed, at least in part, to counterbalance the teeming and often corrupt political atmosphere in large cities in the early part of the 20th Century. Planning was too important to leave to the politicians, or so believed the old-line business leaders and power brokers who didn't trust the political machines that thrived in immigrant neighborhoods. Therefore, planning would be removed from politics and placed in the hands of non-partisan citizens (planning commissioners) and impartial experts (the planners themselves).

Planners and civic leaders often constituted an oligarchy that governed the development and redevelopment of their communities without much involvement from the citizens. Many of our most handsome communities (Santa Barbara, Pasadena, Carmel) were created by these oligarchies, who were able to impose strict aesthetic standards without much regard for the democratic process. In time, however, the unrest of environmentalists, homeowners, preservationists, and others forced a democratization of planning. The goal of planning is neat and orderly development; democracy, on the other hand, requires messy processes. And these conflicting requirements still do not rest comfortably next to each other in most planning processes.

## EARLY HISTORY OF LAND-USE CONTROLS

Traditionally, the land-use system involved both planning and zoning. Their purposes are very different. Planning is prospective, using broad policies to anticipate and plan for the orderly development of land in the future. Zoning is prescriptive, dividing land into categories of use and setting parameters for development. In theory, zoning is supposed to implement planning. (In California, zoning is supposed to implement the general plan.) In the early part of this century, however, zoning developed as a legal system more rapidly than planning, and the connection between the two has always been more tenuous in practice than in theory.

The first zoning ordinances appeared in the early years of the 20th Century, having evolved from common law principles that permitted restriction of neighborhood nuisances. Los Angeles passed a zoning ordinance in 1907, but the most famous early zoning ordinance was New York City's, which was passed in 1916. These early ordinances had many purposes, both overt and covert. Some were merely codification of so-called "nuisance" laws, separating supposedly noxious land uses from quiet residential neighborhoods. Others were designed to keep neighborhoods from getting overcrowded and overbuilt by restricting the number of dwelling units and requiring the preservation of light and air. Still others were meant to "stabilize" neighborhoods — often upper-middle-class, single-family neighbor- hoods — faced with the encroachment of nearby tenements

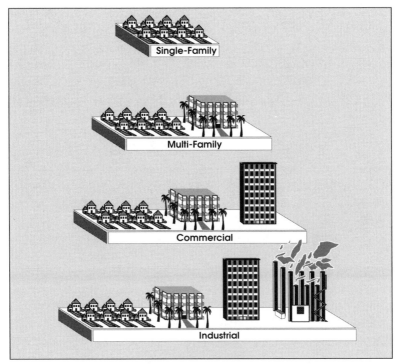

**Cumulative zoning**

and, supposedly, a corresponding decline in property values.

From the very beginning, however, most of these zoning ordinances shared a common goal that is important to note: the preservation, above all else, of the single-family neighborhood. All early zoning ordinances called for a separation of land uses, but the system — called "cumulative" zoning — was really a pyramid, with industrial property at the bottom and single-family homes at the top. Any land-use zone could accommodate uses above it on the pyramid, but not those below it. Thus, anything could be built in industrial zones: commercial development, apartments, even single-family houses. In commercial zones, located just above industrial on the pyramid, anything could be built except industrial buildings. At the top of the pyramid stood the single-family zones, which permitted no construction of any kind except for single-family homes.

Planning documents evolved on a separate track, one much more closely allied with architecture and urban design than with law. The early master plans, such as Daniel Burnham's famous 1909 plan for Chicago, carried no legal force nor even, usually, official government sponsorship; rather, they were the grand visions of private civic leaders, suggesting a possible course for the physical development of their communities.

The great leap forward for both planning and zoning came in the 1920s, when Herbert Hoover, who at that time was the highly respected Secretary of Commerce, engineered the passage of the Standard State Zoning Enabling Act (SZEA) in 1922 and the Standard City Planning Enabling Act (SPEA) in 1928. Neither of these federal laws imposed any enforceable requirements on states or cities. Rather, they laid out model ordinances that states and localities might adopt or adapt, and in so doing stamped the federal government's symbolic imprint on the idea comprehensive plans and zoning ordinances.

SZEA sanctioned the idea of local governments dividing their territory into zones, with uniform regulations in each zone — a key characteristic of what later became known as "Euclidean" zoning. SPEA created a model ordinance dealing with what today's Californians would call the general plan process — laying out the powers of a planning commission, content of the plan, and so on — as well as a municipality's subdivision powers.

The passage of both these laws created a tidal wave of activity in state legislatures and local governments throughout the country. Using SZEA as a model, state legislatures passed their own enabling legislation, formally confirming that local governments' police powers extended to zoning. In response to SPEA, many states also passed planning laws, encouraging or requiring local governments to draw up comprehensive plans.

California had entered the land-use field some 20 years earlier in 1907, when the legislature passed the first Subdivision Map Act. But, like other states, California did not pass the first laws dealing with planning and zoning until the 1920s. In 1927, just prior to the passage of SPEA, the state legislature passed the first law authorizing cities and counties to prepare "master plans." (This law was among the first in the country dealing with comprehensive plans.) Two years later, shortly after the passage of SPEA, the general plan law was amended to reflect its provisions. Most significantly, any city or county which had established a planning commission, as SPEA had called for, was now required to prepare a general plan. In 1937, the state amended the law again to require all cities and counties to prepare general plans. This step was remarkably ahead of its time; even today, local planning and zoning is not required in all states.

The '20s was a time of enthusiasm for zoning and planning in California and throughout the country. However, the quick passage of so many laws in so many states and cities brought problems as well.

For one thing, zoning and planning were rarely used together, even though they dealt with the same area of public policy. SZEA and many state zoning enabling acts called for zoning ordinances to be prepared "in accordance with a comprehensive plan." By and large, however, they were not. Urban designers and civic visionaries went about the business of preparing "end-state" comprehensive plans, which showed how a city was supposed to look at some endpoint in time 20 or 30 years down the road. Meanwhile, in the day-to-day business of city-building, lawyers worried about zoning and ignored plans.

"If a plan was thought of, more often than not it consisted of a map of blobs vaguely suggesting how the community should look in 25 years," wrote the eminent planning lawyer Richard Babcock in his chapter on zoning in *The Practice of Local Government Planning*. "Once drawn, such a 'plan' was tacked on a wall and was forgotten while the local planning commission and city council went about the business of acting upon innumerable requests for changes in the zoning map."

In California, state law did not require consistency between general plans and zoning until 1971 — more than 40 years after the passage of the first general plan law. Although the courts now take this legal requirement seriously, many cities and counties were slow to comply with it. Los Angeles did not undertake a reconciliation between planning and zoning until forced by court order to do so in the late 1980s.

The other problem that arose in the midst of the land-use planning euphoria of the 1920s was legal in nature. The '20s was perhaps the zenith of private enterprise in the United States, and property owners often regarded these new regulations as an unconstitutional infringement of their rights. There were several different constitutional arguments (and they have gone in and out of fashion ever since), but, in general, they fell into three categories: due process, equal protection, and just compensation.

Due process, in particular, was a sticky legal point, because in the latter half of the 19th Century, as government regulation grew, the courts had created a concept called "substantive due process." A government might violate an individual's constitutional rights to "procedural" due process by not according him a fair hearing in some way. But government regulation might also be unconstitutional in the sense that it does not advance a legitimate governmental purpose. In the '20s, many landowners argued that zoning was not a legitimate use of the police power, and therefore their property had been "taken" through a violation of substantive due process.

The equal protection argument was easier to understand but no less important. By dividing land into different use categories, the argument went, a zoning ordinance favored some landowners over others, and therefore denied some landowners equal protection under the law. The constitutional questions cast a shadow over the legality of zoning ordinances, even after the passage of SZEA in 1922, as literally thousands of lawsuits were filed challenging the ordinances.

The just compensation argument arose from the Fifth Amendment to the Constitution, which prohibits the government from "taking" a citizen's property without paying that citizen just compensation; it would not emerge as the leading issue in constitutional land-use law until the 1970s. In the 1920s, the arguments were associated instead with the Fourteenth Amendment's guarantees of due process and equal protection.

## EUCLID V. AMBLER

The legal issues finally came to a head in 1926, when the constitutionality of zoning power was debated by a conservative United States Supreme Court that could not, in advance, have been expected to uphold it. As Seymour Toll explained in his fine account of the case in the book *Zoned American,* the case of *Village of Euclid, Ohio, v. Ambler Realty Co.**  was a test case brought by the real estate industry, selected because it provided a strong and clear-cut attack on zoning.

Euclid was a pleasant "streetcar suburb" of Cleveland that had enacted a zoning ordinance in 1922 to forestall the encroachment of industry and apartment buildings. Ambler Realty owned 68 acres of land in Euclid. Most of Ambler's property was zoned for broad commercial and industrial use, but some of it was restricted to one- and two-family houses.

Ambler claimed that the zoning ordinance took its property without due process of law and denied the company equal protection under the law. Ambler's prospects looked good. There was little doubt that the zoning ordinance had reduced the value of Ambler's property, and the Supreme Court in the 1920s, under the leadership of former President William Howard Taft, was perhaps the most reactionary of the century.

Yet the court upheld the Euclid ordinance on a 6-3 vote. In part, this decision arose from a recognition of "the complex conditions of our day," as compared with the "comparatively simple" urban life that had existed only a few decades before. Crowded cities, the justices seemed to suggest, provided a legitimate rationale for more regulation.

At the same time, there can be no question that the elitist nature of zoning in suburban communities also appealed to these conservative justices. The decision is littered with remarks that seem to reveal a certain prejudice against the lower classes and a sympathetic attitude toward keeping them out of the suburbs. In the course of their opinion, the justices attribute nerve disorders, street accidents, and assorted other social maladies to apartment life, and call the apartment house "a mere parasite, constructed in order to take advantage of the open spaces and attractive surroundings created by the residential character of the district'' — as if only single-family neighborhoods, and not apartment blocks, could be deemed "residential."

*Euclid v. Ambler* upheld the constitutionality of zoning. But just as

*Euclid v. Ambler Realty Co., 272 U.S. 365 (1926).

important, it helped to legitimize zoning's hidden and somewhat elitist agenda. The U.S. Supreme Court reaffirmed the belief, embedded in many zoning laws, that the single-family home provided a particularly healthful way of life, and that single-family neighborhoods (and their property values) were singularly entitled to legal protection. After a clarifying ruling two years later, the Supreme Court departed from the land-use scene for close to 50 years, returning to deal with the issue of "takings" only in the 1970s and '80s. In the meantime, affluent suburbanites used zoning aggressively to reinforce the social values the Supreme Court had laid out in Euclid.

## POST-WAR PLANNING: EXCLUSIVE AND EXCLUSIONARY

With Euclid in hand, planners and land-use lawyers set out to apply the case's legal principles to zoning ordinances throughout the country. The two most important principles were the division of all of a municipality's land into use districts and the more or less equal treatment of property owners within each district. Both of these principles were meant to ensure that police powers advanced a legitimate governmental purpose — protecting substantive due process rights — and also to provide landowners with equal protection under the law. Together they formed the basis of what became known, both for its connection with the Supreme Court case and its geometric appeal, as "Euclidean" zoning.

Procedural due process was supposed to be ensured by fair and expeditious hearings on zoning and planning issues, but as Babcock pointed out in *The Zoning Game*, from the '20s on, local governments and their planners frequently undermined due process by "our medieval hearings, our casual record-keeping, and our occult decision-making."

When the postwar prosperity led to the construction of massive housing tracts in the suburbs, however, one early tenet of zoning fell by the wayside: cumulative zoning. In its place, planners created "exclusive" zoning, a system which permitted one — and only one — use in each zoning district. Thus, just as only single-family homes could be built in single-family zones, now only industrial buildings could be built in industrial zones, or apartment buildings in apartment

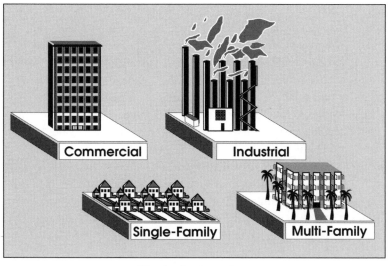

**'Exclusive' zoning**

zones. Such separation was facilitated, of course, by the automobile, which permitted easy mobility from one zone to another (at least in those days!).

In the same way that an earlier generation of zoning laws had reinforced the idea that single-family living was a superior way of life, "exclusive" zoning cemented in the public consciousness the notion that any mixing of land uses was unhealthy. In the post-war era, suburban jurisdictions throughout the country were able to use their zoning powers — along with these two widely accepted principles of planning philosophy — to create "exclusionary" zoning policies. Large lot requirements, setback standards, and a general reluctance to zone land for anything other than single-family residential use ensured that teeming cities would not spill over into affluent, pastoral suburbs.

As new legal techniques were added to the zoning arsenal, they were deployed for the same purposes. The variance had been created early in the history of zoning to deal with pieces of land that, for some reason or another, could not conform to standard zoning requirements. But the bosses of big-city political machines quickly recognized zoning's value in rewarding or penalizing developers, depending on their political loyalties. In the suburbs, the emergence of the special permit, sometimes called the conditional use permit, allowed local governments to deny a landowner permission to build even if his project otherwise met all legal requirements. This additional discretionary power was used frequently against supposedly "undesirable" land uses — however they might be defined by a particular local government.

The '50s also saw the emergence of another legal technique that would become a powerful tool of discretion in land-use matters: urban renewal. First authorized as a "slum clearance" program in the federal Housing Act of 1949, urban renewal — or redevelopment, as it is called today — permitted local governments to acquire blighted land via eminent domain, then turn it over to another private developer who promised to clean it up. California's Community Redevelopment Law was first passed in 1945 and substantially revised in 1951. Fueled by federal dollars, massive redevelopment programs were in place in Los Angeles, San Francisco, and other large California cities by the end of the decade.

The decade of the '50s also brought the beginnings of the modern general plan in California. As noted above, California's first planning requirements, imposed in the '20s and '30s, were way ahead of their time, and laid the groundwork for a modern body of law unmatched by any other state. While some other states have no state planning or zoning requirements (two-thirds of Georgia's counties had no zoning at the end of the '80s), all of California's cities and counties must establish a planning agency and prepare and adopt a general plan. These requirements were first centrally organized in the state's government code in 1953 (Sections 65000 et seq., where they remain today as the so-called Planning, Zoning & Development Law), and two years later the state imposed its first specific requirements on general plans: all plans had to contain at least two "elements," one dealing with land use and the other dealing with circulation. Thus, a general plan prepared in the late '50s would bear at least a passing resemblance to a general plan of today.

These general plans were far from perfect. They were virtually unconnected to zoning ordinances, which established the precise nature of a city's development patterns. Rather, they were usually regarded merely as guidebooks for the general pattern of a community's future growth — more useful, probably, to the public works department than to the zoning administrator. And they still envisioned a community's future in static, "end-state" terms, rather than recognizing the fact that communities are always changing and evolving. The '60s and '70s, however, brought a series of profound changes — changes that challenged virtually all of the long-standing tenets of law and practice in land-use planning.

## THE DEMOCRATIZATION OF PLANNING

The tumultuous social changes of the '60s and '70s created a new set of public-policy priorities which, while they did not always affect land-use planning directly, had a major impact on the field indirectly. These new priorities were characterized by a greater sensitivity to environmental damage and a much more open and inclusive decision-making process. As a result, such traditional staples of planning as uniform zoning requirements, the end-state plan, and broad use of the police power were first altered and then dramatically changed.

In general, these changes can be traced back to four somewhat related trends: stricter environmental laws, greater citizen power, the fiscal problems of local government, and the rise of the modern property-rights movement.

### THE GREENING OF AMERICA: ENVIRONMENTAL LAWS

"There is a new mood in America," the Rockefeller Brothers Fund Task Force on Land Use and Urban Growth reported in 1973. "Increasingly, citizens are asking what urban growth will add to the quality of their lives. They are questioning the way piecemeal urbanization is changing their communities and are rebelling against the traditional processes of government.... They are measuring new development proposals by the extent to which environmental criteria are satisfied — by what new housing or business will generate in terms of additional traffic, pollution of air and water, erosion, and scenic disturbance."

This "new mood" helped force passage of two landmark environmental laws: the National Environmental Policy Act, or NEPA, passed in 1969, and the California Environmental Quality Act, or CEQA, passed in 1970. Both (but especially CEQA) had a profound effect on planning by establishing systems of environmental review for development projects in California.

In a sense, these new laws tried to stand traditional planning principles on their head. Unlike zoning, these laws did not constitute a set of development limitations intended to ensure that all pieces of property dedicated to similar uses were treated the same. Quite the opposite: They established procedures, such as preparation of "environmental impact reports," also known as EIRs (or environmental impact "statements," or EIS's, in federal jargon), designed to assure that each piece of land's differences were taken into account. The same project built on different pieces of land might affect the environment and the surrounding communities in entirely different ways, and therefore might be subject to completely different regulations. Thus, a procedure that stood somewhat in conflict with traditional land-use planning system was simply grafted onto that system.

## CITIZEN POWER

Up until the '60s, "public participation" in the planning process rarely consisted of much more than perfunctory public hearings before the local planning commission. The real decisions about planning in a community were still made largely behind closed doors, by elected officials, developers, public works officials, and planners. The '60s and '70s, however, saw the rise of "citizen power" — a term that can be applied loosely to encompass the empowerment of slum dwellers, consumer activism, neighborhood organizing, and the birth of both the environmental movement and the historic preservation movement.

In part these organizations obtained power over the land-use planning process simply by grabbing it — through direct action such as street demonstrations, political organization, and use of the media. When politicians and courts didn't respond, citizens were able to take large-scale political action that sent a ringing message to the authorities. Perhaps the most dramatic example in California was the passage of Proposition 20, the 1972 coastal initiative, which took land-use planning power along the coast away from local governments and gave it, instead, to a new state coastal commission.

In time, however, both politicians and the courts responded to these demands for power by creating a much more wide-open process. And this process contained many levers that citizen groups could use to their advantage. CEQA, for example, was designed mostly as a law to empower ordinary citizens; its chief function remains to bring lots of information about a project's environmental impact out into public view. Under CEQA, public access to the information is just as important as the information itself, meaning that citizen groups have many legal steps at their disposal to flush the information out if they can't get it any other way.

In this environment of citizen activism, even the long-ignored general plan took on a new importance. In the '60s, California courts began taking seriously the language contained in state law about the general plan's significance. In 1965, an appellate court first called the plan "a constitution for all future development in the city."* Six years later, the legislature required — at last — that zoning ordinances be consistent with their accompanying general plans.** These changes made the general plan a significant lever for citizen groups seeking to hold local governments and developers accountable.

Thus, by the mid '70s, citizen activists had forced onto the land-use agenda the social and environmental costs of development that zoning had never addressed. Just as important, the rise of citizen power encouraged a kind of flexibility that land-use planning had never seen before. No longer was certainty and consistency the system's goal; instead, the goal was to minimize social and environmental costs and mollify the citizen groups that could stop a project. Thus, for the first time since the inception of zoning, landowners did not always know in advance what they would be able to build. In this environment, the "end-state" plan seemed less relevant than ever.

* * *

* *O'Loane v. O'Rourke*, 231 Cal.App.2d 774 (1965), at page 782.
** Government Code Sections §65860, 65587, 65910.

## FISCAL PROBLEMS

The rapid urban growth of the '60s and early '70s brought about a voracious need for new public facilities like roads, sewers, police stations, schools, and libraries. In time, an elaborate financing system sprung up to provide these facilities — a combination of federal grants (for water and sewer systems), state grants (for roads and schools), and local bond issues (for the rest of the facilities).

In the '70s, however, this system came crashing down. Federal and state budget cuts virtually eliminated local grants. And the passage of Proposition 13 in 1978 cut local property taxes by two-thirds, and made it virtually impossible for local governments to raise those taxes again in order to pay debt service.

These financial problems have probably helped to shape California's development patterns in the last decade almost as much as the land-use planning system itself. Strapped for capital funds, most cities and counties demanded that developers provide the money needed for public infrastructure — a trend that has altered the scale and price of new buildings of all sorts. Also, financially strapped communities, which might once have purchased land for open space or parks, are now more inclined to place severe land-use restrictions on it in order to preserve it, or to demand dedications of park lands in return for development permits.

Just as important, California's communities entered into a brutal economic competition for new development, which was virtually the only way of obtaining new tax revenue. Many communities engaged in "fiscal zoning" — encouraging construction of tax-rich projects (shopping malls, auto dealerships, hotels), while discouraging construction of tax-poor projects (principally housing and especially lower-cost housing). Many more have used redevelopment aggressively to subsidize tax-rich projects. The result is an "imbalance" of land uses in many communities because of financial considerations.

## PROPERTY RIGHTS

Toward the end of the '70s, the dramatic changes of the previous 15 years created a counter-reaction: the "property rights" movement.

Especially in California, landowners and developers felt ravaged by uncertainty, by fiscal demands, and by the opposition of citizen groups. So, for the first time since the '20s, they launched a broad-based counterattack, claiming that modern land-use regulation had gone so far that it had actually become confiscatory and, therefore, unconstitutional.

At first the property rights movement fared poorly. In the '70s, developers lost a series of cases on the issue of "vested rights," and the result was that it was harder for a developer to "vest" his right to build in California than in any other state. In 1979, the California Supreme Court ruled against developers in *Agins v. Tiburon*\* by ruling that a landowner who claimed his property had been "taken" by regulation was entitled only to an invalidation of the ordinance, not to just compensation. (As a result, for years most California landowners could not even get a court hearing in a regulatory taking case.)

As the political winds shifted to the right, however, the property rights movement began to score some victories. In 1981, the legislature passed the "development agreement" statute, which permits developers to enter into long-term contracts with local government that secure the developer's vested rights. And in 1987, the U.S. Supreme Court issued two important rulings — both in cases from California — that constituted a victory for the property rights movement.

The first, *First English Evangelical Lutheran Church v. County of Los Angeles,*\*\* was the most important ruling since Euclid v. Ambler. The Supreme Court overturned the Agins decision and ruled that a property owner whose land was taken by regulation is entitled to just compensation, even if the taking was only temporary. (The question of under what circumstances a regulatory taking actually occurs, however, remained open.) In the second, *Nollan v. California Coastal Commission,*\*\*\* a divided (5-4) court ruled that exactions and other

---

\* *Agins v. City of Tiburon,* 24 Cal.3d 266 (1979). The U.S. Supreme Court later declined to take the case, concluding it was not ripe for its judicial review. *Agins v. City of Tiburon,* 447 U.S. 255 (1980).
\*\* *First English Evangelical Lutheran Church of Glendale v. County of Los Angeles,* 482 U.S. 304 (1987).
\*\*\* *Nollan v. California Coastal Commission,* 483 U.S. 825 (1987).

conditions of approval placed on a development permit must be directly related to the project under consideration. While these two decisions did not lead to a flood of litigation, as some predicted, they have moved the pendulum of regulation back toward property owners for the first time in 60 years.

## A SYSTEM FILLED WITH FRICTION

Because of all these dramatic changes, planning in the '90s is characterized by friction everywhere. There is friction between traditional zoning, in which like landowners are treated alike, and environmental review, in which each piece of land is dealt with differently. There is friction between the power of citizen groups, which breeds uncertainty, and the renewed property rights of landowners. There is friction between those same property rights and the fiscal demands cities and counties place on developers. And there is friction between the uncertain and somewhat flexible nature of current land-use planning — created by all of the above conditions — and the traditional concept of the end-state general plan.

In short, over the past 70 years, generation after generation of planning tools and techniques have been added to the pile, with little thought to how they all work together. In the next several chapters, we will discuss these tools and techniques individually. But it is important to remember that many of California's planning problems are inherent in the conflicts among these competing planning tools.

# CHAPTER 3

# THE BASIC TOOLS, PART 1: THE GENERAL PLAN

On a day-to-day basis, planning in California is carried out through the use of three basic tools: the general plan, the zoning ordinance, and the subdivision ordinance. These three are not the only tools at the disposal of local government; there are also several more sophisticated tools, which will be discussed in Chapter 6. Nevertheless, these three tools do most of the work, and no one can truly understand California's planning system without understanding what they are and how they operate.

The *general plan* (required by Government Code §65300 *et seq.*) is California's version of the "master" or "comprehensive" plan. It lays out the future of the city's development in general terms through a series of policy statements (in text and map form).

The *zoning ordinance* (authorized by Government Code §65850 *et seq.*) is, at least theoretically, the "beast of burden" for the general plan, designed to translate the general plan's broad policy statements into specific requirements on individual landowners. The zoning ordinance divides all land in the city into zones and specifies the permitted uses and required standards in each zone.

The *Subdivision Map Act* (Government Code §66410 *et seq.*) is a state law that establishes the procedures local governments must use when considering the subdivision of land. The Map Act is intended to ensure, among other things, that adequate public services will be provided to these new subdivisions.

Some overlap exists among these three tools. Generally speaking, however, they are meant to be used together to ensure the orderly development of communities in California.

## GENERAL PLANS

Over the past 20 years, the general plan has emerged as the most important document in local planning in California. Though the state government required every city and county to produce a general plan beginning in 1937, more than 30 years later the plan remained little more than an advisory document. In fact, as prominent land-use lawyer Daniel J. Curtin, Jr., points out in his book *California Land-Use and Planning Law*, up until 1971 state law even permitted local governments to adopt a zoning ordinance before they adopted a general plan.

In 1971, however, the state legislature passed a law requiring counties and most cities to bring their zoning ordinances and subdivision procedures into conformance with their general plans. Ironically, this law was originally drafted with the narrow purpose of controlling second-home subdivisions. Nevertheless, the "consistency" law, as it is usually known, became one of the most important planning laws in California history, because it essentially reversed the legal power of the general plan and the zoning ordinance.

In the past, the zoning ordinance usually had the most "teeth," but today its legal function is to serve as a tool by which the general plan is implemented. As one appellate court wrote, the consistency law "transformed the general plan from just an 'interesting study' to the basic land-use charter governing the direction of future land use in the local jurisdiction."* (The consistency legislation applies only to counties and general-law cities. But a later state law specifically required Los Angeles's zoning to be consistent with its general plan, and some legal opinions suggest that other charter cities are subject to the provisions

---

* *City of Santa Ana v. City of Garden Grove*, 100 Cal.App.3d 521,532 (1979).

as well. In addition, according to the state Office of Planning and Research, at least 60 of the state's 83 charter cities have local ordinances requiring consistency.)

Perhaps the best way to understand the general plan is to think of it, as many court rulings have done, as the "constitution" for the future development of a community. As the constitution, the general plan is the supreme document from which all local land-use decisions must be derived. Its constitutional nature also gives the general plan two other characteristics that are important to note as well:

• Like a constitution, it is truly "general." The general plan contains a set of broad policy statements about the goals for future development of the city. But usually it does not contain specific implementation procedures. That's why the zoning ordinance and other implementation tools are needed. (Occasionally the general plan and zoning ordinance are combined as one document, but more typically the zoning ordinance is written after the general plan has been adopted.)

• Also like a constitution, it may be amended and revised, and these amendments and revisions often create an important forum for debate about the future of a community. Generally speaking, specific amendments (which are usually designed to accommodate a particular new development project) are limited to four per year. Large-scale revisions typically take place once or twice per decade. The process of drawing up and adopting these revisions often becomes, essentially, a "constitutional convention," at which many different citizens and interest groups debate the community's future.

## WHAT THE GENERAL PLAN CONTAINS

General plans come in all shapes and sizes. Some are slick and colorful; others consist of little more than some typewritten text and a couple of rudimentary diagrams. But all general plans share certain characteristics.

Most important, all general plans are supposed to contain a vision for the community's future. At its best, the general plan identifies a community's hopes and aspirations and translates them into a set of policies laying out the community's physical development. Considering how few restraints the state really imposes on the content of general plans, it is remarkable how rarely a general plan actually contains a thoughtful vision of its community's future. Most contain a preamble that includes a set of inspirational comments. But the policies that generate widespread public debate usually revolve around some quantitative measurement of the future: the eventual population, the number of housing units to be added, the amount of commercial square footage that will be permitted. In most general plans, remarkably little attention is paid to design, quality of life, and the likely patterns of day-to-day life that will emerge as a result of the plan's policies.

Many general plans also encompass "area plans," which are more specific versions of the general plan dealing with smaller geographical areas. Area plans, sometimes known as community plans, have the same force of law as the general plan. (They are different, however, from "specific plans," which will be dealt with in Chapter 4.) Most general plans also include some kind of "technical background report," consisting of quantitative information about the city's demography, housing stock, economic make-up, and other aspects of the community. This information is used as documentation to support the policy direction laid out in the general plan. Also important in shaping policy direction for the general plan are the circulation element and the soils, slopes, and seismic subsections of the safety element, which are — or should be — the primary determinants of any limitations on the use of land and on the pattern, location, and character of development. These are the constraints which, if properly identified and mapped, form the "reality check" around which land-use preferences are expressed in the land-use element.

The general plan also must follow certain state requirements contained in the state Planning, Zoning, and Development Law.* The fact that the general plan is the "constitution" — the supreme local land-use document — does not mean it is exempt from state laws.

As one might expect, the state's general plan requirements do not attempt to force local governments into specific policy conclusions. Nor is a city's layout, mix of uses, height limitations, character, economic development, or any number of other matters the concern of the

---

* Government code §65030 *et seq.;* general plan requirements begin with §65300.

state. Rather, local governments are required to follow certain procedures and cover certain subject areas (called "elements") in the general
plan. Similarly, the state does not, generally speaking, review general
plans for compliance with state law; such compliance is ensured only
through litigation. (The housing element is something of an exception
to both of these statements, and for this reason will be dealt with in a
separate section later in this chapter.)

Under state law, every local general plan must include seven "elements," or sections. These include the following:

• *The land-use element*, the most basic part of the plan, deals with
such matters as population density, building intensity, and the distribution of land uses within the city or county.

• *The circulation element* must deal with all major transportation
improvements. It serves as an infrastructure plan and also must be
"correlated" with the land-use element specifically — that is, the
infrastructure laid out in the circulation element must correspond with
the needs required by the development patterns expected by the land-
use element.

• *The housing element* must assess the need for housing for all
income groups and lay out a program to meet those needs.

• *The conservation element* deals with the need to address natural
resource issues such as flood control, water and air pollution, agricultural land, and endangered species.

• *The open-space element* is supposed to provide a plan for the long-
term conservation of open space in the community.

• *The noise element* must identify noise problems in the community,
as well as measures for noise abatement.

• *The safety element* must identify seismic, geologic, flood, and
wildfire hazards, and establish policies to protect the community from
them.

These seven elements are not etched in stone by the state. The legislature may amend the general plan law to add or subtract required elements whenever it wishes. From 1970 to 1984, for example, the state
required separate elements to deal with scenic highways and seismic
safety, but then folded those requirements into other elements. Recent
legislative proposals have called for a revision of the circulation ele-

ment (renaming it the transportation element) and the addition of a separate air-quality element, though at this writing these proposals have not been enacted into law.

Communities may add other elements to the general plan if they wish, and most cities and counties do add at least three or four more. The specific mix of elements will vary depending on the needs of each community, but typical additional elements include human resources, economic development, historic preservation, and community design. Virtually any area of community concern may be addressed in a sepa-

rate element, but once an element is included in the general plan, it carries the same force of law as the seven elements required by the state.

It is also permissible to combine elements, and many communities do so. A particularly popular technique is a combined land-use and circulation element, because the distribution of land uses and the construction of roads and transit lines are closely related, and because state law requires a specific correlation between them anyway.

Perhaps the most important legal principle concerning the general plan's elements is that they must be consistent with each other. Not only must the zoning ordinance and other planning documents be consistent with the general plan, the general plan's provisions must be internally consistent as well. (Under law they are all regarded as equally important.)

The reasons for this requirement are obvious. A city council intent on pleasing all interest groups could be tempted to pass conflicting policies. For example, the city may enact an open-space plan that says 80 percent of the city's land will be set aside for open space, and at the same time approve a housing element that says 80 percent of the city's land will be set aside for housing. The internal consistency requirement is meant to assure that the general plan is not only visionary, but also realistic.

It is probably impossible, however, to draw up a general plan that is totally free of internal inconsistencies, meaning that most general plans are, at least theoretically, vulnerable to legal attack. Indeed, the consistency requirements — both zoning consistency and internal consistency — have been a favorite tool of builders in trying to strike down growth-control initiatives.

## THE LAND-USE ELEMENT

Although the general plan deals with many aspects of a community and its future, perhaps its most basic job is to chart a course for the community's future physical development. And for this reason the land-use element is the broadest-ranging, the most important, and — usually — the most highly publicized aspect of the general plan.

At its core, the land-use element must lay out a vision of the distribution, location, and intensity of all land uses in the city — not just what they are now, but what they will be in the future. Perhaps the most important piece of the land-use element is the diagram (or diagrams) that accompany the text. This diagram is, in essence, a graphic representation of the policies laid out in the land-use element, and it must be consistent with the written text.

Because it looks like a map, the land-use diagram often becomes the focal point of discussion. Residents can relate much more directly to the diagram than to the written text. They can identify the part of town where they live and see what the land- use element calls for in that area. In many ways, this is good, because it sparks discussion and gets the residents involved in the process of preparing the land-use element. In some ways, however, it is not so good. The diagram and its vivid graphic elements — bright colors, geometric shapes, and so forth — can confuse residents into thinking that the map's potential will be fully realized — especially if they see something on the diagram that they don't like.

For this reason, it is important to note that the land-use diagram is not necessarily a map, nor is it required to be by law. Unlike a zoning map, it does not have to show the impact of the city's regulations on every single parcel of land. Rather, it is merely a graphic representation of a series of policy statements. The diagram does not say, "We are going to put this building on this parcel." Instead, it says, "Generally speaking, in this part of town we're going to permit and encourage these kinds of developments." The diagram doesn't even have to look like a map; it could be a schematic diagram or even something more abstract, as long as it gets the message across to the citizens.

Aside from the diagram and the general statements about "location and distribution" of land uses in the city, the land-use element is required by state law to deal more specifically with certain aspects of land-use planning in in the community:

*Distribution and location of uses.* State law requires the land-use element to discuss the general distribution of some land uses and the specific location of others.

The land-use element must address the distribution of: housing, business, and industry; open space and agricultural land; mineral resources; and recreational facilities. As with the land-use diagram, these discussions do not have to identify the specific parcels where these uses are or will be located. Rather, they must reveal general patterns in the community.

The question of specific location must be dealt with, however, for certain land uses — mostly uses that require the intimate involvement of public agencies: educational facilities; public buildings and grounds; and future solid and liquid waste facilities. The land-use element must also identify flood plains, and, in high-altitude cities, timber lines.

The reasons for these requirements should be clear. The basic role of the land-use element is to lay out the general patterns of development in the community. If local governments have to identify the probable future location of public facilities, as well as the current location of flood plains and timber lines, they are much more likely to consider whether the broad land-use patterns they are establishing bear a relationship to their own public works projects, and to natural barriers to development.

*Standards for density and intensity.* The land-use element must lay out standards for population density and building intensity.

Many communities deal with population density by including a projected "ultimate" population for the city or county, and perhaps even for sub-areas as well. A city does not regulate the actual number of people moving in or out of it; rather, the population density projections are translated into dwelling units per acre. Each neighborhood is assigned a "standard" in terms of dwelling units per acre (between four and eight, say, in a single-family neighborhood; 35, 50, or even more in a multi-family neighborhood). Collectively, these standards will be used to create both the density and distribution of population called for in the land-use element's broad policy statements.

Standards for building intensity are required to avoid the problem of using vague terms in drawing up land-use policies. The land-use diagram, for example, may call for "regional commercial" development along a local freeway, "service and neighborhood commercial" projects adjacent to residential neighborhoods, and "very low-density" residential development on the edge of town. But these general terms must be defined more specifically somewhere in the general plan. For example, while the diagram may earmark an area for "very low-density" development, a section of the land-use element dealing with standards may define "very low density" as meaning, specifically one unit for every two acres of land.

*Relationship to other elements.* The land-use element, of course, must be consistent with all other elements of the general plan, as well as with the general plan's other provisions. Nevertheless, two specific relationships are worth noting.

The land-use element must bear a close correlation to the circulation element. That is, the circulation element must explicitly call for the creation of a transportation system that is capable of handling the circulation needs of the community being constructed under the provisions of the land-use element. Though the land-use element must be consistent with other elements, the correlation with the circulation element is regarded as particularly important. It would be counter-productive to earmark an area for future development without also identifying the transportation facilities that would be required to accommodate that growth.

The land-use element must also maintain a close relationship to the noise element. This requirement means that the noise "contours"* and standards developed in the noise element must be used in the land-use element to determine what the land-use patterns will be. For example, if a vacant district lies next to a freeway, the land-use element must recognize that noise from the freeway will have an impact on the adjacent land. Thus, the land-use element might call for industrial buildings or warehouses on the vacant property, or else require the construction of sound barriers if it is to be part of a residential district.

Generally speaking, while the land-use element must meet certain general requirements, the specifics are up to each individual community. While the state planning law requires that a land-use element must identify the location of future schools and public buildings, it imposes no standards. The law does not say the schools must be located in a particular part of town. The law does not even say that the schools must be located near the houses where the students will live. The law merely says that the land-use element must specify the location of the schools. This approach is different from that of several other states, notably Oregon and Florida, which review local plans and require that they be held strictly to state goals and standards. Nevertheless, the approach is in keeping with California's general attitude toward local planning, which is to set up the process and then stay out of it.

* * *

* Noise "contours" are similar to topographical contours. Noise specialists measure decibel levels in many locations and then map the resulting "contours" at which those decibel levels occur.

## THE HOUSING ELEMENT

The one area of the general plan where the state does not take a passive role is the housing element. The state legislature has declared that the provision of housing for all segments of the community is a matter of statewide concern, not merely a local problem. Therefore the state has more specific requirements in the preparation of housing elements — requirements that seek to ensure that the state's own goals are met.

Even in the area of housing elements, however, the state has only limited power to push local governments in a specific policy direction. Unfortunately, communities often abuse the process by using the housing element to avoid building a range of affordable housing, rather than to facilitate its construction.

In the housing element, each local government is supposed to assess the need for housing in the community (with the state-imposed goal of providing housing opportunities to all segments of the community and all income groups) and then establish policies to ensure that this housing need is met.

The "needs assessment" portion of this requirement begins with the regional council of governments, such as the Southern California Association of Governments (SCAG) or the Association of Bay Area Governments (ABAG). These agencies calculate the regional need for low- and moderate-income housing and then calculate each local government's "fair share" of that housing.

Local governments are not required to adopt this "fair share" figure, however. Cities and counties may also conduct their own "needs assessment" to determine the extent of their low- and moderate-income housing needs. They may adopt the COG figures, but they can also select a different (usually lower) figure if they believe their own research justifies it.

Suburban communities often use this technique to avoid setting up an aggressive affordable housing program. Communities that do so are theoretically vulnerable to a legal attack, since they are impeding the achievement of a goal embodied in state law. But it is very difficult for poverty lawyers or homebuilders (the typical plaintiffs in such cases) to nail an offending city. Legally, local governments have great leeway to enact growth-control ordinances that restrict the supply of housing, especially if such ordinances are adopted by initiative. In one notable example, the Court of Appeal upheld an open-space ordinance in the Town of Moraga, even though the justices acknowledged that the ordinance would have a detrimental effect on the supply of housing in the Bay Area.*

Because state goals are involved, the state Department of Housing and Community Development (HCD) holds some review power over local housing elements. But this "power" is not very effective. All cities and counties must submit their draft housing elements to HCD for analysis and comment. Even though HCD specifically identifies the housing elements that do not comply with state law, however, local governments are not required to make any changes based on HCD's analysis.

The state's review of local housing elements does achieve some results, at least on paper. A 1988 survey by HCD found that while only about 45 percent of draft housing elements complied with state law, the figure for adopted elements (after HCD review) was close to 60 percent.

While this survey suggests that HCD does have some influence over local governments, it also reveals the department's limitations. More than 40 percent of the adopted housing elements in the state do not comply with state law. (And the state cannot force local governments to make changes unless the attorney general decides to file a lawsuit against the offending city or county.) But even if the state had more power to enforce the law on housing elements, it's questionable whether it would make much difference. The state's limited review power causes virtually every interested party — local governments, state bureaucrats, builders, and poverty advocates — to focus on the question of whether the housing element complies with state law, rather than the question of whether enough housing is being constructed. This "paper chase" attitude pervades planning in California, as local governments must concentrate on fulfilling paper requirements imposed by the state, to the detriment of broad-based discussions about what's good for their communities.

---

* *Northwood Homes v. Town of Moraga*, 216 Cal.App3d 1197 (1989).

## CRAFTING THE GENERAL PLAN

As such things go in California, the legally prescribed process of creating and adopting a general plan is relatively simple. In its *General Plan Guidelines*, the Governor's Office of Planning and Research, usually known as OPR, recommends an eight-step process (beginning with "identifying issues, opportunities, and assumptions" and concluding with "monitoring implementation and amending the plan"). In fact, however, state law imposes only a few procedural requirements — notably, one public hearing before the planning commission and one before the city council.

In practice, of course, crafting the general plan is not as purely rational as OPR suggests, nor as simple as state procedures permit. If the general plan is the "constitution" for the future development of a community, then the process of writing or revising the general plan is really the "constitutional convention." For most cities, it is a long, expensive, messy, often frustrating, and often exciting process. General plan revisions can take years and, even in a mid-sized city, they can cost several hundred thousand dollars of tax money. But if they are organized properly, they create an ideal forum for everyone to debate the community's future.

Adopting a general plan is, of course, legally regarded as a "legislative" act by local government, and in cities with well-organized citizen groups, the general plan process closely resembles the legislative wrangling that goes on in Washington and Sacramento. Elected officials are heavily lobbied on particular issues. Interest groups decide which issues they can compromise on and which they must "go to the mat" for. And, in the end, a general plan, just like a law or a constitutional amendment, will succeed only if all the important political constituencies are satisfied.

A proposed general plan (or general plan revision) usually doesn't leap forward into public hearings fully formed. In most cities, the process begins with two steps: the creation of an advisory task force, often known as the "general plan advisory committee," and the selection of an outside general plan consultant. (In some cities, a general plan may be prepared entirely by city staff, but that's the exception rather than the rule.)

A citizens advisory committee is usually made up of between 20 and 30 citizens who represent various neighborhoods, industries, and other interest groups that operate in the city. Membership will vary from city to city, depending on the political climate. In many cities, the real estate industry will be amply represented on the committee; perhaps even a certain number of seats will be set aside for brokers, commercial property owners, developers, and other real estate experts. (Architects, planners, engineers, and others familiar with the land-use process may also be represented.) In slow-growth cities, on the other hand, it may be politically difficult to include more than a few representatives of the real estate industry, and the emphasis is likely to be on broad representation from neighborhood and homeowner groups around the city.

Over a period of several months, the consultant and the citizens committee will craft a draft of the general plan. In most instances, the consulting team will provide the committee with technical background and make recommendations, while the committee will make the initial policy choices. After committee approval, the general plan will then move on to the planning commission and the city council. Either or both of these bodies may alter the basic document or even change it completely. (As a major policy statement affecting the environment, the general plan also requires the preparation of an environmental impact report before approval. EIRs will be discussed in more detail in Chapter 9.)

The rise of citizen power has changed this process considerably in recent years, making it longer, more expensive, in many ways more cumbersome, and in other ways more democratic. City managers and council members in many cities still resist broader public participation, believing there is nothing wrong with the "old-fashioned method" of a decision-making elite. However, leaders in many other cities recognize that the power of organized citizen groups cannot be ignored, and many welcome citizen participation.

Typically, an active citizenry is created as a response to a series of development disputes within a community — when ordinary people feel that their neighborhoods are threatened and organize to protect themselves. Once "politicized," these people rarely return to the role of passive citizens. If the group's members have interest and dedication, such a group becomes a permanent part of the city's decision-making "infrastructure," monitoring and commenting on the general plan as it proceeds from the advisory committee to the city council. And members of neighborhood groups and citizens committees often graduate to planning commissions and political office on the strength of their newfound exposure. In a few cities, the city council has even tried to foster citizen participation by providing neighborhoods (especially poor neighborhoods) with funds to help the process of organization.

In highly organized cities, where virtually all citizens are represented by one interest group or another, the general plan process evolves into classic political "pluralism," with the community's various groups making "trades" with each other on contentious issues in order to reach consensus on the entire general plan. In cities where citizen power is very strong, businesses and property owners have sometimes organized as well, creating their own "pressure groups" and hiring their own planning consultants.

Generally speaking, it is easier for a smaller city to become highly political about planning issues, and affluent citizens are more likely than poor citizens to become active participants in the debate. This is not always true, of course. San Francisco is one of the state's largest cities and the level of citizen participation is remarkably high. And citizen groups in poor neighborhoods sometimes carry considerable political weight. Nevertheless, political organization is more likely to occur in a smaller community with an affluent — or, at least, educated — populace.

Even in a highly organized city, however, a political consensus among organized groups does not guarantee the smooth passage and implementation of the general plan. Most citizens are mobilized only by an immediate threat, such as the appearance of a bulldozer on a nearby piece of land. A general plan, by contrast, is an abstract process laying out a broad-brush vision of a community's future. Average citizens won't care much about the general plan unless they understand how the process works and how the general plan's provisions are going to affect the likelihood of a bulldozer turning up in their neighborhood at some point in the near future. Even if a city tries to solicit citizen participation, many citizens simply won't pay attention until a specific development proposal arises — long after the general plan is done. By contrast, developers are more sophisticated in their understanding of the importance of the general plan to their interests, and they are often major participants in both the crafting and hearing process.

## COURT CHALLENGES

As with so much of California planning law, state laws regarding general plans are enforced only by litigation. With the minor exceptions noted above, no state agencies hold the power to review local general plans and penalize cities and counties if their general plans are inadequate. Only a court can do so. For this reason, citizen groups and others with an interest in land-use regulations, such as the building industry, hold considerable legal power over general plans because of their ability to sue.

Thus, the planning process depends heavily on "citizen enforcement" to hold local governments accountable. Typically, if citizen groups or building industry leaders dislike the results of the general plan process (or a general plan amendment), they will sue to have the general plan declared invalid. In essence, a court that finds a local general plan invalid can strip that locality of all of its land-use power. If their general plan is invalid, cities and counties cannot enact a zoning ordinance or approve new developments. They cannot approve a project under their subdivision review procedures. Their environmental impact reports are not binding, and in all probability they may not be able to proceed with public works projects. In other words, the entire planning process can be shut down by the court, at least until the city or county approves a new (or amended) general plan that passes legal muster. The threat of shutting the city's planning process down (or even of forcing the city to undertake a costly and time-consuming general plan revision) is a powerful incentive to local officials to do things right.

A lawsuit challenging the general plan usually challenges one of three areas: consistency with other planning documents, internal consistency, and compliance with state laws governing general plans.

*Consistency with other planning documents.* Perhaps the most popular general plan lawsuit is an attack on the consistency of the general plan and the zoning ordinance. This became particularly popular in the late '80s, when so many growth-control initiatives were written as amendments to the zoning ordinance.

The first important court case of this sort involved a growth-control initiative in the city of Norco, a fast-growing city in Riverside County. The initiative was written as an amendment to the zoning ordinance, but did not seek to change the general plan. The building industry sought to stop the election on the grounds that the initiative would create a zoning ordinance inconsistent with the general plan.*

This concept was later ratified by the California Supreme Court in a case from Walnut Creek. In 1985, voters there approved a growth-control initiative that sought to limit development in areas with heavy traffic congestion. A prominent landowner sued, claiming the initiative was a zoning ordinance that was inconsistent with the general plan, which called for Walnut Creek to develop into a regional center. The Supreme Court eventually ruled that the initiative was invalid because it was inconsistent with the general plan.**

Because initiative and referendum powers are protected by the California Constitution, the courts accord them great deference. For this reason, judges usually permit a measure to appear on the ballot even if there is a legal challenge, thereby postponing a discussion on the merits of the case until after the election. In the case from Norco, however, the Court of Appeal stopped the election. The court ruled that because the initiative changed the zoning ordinance but not the general plan, it would create a zoning ordinance that was, on its face, inconsistent with the general plan. For this reason, most growth-control initiatives in California are now written as general plan amendments, sometimes directing local officials to amend other planning documents to retain consistency.

In the City of Los Angeles, a special state law and a highly publicized court case were required in order to motivate the city to create consistency between the general plan and the zoning ordinance. In the 1970s, the city planning department undertook an ambitious effort to

---

* *deBottari v. City Council,* 171 Cal.App.3d 1204 (1985).
** *Lesher Communications v. City of Walnut Creek,* 52 Cal.3d 531 (1990).

create a new general plan, with the participation of 60,000 citizens in 35 community planning areas. The city's zoning, however, remained much as it was in 1946, when a much more densely populated city was envisioned. In the late '70s, the state legislature enacted a special law requiring Los Angeles, alone among charter cities, to make its zoning ordinance consistent with its general plan.

Despite the entreaties of the city planning director, the Los Angeles City Council never allocated much money for this purpose; as a result, the zoning ordinance and the general plan remained flagrantly inconsistent well into the 1980s. Eventually, a coalition of homeowner groups sued, forcing the city into a consistency program supervised by a local judge. The end result was not the massive "downzoning" in all parts of the city that the law would seem to require; in some places, the general plan was amended so it would be consistent with the generous zoning.

*Internal consistency.* Another favorite legal strategy is to attack the internal consistency of a general plan. While most general plans do not contain flagrant internal inconsistencies, most plans are long and complex documents and any judge is virtually certain to find some inconsistency if he or she looks hard enough.

The internal inconsistency argument is so fertile that both citizen groups and landowners are likely to continue using it for years to come — especially in the context of growth-related ballot measures.

*Compliance with state laws.* A general plan may be the supreme document from which all other local land-use policies must flow, but it still must comply with state planning laws. A general plan that does not comply with some aspect of state law may be legally vulnerable.

For example, if a city or county prepares a general plan without including the seven required elements, the plan will surely be struck down as inadequate. (Believe it or not, some cities and counties do not have the required seven elements in their general plans — including the many localities that have not revised their general plans since the 1970s.) Just as important, however, is the fact that a general plan may be legally vulnerable if it does not contain the standards required in state law.

The most significant case along these lines involved Mendocino

County's noise element. The general plan was challenged on the grounds that the noise element contained no technical background information about the impact of noise on land within the county. Mendocino County's response was simply that such a detailed technical analysis was not necessary for "a quiet rural county such as Mendocino." Nevertheless, the Court of Appeal found the noise element inadequate, saying the technical requirements in state law were mandatory, not optional, even if local decision-makers didn't feel they had a noise problem. If the county had not revised the noise element, it would have been prohibited from issuing any building permits.*

Sometimes even the simplest error can lead to legal problems. In challenging the general plan for the City of Riverside, lawyers for a group of landowners sent one of their clerks to City Hall to pick up a copy of the plan. However, the clerk returned empty-handed; the city was unable to produce a current copy of the plan and all its elements under one cover. Because state law requires the general plan to be readily available to the public, the lawyers made the unavailability of the Riverside plan one of the causes of action in the lawsuit. And the courts subsequently declared the plan invalid, partly because it was unavailable.

*Tests for an adequate general plan.* In his book *California Land-Use and Planning Law*, Daniel J. Curtin, Jr., lays out several questions to ask in order to determine whether a general plan is legally adequate. The list is so good that it bears reprinting here:

1. Is it complete? (seven elements)
2. Is it informational, readable, and public?
3. Is internally consistent?
4. Is it consistent with state policy?
5. Does it cover all territory within its boundaries?
6. Is it long-term in perspective?
7. Is it current?
8. Does it contain the statutory criteria required by state law as demanded by the courts? For example:

---

* *Camp v. Board of Supervisors,* 123 Cal.App.3d 334 (1981).

- Does the land-use element identify areas which are subject to flooding?
- Are noise contours shown for all of the listed sources of noise?
- Does it contain adequate standards of population density and building intensity?
- Does the circulation element responsibly list sources of funding for new transportation facilities?
- Is the circulation element correlated with the land-use element?
- Does the general plan clearly specify allowable uses for each land-use district?
- Are the density ranges specific enough to provide guidelines in making consistency findings where necessary?
- Does the housing element contain a program to conserve and improve the condition of the existing affordable housing stock?

9. Are the diagrams or maps adequate? Do they show proposed land uses for the entire planning area? Is the land-use map linked directly to the text of the general plan? Are the maps and text consistent?

10. Does it serve as a yardstick? Can you take an individual parcel and check it against the plan and then know how you can use your property?

11. Does it contain an action plan or implementation plan?

12. Finally, but most important, is it procedurally correct? Was it adopted properly? Did it receive proper environmental review?

## STRENGTHS AND WEAKNESSES OF THE GENERAL PLAN PROCESS

The general plan has changed planning in California for the better by imposing a "rational" process on communities. Instead of a set of "good ol' boys" charting the future for their own benefit, general planning is now an open and well-debated process that requires the laying down of rules before the laying down of concrete. In effect, it holds everyone accountable to the same rules and the same procedures — a major step forward.

Yet, very often, general plans represent missed opportunities. Usually they are ponderous and boring, or they lack vision, or they're full of glorious rhetoric that goes largely ignored. What visions there are remain visions on paper, and the issuing of permits goes on as before. Traffic increases, open space vanishes, the homeless are uncared for, and so on. The state's procedural mandates have been acknowledged and adhered to, and all the required elements are there; but the promise of the general plan in actually shaping communities often goes unfulfilled. General plans probably serve their inward-looking and self-preservation functions well. But they serve only as limited tools as things now stand in the context of a vast state, where local governments often work at cross-purposes and larger problems usually go unsolved.

## CHAPTER 4

# THE BASIC TOOLS, PART II:
# ZONING

Zoning is the most widely used land-use regulation in the country. Even communities that perform only perfunctory planning (or none at all) often have a zoning ordinance that divides the community into "use" districts. In California, of course, zoning is supposed to be a tool to implement the general plan — that is, the general goals and precepts of the plan are supposed to be translated into parcel-specific regulations by the zoning ordinance.* As the history of California planning law shows, however, this is not always the way it works out in real life. In some cities the zoning ordinance does, in fact, serve as a "beast of burden" for the general plan. In many other cities, however, the zoning ordinance remains the primary tool of land-use planning even today. A general plan may exist, but if no one objects, it is largely ignored. Meanwhile, the zoning ordinance and the zoning map, which are more easily bent to meet the political needs of any given moment, are frequently changed without much consideration for overall planning issues.

The legal basis for zoning, as for most land-use regulations, is the

---

* Zoning ordinances are authorized by Government Code §65850 *et. seq.*

local government's "police power." A zoning ordinance must serve to protect the public health, safety, and welfare, and it cannot be, to use a legal phrase, "arbitrary or capricious." To meet the constitutional tests laid out in *Euclid v. Ambler*, a zoning ordinance must be both comprehensive and fair. Comprehensiveness means the ordinance must cover every piece of property within the jurisdiction. Fairness means that while different pieces of property may be assigned to different zones, each piece of property within the same zone must be treated alike.

The typical zoning ordinance is a set of regulations that prescribes or restricts what landowners can do with their property. Usually, regulations have three dimensions: use, bulk, and impact or performance.

*Use.* The use dimension is the most basic characteristic of zoning. Each piece of property falls into a "use" district, which restricts the type of development that may be built there: single-family residential, multi-family residential, neighborhood commercial, regional commercial, industrial, agricultural. Some local jurisdictions have 30 or more districts; in residential areas alone, a city or county will typically have zones such as R-1 (single-family), R-2 (two-family), and so on. Other jurisdictions have only a few zones. But every piece of property must be assigned to a district, and the uses permitted in each district must be explicitly laid out. And it is important to keep in mind that the true purpose of many zoning ordinances remains the protection of the single-family neighborhood from any intrusions. (In some cases, the stated purpose is the promotion of economic development in commercial and industrial districts, though, in part, this segregation of uses is also meant to protect single-family neighborhoods.)

Though the use district has been the foundation of zoning for more than 60 years, the remarkable fluidity of today's economy may be making it obsolete. Already, developers who build low-rise suburban business parks rarely do so with a fixed idea of what type of use it will contain; it could include anything from a warehouse to a research lab to an office center. (Increasingly, we are seeing not one or another but a combination of all three under the same roof.) Planners in Irvine have wrestled with this issue in recent years, as they have tried to figure out how (or even whether) to apply parking ratios and other commercial and industrial requirements to these business parks. If, as expected, more people work at home in the future (on a full- or part-time basis), then the once-bright line between use districts will break down even more.

*Bulk.* Zoning ordinances typically also create a so-called "envelope" within which any building must fit. This envelope is created by specifying setbacks, height limits, and sometimes limits on the percentage of a site that may be covered by buildings, other structures, and paving. For example, a typical single-family zone may require a 15-foot front yard, a 20-foot back yard, a five-foot setback from the prop-

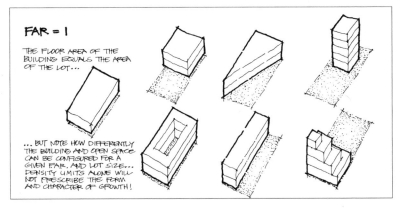

**Floor-Area Ratio**

erty line on either side of the house, and a building height of no more than 25 feet. The landowner must construct his or her house within the resulting "envelope." A commercial property envelope will be dictated not only by height and setback limitations, but also by the square footage allowed under a maximum "floor-area ratio."

The floor-area ratio, or FAR, is expressed as a ratio of building square footage to square footage of land — i.e., an FAR of 3:1, meaning that for every square foot of land, the landowner may build three square feet of building. Thus, a 3:1 FAR on a 10,000-square-foot commercial lot means that the landowner may build a 30,000-square-foot building. But this does not mean the result will always be a three-story building. Because of setback and lot coverage requirements, the landowner might have to build a taller building — four, five, six stories — to obtain the 30,000 square feet.

Envelopes vary from use to use. Pedestrian-oriented retail districts may not need setbacks; such a district may, in fact, require buildings to run from lot line to lot line and all the way up to the sidewalk. But industrial zones often specify a maximum "lot coverage" so that factories are buffered from surrounding neighborhoods, and increasingly commercial and multi-family districts have similar requirements.

*Impact/Performance.* The last set of requirements tries to regulate how a building will "perform" in the context of its neighborhood. Ideally, these requirements seek to minimize the negative side-effects a building and its uses will have. For example, virtually no modern zoning ordinance permits the construction of any building without parking. Parking requirements will vary from zone to zone; a single-family residence may require one or two parking places, while an office building may need four per 1,000 square feet of space.

The only exception would be the zoning ordinance for a dense urban area with a good transit system. San Francisco, for example, actually discourages the provision of off-street parking places in some parts of the city. (Though, increasingly, developers in San Francisco and densely built sections of Southern California may be required to contribute funds to a parking authority that constructs parking garages serving an entire business district.)

Similarly, in industrial zones, builders may be required to provide heavy landscaping and berms in order to shield industrial activity from public view.

Obviously, all three types of requirements play an important role in shaping what a new development will look like. The use requirement will dictate that a piece of property in a multi-family zone will be an apartment building rather than a store or a factory. The bulk requirements will set the zoning envelope, establishing, in essence, the size and shape of the building. And the impact requirements will assure that the building will provide a certain number of parking spaces. Increasingly, however, the impact requirements drive the entire development process — not the use of the project, necessarily, but often its bulk and height.

Take the example of a high-density apartment project in an already built-up area. Perhaps the property is zoned for 30 apartment units per acre. Theoretically, building a 30-unit apartment building on a piece of land already zoned for such a purpose should be easy. However, most zoning ordinances require two off-street parking spaces per unit, plus additional parking spaces for guests or visitors (usually about one space for every two to four units). Suddenly, the owner of a one-acre site must build not only 30 apartments but also 68 parking spaces. This is a much harder task — probably meaning the developer must forgo surface parking and provide the spaces within or underneath the apartment building itself. Furthermore, if the area in question has a three-story height limit, the only alternative is to provide the spaces underground, which doubles their cost of construction.

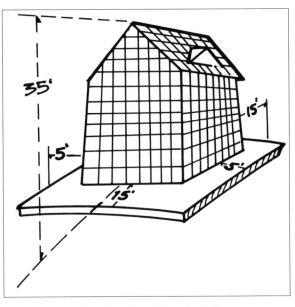

**The Zoning 'Envelope'**

A developer boxed in by this kind of zoning "envelope" — and a substantial impact requirement, such as 2.25 parking spaces per unit — may discover that it is simply too expensive to build the largest project permitted by zoning. In order to cut the cost of providing the parking facilities, the developer may have to reduce the size of the project. In this example, the size of the project is driven by the parking requirement, not by the allowable density or the setback requirements. The landowner is often placed in the same situation when different uses permitted in the same zone — a restaurant and a retail shop, for example — have vastly different parking requirements. A restaurant will usually be required to have far more parking available than a retail shop. The ability of the landowner to open a restaurant will depend not on the zoning, but the landowner's ability to build or secure enough parking. If the parking can't be worked into the project, the landowner may be forced into opening a retail shop instead of a restaurant.

Sometimes, "performance standards" alone may dictate the type of building or business a particular parcel of land can sustain. Rather than identifying uses, setbacks, or even specific standards, some cities simply require that a building "perform" to a certain level — for example, producing no more than a certain number of vehicle trips, no matter what the use. Sometimes uses may be permitted conditionally, but only if these performance standards can be met. Performance standards were regarded as a "new wave" of zoning techniques in the '70s. But they are more difficult and expensive to administer, so most cities have stuck with older, more familiar zoning methods.

## ZONING TOOLS

Within the concept of zoning are many tools that landowners, developers, and cities may use to accommodate projects that otherwise would be unacceptable, or to stop projects that otherwise would be allowed. Traditionally, these tools have permitted developers and elected officials to exert political power over the land-use process, whether or not the project in question conforms with local plans. The growing strength of the slow-growth movement and the power of the general plan have made this kind of political manipulation more difficult to achieve, though it still exists. More frequently today, some of these tools (principally discretionary review) are used to make otherwise acceptable projects more difficult to build.

### ZONE CHANGES

The most obvious method of permitting a project that otherwise would not be allowed is to change the zoning on the parcel of land in question. And, indeed, this is the classic route for landowners to take. City councils and boards of supervisors have always shown a willingness to change zoning if the project proposed is something they really want built. (This is true not only of projects proposed by developers with political influence, but also of projects desirable because they would bring tax revenue or some measure of prestige to the community as well.) Zone changes are legislative in nature under California law, even if they involve only one parcel of land. This designation means all zone changes are, essentially, policy statements by the city or county. Therefore, they must be approved by the legislative body — the city council or board of supervisors — after a public hearing, and they are subject to initiative and referendum.

Perhaps the most abused type of zone change over the years has been *spot zoning*, a practice which essentially grants one parcel of land a zoning designation that is incompatible with the rest of the neighborhood (but probably affords the landowner with an economic windfall). Spot zoning, for example, might designate one house in a residential area for retail use, or one commercial parcel along a pedestrian-oriented strip for an automobile body shop. In theory, spot zoning is legally vulnerable, because all parcels in a zone have not been treated alike — one has been moved into a new zone while others have not.

In practice, the strengthened legal

## FINDINGS

One of the most important — but abused — concepts in planning is the concept of "findings."

"Findings" simply constitute the rationale that a city council or planning commission uses in making a decision — or, in the words of a landmark court case on the subject, findings "expose the agency's mode of analysis" and "bridge the analytical gap between raw data and ultimate decision." (*Topanga Association for a Scenic Community v. County of Los Angeles* (1974), 11 Cal.3d 506, 511, 516.) In short, findings should discuss the reasons why a city or county has decided to take a certain action.

The legal purpose of findings is to give judges a way of assessing the local government's decision if that decision is challenged in court. With a few exceptions, localities don't need to draw up findings for legislative actions such as zoning ordinances and general plan amendments, because these are presumed to be policy statements. But quasi-judicial decisions must be supported by findings, so that it is clear how a city or county is applying its policy to a particular case. Thus, findings are required for such actions as conditional use permits, variances, subdivision approvals, and other development permits.

State law requires findings for a variety of other actions, such as general plan consistency, moratoria on residential construction, and growth control ordinances. (However, findings are not required for initiatives that impose growth control.)

Findings are also required under the California Environmental Quality Act when a project is approved even though it has significant environmental effects. (For a further discussion of CEQA, see Chapter 9.) Ideally, findings will lay out the "evidence" a city council or planning commission considered and then explain how that evidence laid the groundwork for the decision that eventually was made. Those findings

status of general plans has made spot zoning and other questionable zone changes more difficult to achieve. In decades past, the zoning designation on a parcel of land could be changed without much consideration for the general plan. Now, however, a zone change that creates an inconsistency with the general plan is legally vulnerable. Therefore, zone changes and general plan amendments are typically processed together in order to avoid inconsistencies. This practice serves to reduce the number of zone changes (since general plan amendments are restricted to four per year) and sometimes also to heighten public awareness of the proposal, especially if the city or county has recently been through a major general plan revision.

## VARIANCES

Perhaps no single aspect of zoning receives more attention (or abuse) than the variance. As the name implies, a variance is a kind of permit that allows a landowner to do something he couldn't otherwise do. Traditionally, zoning has encompassed two types of variances: The so-called "use variance," which permits an otherwise unacceptable use on the property without changing the zone, and the "variance from standards," which permits the landowner to construct a building or open a business without having to comply with the standards required of other landowners in the same zone. Use variances are not permitted under California law, but variances from standards are common.*

On paper, the variance serves a useful purpose by providing for the "hardship" exemption. It permits a landowner to make use of his property even if there is something about that property which makes it impossible for the landowner to comply fully with the zoning ordinance. Such a hardship should be associated with the land, not the owner. The classic example involves a residential lot that is identical in size and shape to the surrounding lots, but suffers from the presence of a large, immoveable boulder on it. In such an instance, a variance to waive ordinary setback requirements may permit the landowner to build a house, even though the boulder makes construction of the house within the normal zoning "envelope" impossible.

Beyond the geologic impediment, however, the legal authority for a variance is vague. California court opinions are split on the question of whether a lot of odd size or shape constitutes a hardship. Under other conditions, variances are not legally acceptable. In particular, "economic

will then be attached to the decision itself as part of the permanent record.

In fact, most findings are woefully inadequate. A typical set of findings will "find" that certain conditions exist which justify the local government's action. For example, the findings attached to subdivision approval for a housing project are likely to "find" that more housing is needed in the community. But only rarely will a community's findings go on to cover what they are really supposed to cover — the evidence on which the decision is based, and the connections between that evidence and the case at hand. In most instances, findings are made up of mere "boilerplate" material.

Even though poor findings are common, they are legally vulnerable. In recent years, a number of Court of Appeal cases have attacked findings as inadequate, especially under CEQA. In the future, judges are likely to hold findings to an even higher standard.

* The legal limitations of variances are contained in Government Code §65906.

hardship" cannot form the basis for a variance because an economic problem, unlike a geologic problem, is self-inflicted.

These legal limitations have not prevented many cities and counties from using the variance when it is politically expedient to do so. In all of planning, probably no tool has been more widely abused than the variance, simply because it is so tempting. If a zone change would be politically difficult to achieve, a variance is likely to attract much less attention. If a favored landowner can almost (but not quite) meet the standards required in a particular zone — and the city wants his project — then a variance provides a convenient solution. In some pro-development communities, planners may actually encourage variance applications, knowing that getting one through the political process is not difficult.

Whether it is difficult to achieve politically or not, the broad use of the variance is wrong because it perverts the process. Unlike zone changes, variances are quasi-judicial in nature, not legislative. This designation means that the planning commission's approval is binding (unless appealed to the city council) and also that a variance cannot be placed on the ballot, via either initiative or referendum. Variances are quasi-judicial because, supposedly, they do not deal with policy issues, but, rather, with the application of city policy to one particular case. They may be passed by resolution, not by ordinance, which means that they may take effect immediately following a short appeals period. (Ordinances must have two readings before a city council or board of supervisors, meaning they must wait 30 days before they are enacted.)

A variance that deals with a geologic problem clearly constitutes nothing more than the application of city policy to an unusual case. But any other kind of variance is simply an insidious way of shielding a policy decision from broad public debate. A variance that permits a use that otherwise wouldn't be allowed — even if it involves nothing more than a slightly trimmed parking requirement — is really a zone change in disguise. A zone-change decision is clearly a political decision, but at least it is made in an overtly political forum — before the legislative body, with voters having the recourse of initiative and referendum.

*   *   *

## DISCRETIONARY REVIEW

Most aspects of the zoning ordinance are designed to yield an answer of "yes" or "no." A landowner may build a house in a residential neighborhood but not a store. A developer may build a 30-unit apartment building on a particular parcel of land if certain requirements are met (setback, parking, etc.), but not if those requirements are not met. In recent years, however, many cities have begun to emphasize one aspect of zoning designed to yield an answer of "yes ... if."

"Discretionary review" is a process that permits local officials, usually the planning commission, to review a specific development proposal and either attach conditions to it or deny it. Thus, even a proposal that conforms to the "paper" requirements of the zoning ordinance must be reviewed by the planning commission, which may or may not approve it.

The concept of discretionary review emerged from the "conditional use permit," or CUP, a device cities have used since World War II to trigger planning commission review of certain projects.* The concept behind a CUP is that some uses may be theoretically compatible with other uses in a particular zone, but only if they meet certain "conditions" that minimize their impact on the surrounding area. An auto body shop in a commercial area would be a good example. In recent years, however, many cities have expanded the boundaries of discretionary review to include not just potentially incompatible uses, but essentially all projects over a certain size. A trailblazer in this area has been the City of San Francisco. The San Francisco city charter contains one line permitting the planning commission to review development projects at its own discretion. The commission and the city planning department have not been afraid to use this phrase as the legal basis to review a vast array of projects, large and small. Other cities have followed suit. West Hollywood, for example, now requires planning commission review of all commercial projects of 10,000 square feet or more. (By contrast, until 1987 the City of Los Angeles required virtually no review of any project that conformed with the city's general zoning ordinance; even 20- or 30-story buildings were approved "over

---

* Conditional use permits are discussed in Government Code §65901.

the counter," though there was a good deal of staff review involved.)

This expanded use of discretionary review is not really a logical extension of the '50s "pig in the parlor" concept of a conditional use permit. Rather, it's a response to citizen demand for a more open decision-making process, since it opens up for public debate many projects that wouldn't otherwise come before a public body. In many respects, the expanded use of discretionary review has been influenced by the California Environmental Quality Act, which encourages a spirited public debate on the environmental aspects of many projects, whether they conform to zoning or not. The case-by-case analytical structure of CEQA has prompted many communities to expand the range of projects they will review with "discretion" — since these projects will be reviewed individually under CEQA anyway. (For more information on how the CEQA review process works, see Chapter 9.)

Of course, local politicians often prefer discretionary review, since it allows them to approve or reject projects depending on the current political situation, no matter what the local codes say. And, in practice, cities also use discretionary review in order to gain more leverage over developers. On complicated projects, a conditional use permit may impose several dozen conditions on a developer. While some of these conditions are associated with the "conditional use" under consideration — a store's hours of operation, for example — many others are really "exactions," imposed in response to political pressures and perceived planning problems. (Exactions are conditions or financial obligations imposed on developers to deal with specific problems arising from the development in question, such as traffic, housing, and open space. Exactions will be discussed in detail in Chapter 6.) Conditions imposed on a development through discretionary review may call for anything "reasonably related" to the project — the planting of a large number of trees, the construction of affordable housing, the payment of a traffic mitigation fee. Design review (sometimes known as architectural review) also falls under the category of discretionary review, and can lead to a separate set of conditions specifying anything from the placement of dumpsters to the color of the building.

Many times, the discretionary review process is really the beginning of a policy cycle. An issue pops up during discretionary review; at first it's dealt with on a case-by-case basis, and eventually requirements based on the case-by-case experience are included in the zoning code. Many exactions and impact fees have become established city policy in this way. Partly because of discretionary review, however, the cycle has become never-ending: New problems (both planning and political) are always discovered in discretionary review, new conditions are imposed, and eventually new exactions are institutionalized in the zoning ordinance.

Discretionary review provides both the city and its citizens with many opportunities that wouldn't otherwise exist. At the same time, it also makes the development process a lot longer and less unpredictable. Developers don't always know what kind of project they'll wind up with in the end or how expensive it will be. It's also hard to predict in advance whether any agreement between developers and city staff (or between developers and angry citizens) will hold up in front of the planning commission or the city council.

## NON-CONFORMING USES

As zoning ordinances change over time, inevitably many structures that don't conform will be "left over" from previous eras — a corner store in a residential neighborhood, for example. In many traditional zoning schemes, these "non-conforming uses" were simply permitted to continue indefinitely, so long as they did not expand or change the nature of their business. More recently, zoning ordinances have been less tolerant of non-conforming uses over the long term, requiring that they be phased out over a period of years. Generally speaking, the courts have permitted this "amortized" approach to phasing out non-conforming uses.

The problem of non-conforming signs, however, has been a much more controversial issue. As more and more local governments have passed strict sign ordinances, for example, the advertising industry has used its clout in Sacramento to restrict localities' ability to eliminate non-conforming signs. (An indication of the advertising industry's influence in this area lies in the fact that while local government power to restrict signs is located in the Government Code, the limitations on that power are included in the Business and Professions Code (§5200-

5486), where laws sponsored by specific industries are typically codi-fied. While the power of local governments to restrict signs is broad, they usually can't require that a non-conforming sign be taken down unless the sign's owner is compensated. Localities can require signs be phased out over a period of time without any compensation, but the amortization periods are specified by the state.*

## EXCLUSIONARY AND INCLUSIONARY ZONING

Zoning is easily manipulated for political purposes, and in the suburbs, it's been used to create many high-income enclaves by mak-ing construction of low-cost housing virtually impossible.

Perhaps the most prevalent form of exclusionary zoning is the sin-gle-family neighborhood, which, by its very nature, limits the amount of development in a community and, indirectly, sets a minimum income requirement for all residents. Most suburban ordinances also establish a minimum lot size, and some even require a minimum square footage for each house. The alleged public purposes of such ordinances vary. Some communities claim that low-density housing will limit the environmental impact of a new development by minimiz-ing traffic, impact on schools, and so forth. Others have produced stud-ies claiming that minimum lot and house sizes are required for public health. In general, though, the citizens of these suburban communities are not unaware that what they are really doing is excluding the poor (and sometimes the middle class as well) and increasing their own property values in the process. There is no question that the high cost of housing in California and elsewhere is due, in part, to exclusionary zoning practices.

Over the years, many courts have accepted a community's right to engage in exclusionary zoning. Minimum lot sizes of up to five acres have been upheld in court. As housing prices have increased rapidly over the last 20 years, however, there has been growing pressure to reverse exclusionary zoning practices and, in fact, give preference in the zoning ordinance to low-cost housing.

By far the most influential events in this trend toward "inclusionary

* Business and Professional Code §5412.1.

zoning" were the two *Mount Laurel* court rulings by the New Jersey Supreme Court. The first case* challenged the zoning scheme of the Town of Mount Laurel in suburban Philadelphia. The ordinance had zoned all land in the city for either industrial use or large single-family lots. The NAACP contended that the zoning ordinance discriminated against the poor by zoning them out of the town. In 1975, the New Jersey Supreme Court ruled in favor of the NAACP, but also went much further, saying that each municipality had a "presumptive obligation" to zone and plan for housing that will accommodate a variety of income groups.

*Mount Laurel* was an earth-shattering decision indeed, but over the next few years it proved ineffective. Mount Laurel and other suburban communities in New Jersey rewrote their ordinances, but only to give the appearance of compliance with the ruling. Remarkably, in 1983, the New Jersey Supreme Court issued a second ruling** that laid down very specific rules about how local governments should provide affordable housing. In essence, the court said that all new housing development must set aside 20 percent of its units for low- and moderate-income residents, and the justices also appointed a three-judge panel of "zoning czars" to oversee all litigation related to *Mount Laurel*. Horrified at such judicial activism, the New Jersey legislature finally stepped in and established an administrative process to deal with inclusionary housing. Today, virtually all large projects in New Jersey must include so-called "Mount Laurel" units, and local efforts at affordable housing are reviewed by a state agency. In practical terms, developers "sell" local governments on the Mount Laurel units by suggesting that they provide homes for teachers, police officers, and entry-level professionals — mostly white — who would otherwise have to commute long distances to local jobs.

In California, the general plan's housing element is theoretically the tool by which the state seeks to force the construction of a variety of housing types. As the discussion in Chapter 3 suggested, however, the housing element has not proven to be an effective tool in enforcing

---

* *South Burlington County NAACP v. Mt. Laurel*, 336 A.2d 713 (1975).
** *South Burlington County NAACP v. Mt. Laurel*, 450 A.2d 390 (1983), sometimes referred to as *Mt. Laurel II*.

state housing policy. And despite repeated attempts by both poverty lawyers and the building industry, the California state courts — and the California-based federal courts — have never been willing to render a *Mount Laurel*-style decision. These legal attacks have challenged the constitutionality of either the housing element of the general plan or a growth management scheme. Despite a few minor victories for housing elements, generally speaking the courts have deferred to the discretion of local governments in this area. The judicial attitude today is still best summed up by the Ninth Circuit's reasoning in upholding Petaluma's growth-control ordinance in 1975: "Although we assume that some persons desirous of living in Petaluma will be excluded under the housing permit limitation and that, thus, the plan may frustrate some legitimate regional housing needs, the plan is not arbitrary or unreasonable."*

Although the judicial activism of *Mount Laurel* has not caught on in California, the trend toward inclusionary housing has. Many cities in California now require that some percentage of new housing units (usually between 15 and 25 percent) be set aside for low- and moderate-income persons. Some cities with an annual cap on permit allocations also give affordable housing projects preference, either by awarding extra points to such projects or exempting them from the cap altogether.

The building industry often opposes inclusionary zoning requirements, saying they merely drive up the cost of the units that are not offered at affordable rates. But the builders have been supportive of density bonuses for affordable housing. In fact, largely at the builders' urging, the legislature passed a mandatory density bonus law. If a builder offers to construct a project that meets specified standards for affordability, the city must grant a density bonus. However, a city may deny the density bonus if it makes written findings that the bonus isn't needed to ensure affordable housing.** The density bonus law is a rare exception to the rule that the state does not meddle in local zoning matters — but despite the clout it gives developers, it is rarely used.

* *Construction Industry v. City of Petaluma*, 522 F.2d 897. For more information on the Petaluma growth management system, see Chapter 6.
** Government Code §65913.4 and §65915-65918.

## CODE ENFORCEMENT

As the number of conditions imposed on developers has grown, so has the importance of code enforcement. Yet, historically, code enforcement has been a virtually forgotten area in land-use planning. Often, code enforcement officers aren't even in the same division of city government with the planners who craft all the conditions. Rather, they're often attached to the building and safety department, because the bulk of their job consists of responding to mundane citizen complaints about code violations — a neighbor who is constructing an addition to his house without a permit, for example.

To many code enforcement officers, the complicated conditions imposed on a modern development project simply constitute an annoying distraction from their bread-and-butter work. At the same time, however, planners don't take responsibility for code enforcement; they rarely follow up to investigate whether conditions are met, assuming instead that such investigation is the job of code enforcement.

Zoning violations are usually misdemeanors, meaning a property owner who is cited is thrown into criminal court. Even if code violators are caught and cited, however, it can be difficult for local governments to motivate property owners to comply with the law. Such property owners may pay a fine and promise to "clean up their act," but in all likelihood they won't change the way they do business — for two reasons. One is that code enforcement officers are usually overworked, and property owners know it will be a long time before they get around to following up. The second reason is that the threat of further punishment usually doesn't exist.

A retail business — a liquor store, for example — that is violating conditions of approval by staying open late can probably make more money by continually paying fines than by closing on time. In order to take any more serious action, most cities must depend on the county's district attorney to press charges. And a busy district attorney's office concerned with murders and rapes isn't going to give high priority to a neighborhood dispute over a liquor store.

Some cities have tried to deal with this problem by downgrading zoning violations from a misdemeanor to an infraction. This action permits code enforcement officers to issue tickets, just as a Highway

Patrol officer does, and places the burden on the property owner to go into court and defend himself. A few cities have experimented with code enforcement by hiring their own city prosecutor who is empowered to take code enforcement problems to court.

But even then there are problems. A property owner charged with a misdemeanor will usually correct the violation prior to his or her appearance in court, which will often lead the judge to dismiss the charge. Furthermore, many cities don't regard a violation of conditions imposed via discretionary review as a true violation of the zoning ordinances. If such conditions are construction-related (using a particular type of window, for example), then the city can simply withhold the certificate of occupancy, which the landowner needs to occupy the building, until the conditions are met. (Of course, for many structures, certificates of occupancy aren't required.) However, if a condition related to the building's operation is violated (no carpooling program five years later, for example), the city may have no recourse if such a violation is not considered a true violation of the zoning ordinance. Compared to neighborhood nuisances and "true" zoning violations (building construction to wrong specifications, improper use for the zone, etc.), discretionary conditions get low priority indeed — and so, often, they are never implemented at all.

## PLANNED UNIT DEVELOPMENTS AND SPECIFIC PLANS

In the 1960s and '70s, perhaps the most popular zoning tool, especially in the suburbs, was the "planned unit development," or PUD. The PUD was essentially a separate zoning ordinance written especially for one development project — usually a large project. A PUD gave cities and developers the flexibility to create zoning standards that were appropriate to the site and the project in question.

In recent years, the PUD has given way to a similar tool permitted under state law, the "specific plan."* Cities and counties often use specific plans to deal with a planning problem in a particular area, especially if citizens are demanding action. Developers often use the specific plan as part of a package of planning documents used to lay

*Government Code §65450-65457.

out development of large new tracts in the suburbs.

A specific plan is not part of the general plan. Cities and counties can prepare "mini" general plans for specific areas, but these documents are usually called "area" or "community" plans. Such documents are often incorporated into a community's overall general plan, and they carry the same legal force as the general plan. In legal terms, the specific plan is more akin to a zoning ordinance — and, especially, to the planned unit development. It is an implementation document — a document designed to implement the general plan (or an area plan) within a certain area. Thus, perhaps the most important part of a specific plan is the set of development standards it contains, which is typically laid out in great detail.

Nevertheless, a specific plan is a hybrid tool in the sense that it may also contain statements of planning policy, so long as they are consistent with the community's general plan. This flexibility is very attractive to both developers and communities, which accounts for the specific plan's popularity.

The legal requirements for what must be included in a specific plan (contained in Government Code §65451) are not unlike the requirements for the land-use element of the general plan, with the added provision that implementation measures must be spelled out. Specifically, the law requires:

• The "distribution, location, and extent of the uses of land," including open space.

• The proposed "distribution, location, and extent and intensity of major components" of public infrastructure, such as transportation, sewage, water, energy, and solid waste disposal.

• Development standards and criteria.

• Implementation measures "including regulations, programs, public works projects, and financing measures" required to carry out the planning program as laid out elsewhere in the plan.

Because the specific plan serves as both planning document and implementation tool for a specific area, it is often used as the focal point of a broad-based planning process for newly developing areas. This is especially true if a large tract is being developed in phases by a single development company. Typically, the specific plan will lay out the overall development scheme, establish the specific development standards the project must follow, and identify the public facilities and capital infrastructure required to support the project.

At the same time, a "development agreement" between the developer and the locality will guarantee the developer's legal right to build the phases when the market will permit and also commit the developer to building the infrastructure, dedicating land for schools or parks, or alternatively paying for those facilities. (For more discussion of development agreements, see Chapter 11.) If necessary, assessment districts will also be established to permit the locality to issue bonds for the public improvements. Thus, a city or county might draw up a specific plan laying out a new development, and then process the specific plan, a development agreement, a subdivision map, a capital improvement program, and a general plan amendment all at once.

Specific plans are not used only for newly developing areas, however. Often they are ordered in response to some planning crisis — if a particular neighborhood or commercial district is suddenly experiencing increased pressure for new development, for example. A specific plan prepared under these circumstances is likely to include development standards that will permit new development, but constrain their size and shape very specifically in response to neighborhood political pressures. In Los Angeles, the city has also sponsored a series of specific plans for depressed areas prepared through a kind of "design charette" process. Under this process, a group of planning and design professionals spent a few intense days in the community, interacting with local citizens and organizations. The resulting document includes planning policy, economic development strategies, and design and development standards.

# CHAPTER 5

# THE BASIC TOOLS, PART III:
# THE SUBDIVISION MAP ACT

One of the most colorful chapters in American history is the story of land speculation in the United States — and, especially, the story of the land swindlers who bought property, subdivided it, and sold it to gullible people who had never seen it. In the 19th Century, huge pieces of the Midwest were purchased, subdivided, and sold by these swindlers, who promised to build bustling new towns but then disappeared with the profits. By the turn of the century, Middle America had been carved up, and these shady characters turned to exotic "resort" areas like California and Florida, subdividing mountains and deserts and swamps into lots that existed only on paper — and in the minds of small buyers who dreamed of retiring there.

Up until 1930, land in the mountains and deserts of California was still so cheap that these lots were sometimes given away. The Los Angeles Examiner, the flagship of Hearst's great newspaper chain, sometimes gave away lots to new subscribers. Some encyclopedia companies gave away building lots as an incentive to buy a set of encyclopedias. Decades later, people all over the country still cherish their 25-by-50-foot "encyclopedia lots," unaware that their parcel might lie on the side of a steep hill eight miles from the nearest road.

From time immemorial, the mere act of "subdividing" land into smaller parcels has been a profitable enterprise, and that is why, in addition to zoning and general plans, state law requires cities and counties to regulate the subdivision of land. The Subdivision Map Act was the first land-use law ever passed by the state legislature (1907). More than 80 years later, it has evolved into a powerful tool used by local governments to exact many concessions from developers related to what the law calls the "design and improvements" of subdivided land.

The Subdivision Map Act* is equal parts consumer protection, real property law, and land-use regulation. The original intent of the Subdivision Map Act was merely to keep track of the subdivision of land, so that real estate titles would not become clouded. In the 1920s and '30s, it was amended to combat the ill effects of land speculation — especially the problem of "paper" subdivisions, in which a landowner might subdivide and sell property but never provide even the roads required to reach the land. (This practice was so popular in the early part of the century that today there are somewhere between 400,000 and 1 million "paper" lots in California.) Whereas the original Subdivision Map Act merely required developers to file subdivision maps so government could keep track of ownership, a 1929 revision of the law permitted local governments, for the first time, to require subdividers to dedicate land for streets and sidewalks, provide utility easements, and conform their subdivision configurations to major roads.

Beginning in the 1930s, however, a series of amendments to the Subdivision Map Act gave local governments progressively more power to control the "design" and "improvements" of a subdivision. These powers had two purposes: first, to prevent the creation of new subdivided lots that were so small or badly configured that they were essentially unbuildable; and second, to give local governments sufficient legal authority to exact from developers the improvements required to serve a new subdivision. Together, these two powers were supposed to permit local governments to assure "orderly" patterns of development and prevent sprawling subdivisions, which were expen-

* Government Code §66410 *et seq.*

sive for the government to serve. By the 1970s, the Map Act had been recodified from the Business and Professions Code to the Government Code, and coordination was required between subdivision requirements and general plan requirements.

Unlike zoning or general plan law, the Subdivision Map Act does not apply to all land within a community. Rather, it comes into place only when a landowner seeks to subdivide his property. (It applies to condominium conversions as well as the more conventional subdivision of land.) But the influence of the Subdivision Map Act is remarkably broad. Because subdivision regulations typically govern the physical layout of new development, it is fair to say that the Map Act affects the physical appearance of a community far more than the zoning ordinance does. And because local governments may regulate the "design" and "improvements" of a subdivision, the Map Act is an important tool in today's exaction-driven regulatory environment.

## PROCEDURAL REQUIREMENTS OF THE SUBDIVISION MAP ACT

Under the Subdivision Map Act, any time land is subdivided in order to be sold, leased, or financed, the subdivision must be approved by the appropriate local government. For this purpose, each local government must adopt subdivision regulations that comply with the state law. Actions under the Subdivision Map Act are quasi-judicial in nature, which means that they are not subject to initiative and referendum. The quasi-judicial nature of the Subdivision Map Act also means that binding Map Act approvals can be granted by a city or county planning commission. However, some jurisdictions require approval by the city council or board of supervisors as well, and in all cases appeals are provided for.

Technically, the document being approved by the local government is the subdivision "map" — a two-dimensional representation of the land in question, showing exactly how the property will be split up and where the lot lines will be. (This requirement goes back to the original purpose of the Map Act, which was to make sure the government had a precise record of subdivided lots for title purposes.) If a property is subdivided into two, three, or four parcels, the landowner needs governmental approval for a "parcel map," which is not subject to all strict state requirements on subdivisions. However, all subdivisions of five or more lots must go through the full Subdivision Map Act procedures, meaning landowners must receive approval for both a "tentative map" and a "final map."

In practice, the essence of the Subdivision Map Act is the horsetrading that goes on between the local government and the developer over the design and improvements of the subdivision — that is, the site layout and the exactions required to permit the subdivision project to go forward. These negotiations typically occur while the landowner is seeking approval of a tentative map. Under the Subdivision Map Act, the tentative map is really the crucial document, because under law it virtually guarantees approval of the final map. To try to smooth out the sometimes rough process of subdivision negotiations, many cities require a "pre-filing" conference — that is, a meeting with the landowner even before the tentative map application is filed.

An application for a tentative map is subject to hearing and notice requirements similar to those for conditional use permits, and also to the provisions of CEQA. Once a city or county approves a tentative map, the jurisdiction must approve the final map if the project has not changed substantially in the interim. An approved subdivision map is valid for two years by state law, though a locality may, by ordinance, extend that period to three years.

## VESTED RIGHTS AND THE VESTING TENTATIVE MAP

One of the most controversial aspects of planning law in California is the question of vested rights. Under California case law, a developer's right to build becomes "vested" — that is, protected against future growth restrictions or other regulatory reversals — only after a building permit is issued and the developer has made a "substantial investment" in the project. (For a complete discussion of the history of vested rights in California, see the section in Chapter 10 on development agreements.)

In response to this harsh requirement for vested rights, the state legislature has passed two laws that will "vest" a developer's right to build earlier in the process. The first is the "development agreement," which will be discussed later in the book. The second, adopted in 1984, is the "vesting tentative map" under the Subdivision Map Act. The vesting tentative map is identical to a tentative map except that the words "vesting tentative map" are printed on it. By law, when such a map is approved by the local jurisdiction, then the developer has received the vested right to build the project laid out in the tentative map.

The law also specifies that a city or county cannot deny a subdivision proposal simply because a vesting tentative map is sought. However, local governments can — and usually do — ask for far more detailed information about the project at the tentative map stage if vesting is requested. In fact, some localities have established an approval procedure for a vesting tentative map that is often completely different from, and far more difficult than, approval of a simple tentative map.

## CONDITIONS OF APPROVAL

Over the past 20 years, the Subdivision Map Act has become a very powerful tool for obtaining exactions from developers via conditions of approval. The general topic of exactions will be dealt with in greater detail in Chapter 6, but a general description of the Map Act's power in this area is necessary here.

Because the Subdivision Map Act permits local governments to regulate the "design" and "improvement" of subdivisions, the law gives these jurisdictions expansive power to require developers to provide land, public facilities, and/or "in-lieu fees" needed for those subdivisions to operate smoothly. Such exactions are subject to many legal limitations that will be discussed in detail in the next chapter — most notably the requirement that the exactions be directly related to the project in question. But probably no other state law provides so many ways for local governments to exact conditions of approval from developers.

For example, the Subdivision Map Act contains a long list of exactions and fees that local governments have specific authorization to collect. Perhaps the best-known exaction of this type is the so-called "Quimby Fee," which permits cities and counties to require that developers either dedicate parkland or pay an equivalent fee that will allow the governmental jurisdiction to buy land for parks. The Quimby Act* lays out a specific set of procedures that localities must follow if they plan to implement the law's parkland requirements. These procedures include setting standards for parkland (how many acres are required per 1,000 residents, for example) and a specific schedule of how the land and/or fees will be used to develop a park system.

The Subdivision Map Act also specifically permits local governments to require land set aside for streets, bicycle paths, and public transit lines; fees for drainage and sewer facilities, bridges, and groundwater recharge programs; and easements that will provide public access to rivers and streams.

Because the Map Act also contains a separate provision requiring environmental review of subdivision projects, the Map Act and CEQA together can provide a powerful legal tool for environmentally related exactions. Essentially, the Map Act forms the legal basis for any exaction required to mitigate a significant environmental effect that has been identified through an environmental impact report (EIR). (EIRs are discussed in more detail in Chapter 9.)

Finally, the Subdivision Map Act also provides cities and counties with the legal power to impose exactions required to bring subdivisions into compliance with the local general plan. These provisions broaden the Map Act's exaction power beyond the mere dedication of land for streets and schools. In fact, local governments can require any physical rearrangement of the project — or any fee — necessary to bring the project into conformance with the general plan. For example, in an important piece of case law known as the *Soderling* ruling, the Court of Appeal ruled that the City of Santa Monica could require the owner of an apartment building to install smoke detectors in order to convert the building to condominiums. The smoke detectors were required to achieve the city's general plan goal of "promoting safe housing for all."**

According to prominent land-use lawyer Daniel J. Curtin, Jr., the *Soderling* case — and, indeed, all the legal provisions linking the Map Act to the general plan — give local governments tremendous power

---

* Government Code §66477
** *Soderling v. City of Santa Monica*, 142 Cal.App.3d 501 (1983).

to impose conditions that would otherwise be outside the scope of subdivision review. These conditions include fees for child-care centers and public art, inclusionary housing setasides, and other exactions not specifically authorized under the Map Act itself.

## GROUNDS FOR DENIAL

Under the Subdivision Map Act, a city or county must deny landowner permission to subdivide property if, in its legal findings,* the jurisdiction finds that one or more of the following conditions is present:

1. *Environmental Damage.* In combination, the Subdivision Map Act and the California Environmental Quality Act give local governments considerable power over subdivisions. If an environmental impact report finds that the subdivision of land may lead to significant environmental damage, the subdivision application must be rejected. As with any action under CEQA, the local jurisdiction may approve the project even under these circumstances if it adopts a statement of overriding consideration with appropriate findings. (For more information on these CEQA procedures, see Chapter 9.)

2. *Inconsistency with Local Plans.* The subdivision of land must be consistent with the local general plan.

3. *Physical Unsuitability of the Site.* A subdivision must be denied if the proposed project is not "suitable" for the site. For example, in a leading court case on this topic, a proposed residential project in Carmel Highlands was rejected because the soils in the area were not suitable for the system of septic tanks proposed by the developer.** However, in such a situation, the local jurisdiction may approve a subdivision map on the condition that the density be reduced to a level that may be sustained by the physical characteristics of the site.

4. *Conflict With Public Easements.* If utility or other easements run through the site, they must not be disturbed by the subdivision. But the subdivision may be approved if the landowner agrees to provide alternative easements.

---

* A discussion of findings is included in Chapter 4.
** *Carmel Valley View Ltd. v. Board of Supervisors*, 142 Cal.App.3d 501 (1983).

## APPEALS

Local planning commissions often have binding approval power over subdivision maps, but their decisions may always be appealed to the local city council or board of supervisors. Historically, the only party interested in an appeal was the landowner, who asked for one if the planning commission turned him down. As citizen power has grown in recent years, however, citizens have often chosen to appeal subdivision approvals to the legislative body. But appeals often require such a large fee (sometimes as much as $1,500) that citizen groups cannot afford them. Sometimes, staff planning directors may to try to appeal subdivision rulings they dislike. The typical situation occurs when a planning director proposes that a subdivision be denied, or approved only with certain conditions, and the planning commission overrules him. Recently, the state Attorney General's Office issued an opinion concluding that planning directors do, indeed, have the legal power to seek an appeal. In a way, such appeals merely provide a way to ensure that controversial approvals make it to the legislative body, not just controversial denials.

# CHAPTER 6

# EXACTIONS AND LINKAGE

At the beginning of the 1980s, when tourism became San Francisco's leading industry, neighborhood activists started clamoring for the city to do something about the rapid intrusion of tourist hotels into the Tenderloin district. The Tenderloin's old residential hotels were San Francisco's last bastion of unsubsidized low-income housing, but their location — just a few blocks from Union Square — was tempting to developers. Some bought the residential hotels and transformed them into tourist hotels. Others planned the construction of new high-rise hotels in the Tenderloin, complete with luxury suites and conference facilities. From the point of view of grassroots leaders, the Tenderloin was in trouble.

Under the gun to satisfy both the tourist industry and the neighborhood activists, then-Mayor Dianne Feinstein and the board of supervisors took two important policy steps. First, the supervisors imposed a moratorium on the conversion of residential hotels to tourist use. Then Feinstein cut a highly unusual deal with Hilton Hotels, which wanted to expand its high-rise hotel in the Tenderloin, and Ramada Inn, which wanted to build a similar hotel nearby. The two chains would be permitted to build their hotels. But in exchange, Feinstein forced them to agree to subsidize four residential hotels in the neighborhood, in order to protect them from real estate speculation and from conversion into something other than low-income housing.

The Tenderloin hotel deal was one of the first examples in California of what later came to be known as "linkage" — a Robin Hood-like approach of forcing large developers to contribute to solving social problems in exchange for permission to build luxury projects. Coming shortly after the passage of the Proposition 13 tax-cutting initiative, the linkage concept was soon hailed as an effective way for local governments to replenish their treasuries. Shortly after the Tenderloin hotel deal, San Francisco applied the same concept to office developers, creating a linkage program requiring high-rise office developers to build housing (or contribute to a city housing fund). Eventually San Francisco also required downtown developers to pay a transit impact fee, an arts fee, and a child-care fee.

By the late '80s, office developers in downtown San Francisco were required to pay more than $13 per square foot in such "impact" fees on new construction. And while San Francisco might be ahead of most other cities in the range of social programs these fees were used for, the concept of linkage or impact fees caught on very quickly among local governments throughout the state. Fees for low-income housing and child care proved very popular among cities and counties, while school districts began imposing fees on new development (with the state's blessing) to help raise funds to build new schools. The age of the "exaction" had arrived.

## EXACTIONS

The concept of exacting concessions from developers in exchange for permission to build is generations old. But only since the passage of Proposition 13 in 1978 has it become a major instrument of planning policy in California. The basic reason for this change is obvious. Proposition 13 dramatically reduced local government tax revenue and virtually eliminated the ability of cities and counties to issue infrastructure bonds. The passage of Proposition 13 also coincided with the decline of state and federal grant programs that had once provided a good portion of the infrastructure money localities needed to finance growth. Thus, local governments have looked to exactions for needed capital funds.

As the San Francisco example shows, however, after Proposition 13 exactions were not merely a fund-raising technique. They also came to represent an unprecedented linkage between land-use regulations and a city's economic and social problems. Prior to the 1980s, land-use regulations had been used simply to regulate the physical development of the community. The pressing financial requirements of the post-Proposition 13 era, however, forced local governments to scramble for funds wherever they could find them. This search for funds led naturally to real estate developers, who were regarded as creators of local wealth — and, of course, over whom local governments had considerable leverage through the planning process. Thus, local governments throughout the state embarked on aggressive exaction programs, imposing development fees on new projects and negotiating extensive concessions in exchange for permit approvals. In time, when both the courts and state law circumscribed the bounds of exactions, local governments also began an aggressive effort to establish the linkage between the projects before them and the exactions they were requiring.

In general, the power to exact concessions from developers is part of a local government's police power — the concept being that exactions, if they are proper, further a legitimate governmental (public) interest. Because it is an exercise of the police power, the process of exacting concessions from developers can be derived from the general plan and zoning ordinance. Probably the oldest arena for exactions, however, is the subdivision approval process. Because subdivision review emphasized the need for responsible site planning, the process recognized that developers had to account for the consequences of their projects. For example, they would have to build roads and sidewalks within the subdivision, or at least set aside the land required. At first even these modest requirements were challenged. A landmark case from the '50s* dealt with the question of whether a taking occurred if a city required developers to provide curbs, gutters, and storm sewers.

* *Petterson v. City of Napierville,* 137 N.E.2d 371 (1956).

(The city's view was upheld.)

At first exactions were permitted only when there was a direct rela-tionship — a direct "nexus" in legal terms — between the exactions required and the project in question. For example, if a locality required developers to dedicate land for streets within new subdivisions, or even to build those streets, the direct nexus was clear; without the subdivi-sion, the streets would not be needed.

In time, however, the legally acceptable definition of nexus expand-ed, especially in California. If a subdivision developer were required to dedicate land for streets because the residents of that subdivision would use them, surely he could be required to dedicate land for a new school, because children from his subdivision would need a school. Similarly, a developer could be required to set aside land for a park to serve the new subdivision. At the same time, a developer need not set aside land, but could instead pay a fee in lieu of land dedication, which the city or county could bank and use later to buy land for parks or schools. (The state legislature specifically authorized both dedication

of land and payment of in-lieu fees for parks in the so-called Quimby Act.* To this day, such fees are commonly referred to around the state as "Quimby fees.")

Furthermore, in the 1970s, the requirement of a direct nexus was broken, and localities emerged with a great deal more legal power in exacting concessions from developers. In a 1971 case known as *Associated Home Builders,*** the California Supreme Court ruled that an indirect relationship between the project in question and the exaction required was legally acceptable. Subsequently, the Attorney General's Office concluded that the 1971 consistency legislation, combined with Associated Home Builders, gave local governments a great deal more power to exact concessions from developers. In essence, any exactions could be imposed, so long as it furthered the implementation of the city's general plan and bore at least an indirect relationship to the development project being proposed.***

After Proposition 13 passed in 1978, local governments began making much greater use of the broad powers they had acquired in the preceding few years. San Francisco's pathbreaking policies — first the Tenderloin hotel deal and then the office-housing and office-transit linkage fees — came in the early '80s. A few other cities, such as Santa Monica, quickly followed suit, though office-housing linkage fees were confined to a few cities until the end of the decade, when they spread to most large cities in the state, including Los Angeles, San Diego, and Sacramento. Fees for child care and public art also became popular in certain cities.

Other types of development fees were not limited to a narrow political spectrum, however. The breadth of governmental power in the field of exactions permitted suburban jurisdictions to piece together a "capital improvement program" by requiring each developer to pay for a small piece of the overall pie.**** This practice was based on a simple extension of the concept, originally contained in subdivision regulations, that development ought to "pay its own way." If a developer

---

* Government Code §66477
** *Associated Home Builders etc. Inc. v. Cit of Walnut Creek,* 4 Cal.3d. 633 (1971).
*** 59 Ops.Atty.Gen. 129 (1976).
**** For a discussion of capital improvement programs, see Chapter 13.

could be required to build all the streets inside a new subdivision, then surely that same developer could be required to build the new freeway interchange nearby — the theory being, again, that if the subdivision weren't built, the interchange wouldn't be needed.

Similarly, that same developer could be required to pay a fee into a highway fund, because the car trips generated by his subdivision would contribute to the need for additional freeway lanes.

Some cities quantified their capital needs down to the last penny. As part of its growth-management program, Carlsbad estimated the need for all public facilities over a 20-year period, then determined how much each housing unit and each commercial or industrial building would have to contribute to the capital fund. Those calculations became the basis for the development fee structure. Similarly, in 1986 the state legislature authorized local school districts to impose development fees (up to $1.50 per square foot on residential projects, 25 cents per square foot on commercial and industrial projects) as part of an overall statewide school construction finance program.*

But fees and exactions added considerably to the cost of new development. Various building industry estimates suggest that fees on new houses now exceed $20,000 in many Southern California jurisdictions. In a hot real estate market, such as California experienced throughout most of the '80s, builders simply passed this cost on to the home buyers. (When the real estate market slumped at the end of the decade, builders began swallowing this cost in order to lower the price of their houses.)

Builders also objected to what they regarded as a cavalier attitude toward fees on the part of many local governments. Not all cities were like Carlsbad; some plucked development fee figures out of mid-air and then simply dropped the proceeds into the general fund. A backlash was mounting among builders, who demanded, if not lower fees, then at least greater accountability. The response to that backlash came in the form of one court case and one state law.

*  *  *

* Government Code §53080 and §65995.

## THE *NOLLAN* CASE

The California courts had given local governments tremendous leeway in imposing exactions on development. This approach was not surprising, given the courts' general deference to local government and, especially, the courts' reluctance to interfere with local exercise of police power.

However, property rights lawyers kept hammering away, hoping to prove that California-style exactions could be so broad as to constitute a taking of private property without compensation. Not surprisingly, they got nowhere in the California courts — but in 1987 they managed to persuade the U.S. Supreme Court to hear what became a landmark case on the law of exactions.*

The case involved a dispute between the California Coastal Commission and the Nollan family, who owned a small piece of beachfront property near Ventura. The Nollans wanted to tear down their small house and replace it with a two-story house that would have the same "footprint" on the ground. The Coastal Commission, which has land-use authority over beachfront areas, agreed to the new house, but only if the Nollans would grant an easement permitting public access along the beach in front of their house. The Nollans built their house anyway (the access issue did not affect site or construction plans) and sued the Coastal Commission.

The Coastal Commission didn't do anything different in the Nollan case than it had done in hundreds of other permit cases up and down the California coast. One of the commission's major charges is to max-imize public access to the beach, and so the commission had made a public-access easement a condition of virtually every building permit it had granted. In fact, more than 40 of the Nollans' neighbors in the Faria Beach area of Ventura had agreed to this same condition. (The idea, in this  particular area, was to create a public "trail" along the beach connecting two neighboring public beaches.) The Nollans, how-ever, argued that there was no reasonable relationship — no "nexus" — between the construction of a taller house and the access along the front of the beach.

---

* *Nollan v. California Coastal Commission*, 483 U.S. 825 (1987).

The local judge in Ventura sided with the Nollans, but the Court of Appeal sided with the Coastal Commission and the California Supreme Court chose not to take the case. The U.S. Supreme Court, however, was filling up with conservative Reagan appointees and the high court agreed to hear the case. The result was one of the most bitterly divided Supreme Court rulings in recent years.

In rebutting the Nollans' charge, the Coastal Commission's lawyers argued that a relationship did exist between the height of the Nollans' house and the ability of the public to walk in front of house. Two-story houses such as the Nollans', the Coastal Commission argued, created a "psychological barrier" between the public driving along the beach and the beach itself. Encountering a wall of tall homes, an ordinary person might not even know the beach was there — and would certainly not understand that, under state law, he or she had a right to walk along it. Therefore, the Coastal Commission took whatever steps it could to break down this "psychological barrier," including obtaining easements along the beach.

The commission almost won. Justice William Brennan, perhaps the most wily of all members of the Supreme Court, wrote that "state agencies ... require considerable flexibility in responding to private desires for development in a way that guarantees the preservation of public access to the coast." Brennan's opinion was clearly meant to be a majority opinion, but he succeeded in gathering only four of the court's nine votes. The other five justices agreed with the Nollans and signed on to a scathing opinion written by a then-new justice, Antonin Scalia. Calling the Coastal Commission's policy "an out-and-out plan of extortion," Scalia said that no nexus, or relationship, existed between project and exaction. "When that essential nexus is eliminated," he added, "the situation becomes the same as if California law forbade shouting 'fire' in a crowded theater, but granted dispensations to those willing to contribute $100 to the state treasury."

Though it struck down the Coastal Commission's ruling in the particular case of the Nollan property, the Supreme Court hardly outlawed exactions in the *Nollan* ruling. Rather, the court merely reimposed the requirement that a direct nexus be established between the project proposed and the exaction required. In fact, Scalia specifically stated in his ruling that the Coastal Commission would have been well within its rights to require the Nollans to build a public viewing deck on their small lot, because such a condition would have been directly related to government's interest in the project. As of this writing, ideological opponents of the exactions doctrine have filed other lawsuits in an attempt to restrict exactions even more than the  Supreme Court did in the *Nollan* case. So far, however, these cases have not made it up to the appellate courts.

As it stands, however, the *Nollan* ruling did not adversely affect many of the far-reaching exaction ordinances passed by local governments in California during the '80s. In fact, subsequent to the Nollan ruling, San Francisco's $5-per-square-foot transit impact fee was upheld in court.*

The city had met the *Nollan* tests by conducting a detailed economic analysis proving the connection between new office construction and transit ridership. The ruling did, however, encourage the use of development agreements to lock in an exactions schedule that would be insulated from legal challenge. (A development agreement is a kind of contract between a developer and a local government, in which the developer promises to fulfill certain exaction requirements in exchange for a vested right to build the projects. For a full discussion of development agreements, see Chapter 11.)

## AB 1600 AND 'GREEN-EYESHADE' PLANNING

The same year (1987) that the *Nollan* ruling was issued, the state legislature passed a law designed to hold local governments accountable when they impose development fees. In many ways, AB 1600** simply codifies the principles contained in the Nollan case. More specifically, it establishes strict rules local governments must follow when they impose development fees.

AB 1600 requires that, before a development fee is imposed,  a city or county must identify the purpose of the fee and the use toward which it will be put. The locality must document the relationship

---

* *Russ Building Partnership v. City and County of San Francisco*, 44 Cal.3d. 839 (1988).
** Government Code §66000 *et seq.*

between the fee and the project on which it is being imposed. The law also requires local governments to segregate fee revenue from other city funds, and to refund the fees if they are not spent within five years for the purposes originally identified.

The *Nollan* case and AB 1600 have not discouraged local governments from imposing exactions and fees on development projects. By all accounts, these fees are still going up, and they are being used for a broader range of purposes than ever before.

Rather, *Nollan* and AB 1600 have ushered in an era of what might be called "green-eyeshade" planning. Local planners and their consultants now spend a lot of time acting, essentially, as accountants — examining the relationship between the development projects they review and the fees they want to impose. Fiscal analysts are now in great demand, as most jurisdictions follow the trail blazed by San Francisco, Carlsbad, and other cities that have conducted detailed economic analyses to justify their fees.

It remains to be seen whether the courts will permit local governments to accept virtually any fiscal analysis as proof that a direct nexus exists between fee and development. (At this writing, the building industry is challenging Sacramento's commercial-linkage fee in court, saying the study did not prove a strong enough connection.) But there is no doubt that these  analyses will undergo great scrutiny in the years to come.

It's true that such studies are strongly rooted in fiscal and statistical analysis. But it's equally true that their results depend on assumptions, policy judgments, and interpretation. One of the earliest nexus studies was conducted in the early '80s by the City of Santa Monica in order to determine the size of its office-housing linkage fee. The basis of the study was a survey of Santa Monica office employees, which consultants used to analyze how additional office construction would increase the competition for housing in Santa Monica.

The consultants tried to determine such factors as what percentage of people who work in Santa Monica also live there, and what percentage of workers own or rent their homes. They also tried to ask questions that would assess what was important to these office workers in determining where to live — ownership opportunities, proximity to the ocean, relative cost of housing, and so on. Armed with the results of this survey, the consulting firm tried to quantify the demand for housing if more office buildings were constructed, and then reduced that demand to a dollar figure per square foot of office space. As many other cities have done, Santa Monica settled on a politically acceptable figure that was lower than the consultant's estimates.

This short description reveals both the plusses and minuses of the fiscal analysis that is now so prevalent among cities. On the one hand, the city probably made valuable use of all the additional information gathered by the consultant — the percentage of office workers who live in the city, the number of workers who would not move closer to work if it meant they had to rent rather than own their homes, and so on. On the other hand, the survey represented just a snapshot of the work force. And the dollar figures that emerged from the analysis were dependent on how much weight the analysts gave to survey responses — i.e., whether "demand" is defined as the number of workers who would move into Santa Monica if price was not an obstacle (obviously very high) or the number of workers who said they would not move in the next two years under any circumstances (obviously a smaller figure). Then there's the question of determining how much new housing would cost to build. And it's possible that new office buildings might attract different types of companies, with different types of employees, rendering the survey results less than valid.

For better or worse, after AB 1600 and *Nollan*, such studies now form the basis for exactions and fees, which are, after all, one of the principal tools of planning policy and infrastructure funding in the state. In any case, the law is clear: the basis for exactions and fees must be objective findings on the one hand and general policies on the other. Mere statements of intent are not enough.

# CHAPTER 7

# GROWTH MANAGEMENT AND GROWTH CONTROL

In 1970, the City of Petaluma, a small community along Highway 101 north of San Francisco, saw the construction of 59 houses. In 1971, the number of houses built grew to 891 — an increase of 1,400 percent. And for 1972, builders proposed the construction of 1,000 more units. The result of this explosive growth was a pattern of events recognizable in fast-growing areas throughout California today: double-session schools, an overloaded sewer system, and political pressure to restrict growth.

The city responded by imposing a cap of 500 housing units per year and an allocation system that awarded those units to builders who met criteria for both aesthetics and public services. Four years later, the Ninth U.S. Circuit Court of Appeals upheld Petaluma's growth restrictions as a proper exercise of police power.* Since that time, countless cities in California have adopted some version of the Petaluma plan in order to slow and/or manage growth in their communities.

Many have instituted growth "control" by actually restricting growth. Some have restricted growth through a Petaluma-like ordi-

* *Construction Industry Association, Sonoma County, v. City of Petaluma,* 522 F.2d 897 (9th Cir., 1975; certiorari denied by the U.S. Supreme Court, 424 U.S. 934 (1976).

nance that permits only a certain number of housing units per year. Others have restricted commercial growth to a certain amount of square footage per year. More recently, some cities have restricted growth by tying development in their communities to the availability of roads and other infrastructure.

Many other cities have tried to "manage" growth by directing new developments into certain geographical locations, and by taking other steps that seek to ensure that new growth does not run too far ahead of needed infrastructure even if development is not restricted on an annual basis. Many cities (and a few counties) have tried to use control and management mechanisms together. And, increasingly, growth restrictions have come about as the result of initiatives or referenda placed on the ballot by disgruntled local citizens. ("Ballot-box zoning" will be discussed in more detail in the next chapter.)

## GROWTH MANAGEMENT

Even when they were subject to the twists and turns of political manipulation, traditional land-use regulatory schemes such as zoning still had, basically, only two dimensions: use and bulk. All the land in a community was divided into use districts, and then height, bulk, and setback standards were devised for each of those use districts. The concept of "growth management," as defined by prominent land-use lawyer Robert Freilich, adds two new dimensions to the land-use regulatory picture. In addition to use and bulk, growth management schemes also regulate the timing and sequencing of development within a community.

The Petaluma scheme, for example, sought to gain control over the timing of development by restricting the number of building permits granted per year. Other growth management schemes have concentrated on "sequencing" by identifying the sequence in which specific areas will be developed and then reinforcing that sequence with the capital improvement schedule. Thus, Section A of the community might be scheduled for development in 1995, Section B in 2000, and so on; and infrastructure would be built to those areas on the same schedule.

Though Petaluma represented one of the earliest growth management systems in California, the growth-management mold was actually cast by a New York City suburb, Ramapo, in the 1960s. Ramapo's plan was actually more sophisticated than Petaluma's, and it was the first plan upheld in court against the building industry's challenges. Even though Ramapo's growth-management plan, and the legal challenge to it, did not take place in California, they merit discussion because they established the patterns and the ground rules that growth-management systems still follow today.

Ramapo was a rapidly growing suburb in the late '60s; in fact, between 1960 and 1970 the town's population more than doubled. Under the guidance of lawyer Freilich, now one of the nation's most prominent growth-management experts, Ramapo devised a multi-faceted growth-management program that included several very important components:

• *Timing and sequencing.* The town placed all development in Ramapo on a timing and sequencing schedule that forced some landowners to wait up to 18 years to develop their property. The plan did not restrict growth to a certain number of building permits per year, as Petaluma's did, but, rather, granted permits to development proposals that garnered the highest score on a point system (which was similar to Petaluma's).

• *Linkage between timing/sequencing and the capital improvement program.* This linkage was built into the point system described above. Developments providing sewer systems, rather than septic tanks, received higher scores; similarly, more points were awarded to developments in close proximity to parks, arterial roads with sidewalks, and fire houses.

• *Integration of planning, zoning, and the capital improvement plan.* This is equivalent to consistency in a modern-day California general plan, with zoning and the infrastructure construction program reinforcing the growth management concepts contained in the plan.

• *Lower taxes for some undeveloped land.* The plan also called for the purchase of development rights from owners of undeveloped land, a practice that has since become popular among environmentalists. Most important, landowners who had sold their development rights would be taxed at a much lower rate than landowners who continued to hold their development rights.

This growth-management system was upheld in 1972 by the New York State Court of Appeals, New York's equivalent of the California Supreme Court.* According to Freilich himself, the Ramapo system was able to withstand constitutional challenge largely because of the 18-year time limit it contained. This permitted Ramapo to argue in court that the growth-management plan did not shut off a landowner's development possibilities forever, but rather permitted "reasonable use" of a landowner's property within a "reasonable period of time."

## GROWTH MANAGEMENT AND
## GROWTH CONTROL IN CALIFORNIA

Because the Petaluma plan contained an annual cap on the number of building permits, it was really a form of growth "control" rather than growth "management." Although the Petaluma plan does seek to manage the timing and sequencing of development, its most basic purpose is to restrict the overall amount of growth that occurs by limiting the number of building permits to a "below-market" figure each year. Such building caps have emotional appeal to angry Californians who are drafting growth-control initiatives, and in this way they have become the basis for many local growth-restricting efforts around the state.

Whether or not they contain a cap on building permits, however, most California ordinances dealing with growth control or growth management contain the basic elements of the Ramapo method — especially if they were crafted by the local city council, rather than through the initiative process. The most carefully constructed growth-management ordinances typically follow the pattern set by the Carlsbad ordinance, which was discussed in the last chapter.

The Carlsbad ordinance does not have an annual cap on the number of building permits. Rather, it sets out the "ultimate" number of dwelling units that will be constructed in the city (in the year 2010); describes where they will be located within the city; and then permits development only when the infrastructure is constructed concurrently. In this way, the ordinances allows for ups and downs in the market

* *Golden v. Planning Board of Town of Ramapo*, 283 N.E. 2d 291; appeal to the U.S. Supreme Court dismissed, 409 U.S. 1003 (1972).

over a 20-year period, rather than tight-ly constricting growth on an annual basis. As discussed in the last chapter, the Carlsbad ordinance also contains a fiscal component, which imposes fees on developers in order to raise the money required for the infrastructure. It should be clear from this description how neatly a well-thought-out growth-management ordinance fits into a city's general plan.

While building caps may control the timing of development, they do not always control the sequencing — that is, they do not control the sequence in which different areas of the city are developed. And, while metering the rate of growth can be important to avoid over-burdening infrastructure and schools, the sequencing of devel-opment can be even more important. Under traditional "two-dimensional" zoning, a developer could build a sub-division adjacent to the existing city or 10 miles away from it if he could obtain the proper zoning. From the city's point of view, this "leapfrog" subdivision would probably not be a good deal. Because of its location, the subdivision would be expensive to serve with infrastructure and public services, and its approval would proba-bly lead to land speculation all around it. But the principle of comprehensive "use districts" would be upheld.

Broad-based growth-management

## GROWTH MANAGEMENT BY THE NUMBERS

When the famous Petaluma "point system" was upheld in the courts some 15 years ago, it touched off a wave of interest in similar growth-management schemes throughout the state. Today dozens of communities in California, most of them suburban, "ration" residential building permits on an annual basis using some similar point system. Here's how the Petaluma system worked:

The city was divided into four areas, each of which was allocated an equal number of building permits. Of course, demand for permits was not the same in all four areas of the city, so the net effect was to encourage developers to move from one part of town to another in order to avoid competition for permits. In the first year of the allocation system, for example, there were 505 applications for the 125 permits in one quadrant of the city, and only 59 applications (all of them obviously approved) in another quandrant.

The point system involved a matrix through which projects were rated in two broad categories (public services and design/amenities).

The public service portion of the matrix was worth 30 points, with up to five points being awarded under each of the following criteria:

*Water Quality*
*Sewer System*
*Drainage*
*Fire Prevention*
*IImpact on Schools*
*Contribution to Roads and Parks*

The design/amenities portion of the matrix was worth 80 points, with 10 points each being awarded under the following criteria:

*Architectural Quality*
*Sound Circulation*
*Landscaping*
*Open Space and Pathways*
*Bike Paths*
*Public Facilities*
*Linkages*
*Orderly "Infill" Development*
*Low/Mod Housing*

The highest scores didn't automatically win. A certain number of points was required to

systems deal with sequencing, as the Ramapo system did, by tying new development to the construction of infrastructure and then strictly controlling the timing and location of the infrastructure. As the Ramapo case proved, such an approach can survive a legal challenge if the sequencing rules are clear and if development is permitted in all areas of the city within a foreseeable time frame. (Of course, what's "foreseeable" to the planner may not be foreseeable to the developer; hence the ongoing legal challenges surrounding such ordinances.)

But other techniques have emerged to reinforce the sequencing aspect of local growth-management programs. Perhaps the most innovative is the "tiered" approach, which specifies areas where development is encouraged and/or discouraged — and backs up these designations with financial incentives. Perhaps the most sophisticated tiered growth-management plan was implemented with Freilich's help in San Diego. This plan divided the city (and areas likely to be annexed to the city) into three categories: urbanized area, planned urbanizing area, and future urbanizing area — or, to put it more simply, urban, suburban, and rural areas. To encourage infill development, fees were waived in the urban area. To discourage development in the rural area, developers were required to pay the full freight of all infrastructure if they wanted to develop, and were also offered tax breaks under the state's Williamson Act farmland preservation law if they kept the land in agricultural use. In the suburban areas, landowners helped finance infrastructure and public facilities through a mandatory assessment district.

The process worked well — too well, in fact. When the tiers were adopted in 1979, only 10 percent of San Diego's growth constituted infill development in the already urban area. Throughout the '80s, however, the urban areas received 60 percent of the growth, with only about 30 percent going to suburban areas and a smattering to rural areas. The result, however, was that the infrastructure in the urban areas was soon overloaded, and the city did not have the capital funds to solve the problem; after all, 60 percent of the developers had not paid any fees. Faced with an infrastructure crisis, San Diego had to revise its growth-management program and begin imposing fees on infill development.

Despite this remarkable success, however, San Diego's growth management scheme was not tough enough to endure the slow-growth environment that emerged in the city during the building boom of the 1980s. In 1987, threatened with citizen initiatives, the city council also imposed an annual

"make the cut," and a city board then made the final decisions.

Three important points must be understood about the concept of such a matrix. First, the criteria chosen (and the weight given each one) are not objective, but, rather, serve as a reflection of the community's values. Thus, in Petaluma, bike paths were given twice the weight of good sewers. Second, while the matrix appears quantitative, in actuality it's merely the sum total of a series of subjective judgments, which again reflect the values of the community (or at least of the planning staff). And third, such a point system often leads developers to build large-scale projects and/or more expensive homes, because developers need both economies of scale and an extra profit margin in order to build all the amenities required to win the competition.

cap on residential building permits (8,000) and began an overhaul of the growth-management system in order to tie all of its elements together.

Though San Diego is one of the few large cities in the state with a building cap, it is hardly alone. Many fast-growing suburban communities have imposed such a cap in recent years, especially in the Bay Area, San Diego County, and Ventura County. A few cities with really active slow-growth movements have also imposed numerical restrictions on commercial growth as well. Under a 1986 initiative, for example, San Francisco is limited to 475,000 square feet of new office space per year downtown. Such communities still number only a handful, however. A more popular trend is toward growth restrictions that tie new development to infrastructure. The pioneering example was Walnut Creek's 1985 initiative ordinance, which prohibited new development if it would increase traffic congestion at certain already overloaded intersections in the city. (This initiative was eventually struck down by the California Supreme Court as inconsistent with the city's general plan, but other communities have passed ordinances of a similar type.) Depending on the city, such an ordinance could either bring development to a halt or motivate the business community to sponsor a massive road-building program.

### LIMITATIONS AND PROBLEMS

Cities and counties in California do not have unlimited power to restrict growth through growth management systems. As always when they are exercising their police power, local governments must prove that their actions further a legitimate governmental (public) interest and bear a reasonable relationship to the public welfare. According to Daniel J. Curtin, Jr., in the 1976 *Livermore* case,* the California Supreme Court said that local growth-management systems must be addressed in light of these three questions:

*1. What is the probable effect and duration of the ordinance?*

*2. What are the competing interests affected by the ordinance (for example, environmental protection versus the opportunity of people to*

---

* *Associated Home Builders etc. Inc. v. City of Livermore*, 18 Cal.3d 582.

*settle where they choose)?*

*3. Does the ordinance, in light of its probable impact, represent a reasonable accommodation of these competing interests?*

Furthermore, the court said that the "public welfare" must include the welfare of all people who would be affected significantly by the ordinance, and not just those people who live within the boundaries of the city or county enacting the measure. This aspect of the court's ruling is especially important because so many growth-management ordinances deliberately restrict the availability of housing in a given city. In the *Livermore* case, the court essentially said that cities which restrict housing must take into account the regional impact of their actions. The *Livermore* test is potentially devastating, because growth management systems, almost by definition, restrict housing construction and therefore limit the regional supply of housing.

But the building industry has not been able to exploit this *Livermore* test to its maximum advantage. Generally speaking, subsequent court rulings have deferred to local governments' own judgment in determining whether or not their growth-management or growth-control schemes severely harm the regional housing supply. Not surprisingly, most local governments reach the conclusion that their efforts have only a miniscule effect on the regional housing market.

Just because growth-management schemes are popular and legal, however, does not necessarily mean they always work. Most of these schemes have, in fact, slowed growth within the boundaries of a particular city and/or channeled that growth into certain areas of the city where the streets, sewers, and other infrastructure could handle it. Just like growth itself, however, growth management has unpleasant side effects — some of which are predictable, most of which are inevitable given the constraints that local governments work under.

The most common complaint about growth restrictions from the building industry is that they drive up the cost of housing and other development. Obviously, there is some truth to this claim, especially in a high-demand situation. The whole point of a growth-management system is to tinker with the private market, and in the case of an annual cap on construction, the local government is blatantly replacing the private market with rationing. But the true impact of a growth-management scheme on real estate prices depends on many factors, including the underlying market demand, the actions of neighboring local governments, and the amount of speculation occurring in the market. If a market is really "hot," prices may go up with or without growth restrictions.

Second, while growth-management systems may, in fact, preserve the character of a community by limiting development, they can also change the character of a community by encouraging development of a different type and scale. Point systems such as those used in Petaluma encourage developers to build larger, more expensive houses, in order to finance all the amenities they must offer to win the competition for building permits. Point systems also work to the advantage of large development companies that hold large tracts of land because their financial power gives them the ability to hold land for the long-term and provide up-front amenities.

Third, because growth management emerged from residential suburbs, often the systems focus too much on restricting residential development only, and therefore create imbalanced communities with too little housing and too many jobs. In the late '60s and early '70s, this was an understandable response; suburban towns like Petaluma and Ramapo were inundated by residential builders almost exclusively. Nowadays, however, most office and industrial development also occurs in the suburbs, even though many growth-management schemes (and most growth-control measures) still deal only with residential growth.

In large part, this continuing emphasis on residential restrictions is a reflection of the prevailing political ethic. Most polls show that local voters see no connection between residential development and economic growth; often, they want to restrict housing construction, yet they oppose restrictions on other types of growth. The San Diego Association of Governments once issued a report pointing out that all of the cities in the San Diego area which had imposed residential building caps nevertheless continued to subsidize the county's economic development efforts — efforts which, presumably, attracted new residents to the area. Growth-management schemes dealing with residential growth alone will fail to address many of the traffic and density issues in suburban communities today. In fact, such schemes may make those problems worse by creating imbalanced communities and imbalanced commuting patterns.

Finally, given the fragmented nature of local government in California, growth-management systems adopted at the municipal level simply don't make much of a dent in the overarching problems created by growth. Indeed, a recent study of growth-control ordinances in California found that the state's overall growth had not been reduced by the hundreds of local ordinances that had been passed. A community that restricts residential  construction is simply channeling that development to a neighboring community, whose new residents will work in the same office buildings, drive on the same roads, shop in the same stores, and perhaps even go to the same schools.

Growth management and growth control have become leading instruments of public policy in the entire state over the past few years. Yet their overall effectiveness is questionable, especially since they are usually imposed on a city-by-city basis. Growth control can restrict the number of houses constructed in a particular city in a particular year, but it certainly does not change the basic growth dynamics that have generated such great demand for houses in the first place. At best, growth control maintains the status quo in certain communities while moving overall development patterns around; at worst, it encourages suburban sprawl.

The city of San Luis Obispo, for example, has had a strict cap on residential construction for many years, and as a result the city's small-town ambience has been maintained. At the same time, however, most of the area's residential growth has been pushed into other parts of San Luis Obispo County, which have had to grapple with a planning crisis of their own as a result. Whether imposed by a legislative body or by initiative, growth control is a blunt instrument applied to a subtle and sophisticated problem. Some growth-management schemes have grasped part of the subtlety — San Diego's system of encouraging infill development, for example, or Carlsbad's infrastructure-driven growth plan. But few growth management efforts deal successfully with the many, often contradictory pieces of the growth puzzle — infrastructure, finance, housing cost, traffic, and environmental issues.

# CHAPTER 8

# BALLOT-BOX ZONING

One of the most cherished rights of California citizens is the right of initiative and referendum — the right, in essence, to circumvent elected legislators and place pieces of legislation on the ballot (state or local) for a direct vote of the people. Since the right of initiative and referendum was first guaranteed in the state constitution some 80 years ago, it has played a large role in shaping state-level politics and governmental policy. For most of the 20th Century, however, initiative and referendum powers played only a marginal role in local government. The few ballot measures that were placed before local voters usually involved arcane changes to a city charter or other obscure matters of government.

When growth emerged as a local political issue in California, however, the power of initiative and referendum emerged as a leading tool of citizen groups seeking to control it. After a modest beginning in the '70s and early '80s, "ballot-box zoning," as the use of initiative and referendum in the planning arena became known, came into widespread use in the late '80s. Simply by moving the debate over growth from the legislative arena to the ballot itself, ballot-box zoning made land-use planning more overtly political than ever before.

Campaigns had to be organized, funds raised, precincts walked, phone banks manned. For this reason, the presence of planning issues on local ballots fueled the emerging slow-growth movement in California, because citizen groups developed unprecedented political organizing skill. In many communities, ballot-box zoning brought widespread attention to the debate over a community's future in a way that a typical general plan revision could never do. At the same time, however, the practice created a scatter-shot approach to land-use planning in many cities by focusing the public's attention on one project or one issue, rather than the overall planning process.

How and why ballot-box zoning emerged as a strong trend in California has a lot to do with the peculiarities of California law and politics. The powers of initiative and referendum (along with the power of recall) were placed in the California constitution in 1911 at the height of the so-called Progressive era.* At the time, the state legislature was in grip of special interests (especially the Southern Pacific Railroad), which held considerable leverage over elected officials. Hiram Johnson was elected governor in 1910 on a reform platform, promising to rid the state government of these unsavory influences. In his inaugural speech, Johnson called for initiative, referendum, and recall, saying that while they were not "a panacea for all our ills," they "do give the electorate the power of action when desired, and they do place in the hands of The People the means by which they may protect themselves."

Perhaps the most important of Johnson's three tools is the power of *initiative*. This power permits citizens to place any legislative matter on the ballot simply by gathering enough signatures. Thus, when environmentalists could not get the proposed Coastal Act through the state legislature in the early '70s, they gathered signatures and placed the act on the ballot as Proposition 20, where it received overwhelming approval. Similarly, in the late '70s, when Howard Jarvis and Paul Gann decided it was time to cut property taxes, they placed a constitutional amendment on the ballot via the initiative process. The voters approved Proposition 13 in 1978 — probably the most significant

---

* Article II, §8-11, of the California Constitution.

political event of its time in California.

The power of *referendum* does not involve the enactment of a law, but, rather, provides for voter review of a law already passed by the legislative body. A good example on the state level was the 1982 ballot measure involving the proposed Peripheral Canal, which would have diverted more water from Northern California for use in the south. The legislature passed the canal proposal and Gov. Jerry Brown signed the bill. Then, however, environmentalists opposed to the project gathered enough signatures to place a referendum on the ballot, and the voters overturned the legislature. Referendum powers have played an important role in ballot-box zoning because they provide citizens with a tool for reviewing controversial development projects at the local ballot box after they have been approved by the local city council.

The third power, *recall*, is unrelated to the placement of issues on the ballot. It permits citizens to vote on the removal of an elected official in the middle of his or her term.

In the case of qualifying either initiatives or referenda for the ballot, the key distinction is whether the proposal is legislative or quasi-judicial in nature. Any legislative act — that is, any action by a city council or county board of supervisors acting in its legislative capacity — may be placed on the ballot, because such actions set a local government's policy. No quasi-judicial act is eligible to be placed on the ballot, either as an initiative or a referendum, because such acts involve the simple application of existing policy to a specific situation. Thus, a zoning ordinance or a general plan amendment may be placed on the ballot as an initiative or a referendum, but a conditional use permit or a variance may not. (The proper venue for a challenge to a quasi-judicial action is the courtroom, not the ballot.)

Ballot-box zoning began on a small scale in the 1970s, mostly in Northern California. San Francisco residents voted on (and rejected) a number of ballot measures dealing with height limitations and other curbs on commercial growth in the '70s. Petaluma voters approved a referendum in 1973 on the growth-management plan discussed in the previous chapter. Perhaps the biggest landmark was Santa Cruz County's Measure J in 1978, which limited population growth in the county to 2.2 percent per year. The ordinance is still in effect, and it has had a significant impact on the county's growth patterns — especially considering the growth pressure Santa Cruz has felt from the Silicon Valley in neighboring Santa Clara County.

Ballot-box zoning was not widely used in Southern California during the '70s, perhaps because the region still had a solidly pro-growth political posture at the time. However, Redlands, near San Bernardino, established a Petaluma-type permit allocation system via initiative in 1978, and the following year the City of Riverside passed an initiative protecting hillsides and citrus groves.

At the time, however, some legal questions remained about just how broadly initiatives and referenda could be used in dealing with land-use issues. Beginning in 1974, the California Supreme Court issued a series of rulings that seemed to indicate that citizens had considerable leeway in placing such measures on the ballot. Clearly, broad policy decisions, such as those in Riverside and Santa Cruz, were legislative acts and therefore properly belonged on the ballot. But what about a general plan amendment or a zone change? There was little question that large rezonings and general plan amendments constituted fundamental changes in a locality's policy and therefore qualified as legislative actions. But small rezoning and general plan amendments often involved one piece of property — sometimes a small one. Many experts considered such actions to be essentially quasi-judicial in nature.

In 1980, the California Supreme Court, in keeping with its populist attitude at the time, ruled otherwise. In a case from Costa Mesa involving the Arnel Development Co., the court ruled that even the rezoning of a small amount of land (in this case, 68 acres held by three landowners) was a legislative act and therefore could be placed on the ballot.* The decision, commonly known today as the *Arnel* ruling, was a landmark. Although subdivision review, conditional use permits, and the like remained quasi-judicial in nature, the court ruled, in effect, that virtually any zone change and general plan amendment could be placed on the ballot.

*Arnel* opened the floodgates for ballot-box zoning in California.

---

* *Arnel Development Co. v. City of Costa Mesa,* 28 Cal.3d 511.

Few ballot measures appeared in the early '80s because a deep recession had slowed building. When the building boom of the mid-'80s hit, however, land-use ballot measures became more popular than ever before. The watershed year was 1986, when voters in both Los Angeles and San Francisco passed growth restrictions at the ballot box. (Los Angeles's Proposition U halved allowable densities in most of the city's commercial zones, while San Francisco's Proposition M restricted office construction in the downtown area to 475,000 square feet per year.) Prior to 1986, no more than 20 measures dealing with land use had ever appeared on local ballots in one year. Since 1986, that figure has hovered between 50 and 100 per year.

Oftentimes, such initiatives have served as a harbinger of political change in a community. If an initiative gains widespread support, that support is an indication of dissatisfaction with the current political regime — and, therefore, suggests the possibility of a political shift. An initiative's drafters often run for city council in the same election that residents are voting on the initiative, hoping to ride the initiative's popularity into office. If dissatisfaction with the city's current growth policies is widespread, these candidates often win.

At the same time, however, the initiative has proven to be a much more effective tool at the city level than the county level, for two reasons. First, when it comes to growth, people are usually motivated to take action only if they feel directly threatened — and they are much more likely to feel threatened by new development in their own back yard. Second, a grassroots campaign is much easier to run within the small confines of the suburban municipality. The typical initiative campaign has little money and relies heavily on volunteers. Mounting a volunteer campaign across an area as vast as one of California's counties is difficult, especially if the development community is organizing a well-financed campaign in opposition. Except for smallish counties like Santa Cruz and Santa Barbara, no countywide growth-control initiative has ever won in California. By contrast, the state is filled with examples of city initiatives that won big even though the opposition outspent the supporters by 10-to-1 or more.

*  *  *

## TYPES OF BALLOT MEASURES

Ballot measures dealing with planning fall into one of four categories: initiatives, referenda, council-sponsored measures, and advisory measures.

*Initiatives* often tend to be a visceral reaction to "too much growth in our town," imposing some kind of cap on building. By contrast, referenda tend to be project-specific, giving the voters veto power over the city or county's approval of a controversial development project.

*Council-sponsored measures* are often placed on the ballot in response to a citizen initiative. For example, a citizen group might draw up an initiative limiting a community's growth to 500 houses per year; subsequently, the city council may pass a more comprehensive growth-management ordinance (which includes infrastructure financing and other elements) and place it on the ballot in competition with the initiative. Local elected officials don't always place competing measures on the ballot, largely because such action leaves the impression that voters should choose one or the other. If members of a city council believe that a citizen initiative will probably lose, most likely they will let it go down to defeat.

Competing ballot measures can also lead to confusion if both receive more than 50 percent of the vote. In Carlsbad, a council-sponsored growth-management measure won, but a citizen initiative calling for an annual cap on building permits also received more than 50 percent of the vote. Because the council measure did not include an annual building cap, backers of the citizen initiative went to court and claimed that the two were compatible and both should be implemented. The citizens lost, but subsequent ballot measures in many communities have contained "killer" clauses preventing implementation of a competing initiative in such a situation.

*Advisory measures* are non-binding measures placed on the ballot by elected officials in order to float an idea without risking much political capital. Oftentimes a measure is advisory because too many legal and political approvals would be required to place it on the ballot as a binding measure. For example, in 1988 San Diego County voters approved Measure C, an advisory measure suggesting the creation of a regional growth-management board that would allocate growth among all cities in the county. Obtaining approval of all San Diego County's cities would have been difficult (if not impossible) to achieve. But with a clear advisory mandate from the voters, the cities knew that a clear political consensus existed.

Ballot measures may also be categorized by the type of regulatory scheme they impose. Sorted this way, they can be separated into five categories: residential caps, commercial caps, density restrictions, infrastructure measures, and measures requiring subsequent voter approval.

*Residential caps* are still by far the most common type of ballot initiative. Such initiatives are usually patterned after the Petaluma model: An affluent suburban community wants to get a handle on growth, so citizens draft an initiative restricting residential construction to a few hundred homes per year. Such measures may set up a permit allocation system or leave implementation up to the local city council. Suburban communities have rarely concerned themselves with restricting commercial development — partly because historically they did not have to deal with it, and partly because of the property and sales tax revenue.

*Commercial caps* are still fairly rare but they are becoming more common. Most are patterned after San Francisco's Proposition M, passed in 1986, which restricted office development in the downtown area to 475,000 square feet per year. As with residential building caps, commercial caps usually allocate the construction permitted according to some merit system. In San Francisco, for example, a three-member panel selects office projects based on architectural quality and market demand. In recent years, Southern California cities such as Pasadena and Santa Monica have also imposed commercial caps.

*Density restrictions* usually downzone certain districts and then make it difficult for developers to restore the former zoning. Proposition U in Los Angeles took this approach, reducing the floor-area ratio of virtually all commercial strips in the city from 3:1 to 1.5:1. Sometimes such ballot measures require another vote to increase the zoning, or require that future zone changes increase the zoning by only one district at a time (from R-1 to R-2, for example, but not to R-3 or R-4.)

*Infrastructure restrictions* permit new development only if the project would not have a significant impact on the community's infrastructure. Ballot measures that tie development to traffic levels are especially popular. Probably the most prominent infrastructure-related initiative was Walnut Creek's Measure H in 1985, which prohibited construction of projects that would worsen traffic congestion at selected intersections around the city. Of course, such initiatives can turn out to be growth restrictions or road-building mandates, depending on a developer's willingness to spend money; in Walnut Creek, a developer could "build his way" around Measure H by providing enough road improvements to eliminate the traffic congestion his project would cause. Such schemes could run afoul of the Nollan case, of course, because, in order to build, developers may be required to clean up traffic problems that they did not create. (The Walnut Creek ordinance was struck down by the California Supreme Court for other reasons. For further information on the Nollan case, see Chapter 6.)

*Measures requiring subsequent voter approval* have become more popular in recent years, and they account for the large number of ballot measures we see today. Such measures permit future development or changes to city plans, but only if those actions are also approved by the voters. Perhaps the best example of this type of measure came in Lodi, where a 1981 initiative removed all land in the city's sphere of influence (outside city boundaries) from the general plan and required another ballot measure to reinstate property to the plan. Thus, Lodi could not even begin planning for future development of property within its sphere of influence unless the voters approved. Over the next decade, more than 20 different property owners placed measures on the ballot seeking re-entry to the general plan, but only four of them won approval. One year, Lodi residents voted on 10 such measures and rejected them all.

## THE INITIATIVE POWER AND PLANNING REQUIREMENTS

Local initiative powers are engaged in a constant legal struggle with the state's planning laws. Initiative powers are guaranteed in the California constitution, and they are supposed to be available to the public free of procedural and legal entanglements that could rein them in. At the same time, state laws, which create many procedural requirements, are supposed to take precedence over local ordinances.

The courts and the legislature have already concluded that local land-use initiatives are exempt from the normal procedural requirements contained in general plan law, such as notice and hearing requirements. Despite tenacious lobbying by the building industry, local initiatives remain exempt from the California Environmental Quality Act. A city council or board of supervisors may, however, "sit" on a proposed initiative for 30 days while studying its impact.* The Riverside County Board of Supervisors used this technique in 1988 in order to bump a slow-growth initiative from the June ballot to the November ballot. (By the time the period was over, it was too late to place the measure on the June ballot.) The move might very well have caused the initiative's defeat, since it interrupted the slow-growthers' momentum and gave the builders more time to organize an opposition campaign.

Still unclear, however, is whether a ballot initiative must abide by the consistency requirements in state general plan law. On this point, the building industry has actually had some success in court. Initiative powers are so jealously guarded that courts almost never stop initiative elections from occurring, preferring instead to let the voters decide on the initiative and then sort out its legality later. However, several years ago, an appellate court actually blocked an election in the City of Norco because the proposed initiative would have created a zoning ordinance that was inconsistent with the general plan.** Needless to say, this motivated citizen activists to write virtually all subsequent initiatives in the form of general plan amendments. (In some cases, two measures have been placed on the ballot — one to change the general plan and one to change the zoning ordinance.)

Nevertheless, the relationship between local initiative powers and state general plan law remains unclear. In the *Lesher* case, decided in late 1990, the California Supreme Court had the opportunity to confront the issue but chose not to. Instead, the high court struck down

---

* Elections Code §3705.5 (pertaining to cities) and §4009.5 (pertaining to counties).
** *deBottari v. City of Norco*, 171 Cal.App.3d 1204 (1985).

Walnut Creek's Measure H by concluding that it was a zoning ordinance that was inconsistent with the city's general plan.*

---

* *Lesher Communications v. City of Walnut Creek,* 52 Cal.3d 531.

# CHAPTER 9

# THE CALIFORNIA ENVIRONMENTAL QUALITY ACT

Probably no state law — not even the general plan law — has had a more profound effect on land-use planning than one particular law that is not, strictly speaking, even a planning law: the California Environmental Quality Act, commonly known as CEQA.*

To understand the full significance of CEQA, as the law is commonly called, imagine what land-use planning in California would be like without it. General plans and zoning ordinances could be written and revised without much consideration for environmental consequences. In reviewing a tall office building or a huge suburban subdivision, local planners would concern themselves only with zoning matters and perhaps the site planning questions that emerge under the Subdivision Map Act. Some projects might be constructed with hardly any review at all, because the trend toward discretionary government review is a result, in good measure, of the approach CEQA takes to development. The same is true of exactions, because our current concept of the purpose and broad use of exactions (to "mitigate" a project's "impact" in CEQA jargon) are derived directly from CEQA. Environmental impact

* Public Resources Code §21000 *et seq.*

reports (EIRs), lengthy review processes, expensive mitigation measures, even the concept of a broad-based public debate over a particular
development project — all are attributable in large part to CEQA's role
in local land-use planning.

Unlike zoning or general plan laws, CEQA is not concerned with
overarching urban planning issues. Rather, CEQA is a single- issue
law concerned with one aspect of public policy — environmental protection — that overlaps with planning.

CEQA is the product of the first wave of environmental consciousness, which swept the United States in the late '60s. Enacted in 1970,
CEQA is patterned after a federal law, the National Environmental
Policy Act (NEPA), which was enacted by Congress the previous
year.* (According to some accounts, NEPA is actually patterned after
CEQA, which was written first but passed second.) They are so similar, in fact, that in deciding CEQA cases, California courts sometimes
look for direction to federal court rulings about NEPA.

Because CEQA is concerned solely with the environment, rather
than with broader land-use planning issues, its regulatory scheme is
different from traditional planning and, in fact, turns many of those
principles upside down. Whereas traditional zoning and planning
schemes treat all property as similarly as possible, CEQA treats each
property and each proposal uniquely. Often, this approach creates conflict with traditional planning processes. Just as often, however, the
CEQA approach has "rubbed off" on local planners, who have undertaken more project-specific review within the context of traditional
planning tools. CEQA's influence is so pervasive that it will be discussed in greater detail than almost any other regulatory tool.

## CEQA'S ROLE

Contrary to popular perception, CEQA's primary function is not to
improve California's environment directly. CEQA does not usurp local
authority over land-use decisions or establish a state agency to enforce
the law. CEQA does not even require local governments to deny all

---

* 42 United States Code 4321.

projects that would harm the environment.

Rather, CEQA's role is primarily informational, and in fact the act is sometimes referred to as a "full-disclosure law." By law CEQA has four functions:

1. To *inform* decision-makers about significant environmental effects.

2. To *identify* ways environmental damage can be avoided.

3. To *prevent* avoidable environmental damage.

4. To *disclose* to the public why a project is approved even if it leads to environmental damage.

In carrying out these functions, the CEQA process is meant to unearth information about the likely environmental consequences of any "project" — from general plan to permit approval — and make sure that those consequences are debated by the public and elected officials before a decision is made.

As we will discuss in much greater detail later, this process begins with an assessment of whether a specific project is subject to CEQA's provisions at all. Then local government planners conduct an initial study of the probable environmental consequences of a project. If those consequences are likely to be significant, then an "environmental impact report" must be prepared, specifying the environmental damage and laying out ways to "mitigate" that damage. The "initial study" and the EIR form the basis for public discussion of the project.

In this sense, CEQA is not unlike many state planning laws, such as the general plan law. The general plan law requires local governments to deal with certain issues in the general plan, such as land use and circulation. The law even specifies that the land-use element of a general plan discuss the distribution and location of certain facilities in the community. But the law does not specify which land uses should be located close to each other or how transportation between those two land uses should work. Such decisions are left up to the local community, which is free to implement the law with virtually no interference from state agencies.

Similarly, CEQA requires that local governments gather information about the environmental consequences of a proposed building project and debate the project in light of this environmental information.

CEQA does not absolutely require that environmentally harmful projects be rejected, nor does it even specify how to minimize environmental damage. Again, these decisions are left up to local governments, which operate with relatively little interference from the state. As with general plan law, the Governor's Office of Planning and Research (OPR) is required to prepare guidelines for CEQA on a regular basis. While the *General Plan Guidelines* are truly advisory, however, the *CEQA Guidelines* are binding on local governments.* These guidelines have grown from about 10 pages when they were first written, in the early '70s, to almost 200 pages today.

## THE ROLE OF THE COURTS IN EXPANDING CEQA

CEQA's procedural nature has made it perhaps the most litigated environmental or planning law in the state. Even environmental law experts agree that CEQA's procedural requirements are so broad, and so expandable, that virtually any CEQA document could be challenged in court with some success. Also, no state agency holds the administrative power to enforce CEQA; it is meant to be enforced by citizens through litigation. (The only significant limitation is that a CEQA lawsuit must be filed within 30 days after the CEQA process is concluded.)

CEQA's litigious nature has had two consequences. First, citizen groups (environmentalists, homeowners, and so forth) have used CEQA litigation to obtain tremendous power over land-use planning and, especially, the review of particular development projects. Whether or not they have true environmental concerns, citizen groups can usually find some hook under CEQA that they can use to take a project to court. As a result, citizen groups often succeed in stopping a project, slowing it down, or forcing changes to it.

Second, the vast amount of CEQA litigation has given the courts an unusual opportunity to shape the law and how it is used throughout the state. Since its passage in 1970, CEQA has generated more than 200 appellate decisions, the vast majority of which have expanded CEQA's scope and requirements. According to planner/lawyer Ronald Bass,

* Administrative Code §15000 *et seq.*

these court rulings have fallen into four general categories:

1. *Whether CEQA Applies.* Especially in the early days of CEQA, developers and local governments often argued that certain projects were exempt from CEQA review altogether. Even in recent years, a few important cases have revolved around this question.

2. *Whether an EIR Should Be Prepared.* This is perhaps the most common area of litigation. Citizen groups often challenge a project's "negative declaration," which declares that an EIR is not necessary. Over the years, whenever a question in this area has arisen the courts have usually ordered the EIR to be done. This line of cases has greatly expanded CEQA's scope by requiring EIRs on a broad range of projects.

3. *Whether the EIR Is Adequate.* Another common legal tactic is to challenge the adequacy of the EIR, arguing that some particular aspect of the discussion is incomplete. Again, over time the courts have greatly broadened the scope of EIRs themselves by requiring more complete discussions of potential environmental damage.

4. *Whether Procedures Were Followed.* CEQA contains a broad array of procedural requirements, from hearings to findings to review processes. Generally, the courts have protected these procedural safeguards zealously.

Though CEQA has been the subject of more than 200 appellate cases, one stands far above the rest in terms of importance: the so-called *Friends of Mammoth*\* case in 1972, in which the California Supreme Court ruled that CEQA applies to private development projects as well as public projects. No other case has had a broader impact on the everyday use of CEQA in the planning field — nor does any other case illustrate the expansive attitude the courts have brought to CEQA cases.

After CEQA was passed in 1970, the law was applied only to strictly governmental projects — the construction of buildings, public works facilities, and other projects in which the government was a direct participant. (As with many other aspects of CEQA, this practice was derived from the way the federal government implemented

---

\* *Friends of Mammoth v. Board of Supervisors,* 8 Cal.3d 847 (1972).

NEPA.) In the *Friends of Mammoth* case, however, environmentalists and the state Attorney General's Office argued that CEQA should apply to private projects that must receive governmental approval in order to build.

At the time, CEQA said that local governments had to undertake environmental review "on any project they intend to carry out ... "* In strict legal terms, then, the California Supreme Court had to determine whether a private development proposal constituted a "project" under CEQA, and whether a local government's issuance of development permits constituted "carrying out" a project. Remarkably, it took the Supreme Court nine printed pages to work through these questions.

The court concluded that the term "project" did indeed include "the issuance of permits, leases, and other entitlements." And after reviewing the legislative history of CEQA (which at one time included the phrase "any project or change in zoning they intend to carry out"), the Supreme Court concluded that if "project" encompassed development permits, then certainly issuing such permits constituted a "carrying out" of those projects. Suddenly, one day in 1972, CEQA applied not just to public building projects but to all private building projects as well. It has been a major element in local land-use planning ever since. (The state legislature subsequently amended CEQA to make the meaning of the *Friends of Mammoth* case clear in the law itself.)

The significant role of litigation in CEQA's development has been both its blessing and its curse. On the one hand, the court rulings have

---

* Public Resources Code §21151.

expanded the discussion of environmental factors far beyond the modest expectations of the legislators who originally passed the bill more than 20 years ago. Probably nowhere else in the world are the environmental consequences of development projects so broadly — and openly — debated as in California.

At the same time, however, CEQA's ever-broadening requirements sometimes make it difficult for planners to determine how much environmental review is enough. Whenever the adequacy of environmental review is challenged, the appellate courts' response is usually that more environmental analysis should have been done. A local planner in Southern California once called the CEQA process "Kafkaesque." "These things go to court," he said, "and the judges tell us how we're wrong. But they don't tell us how we can be right." In practice, the result is one of two very different attitudes toward projects under CEQA. Cautious local governments suffer from "paralysis by analysis" because they fear litigation. By contrast, localities hoping to push an important project through are often tempted to cut corners under CEQA, either by underestimating likely environmental damage and therefore avoiding the EIR process altogether; or by trying to minimize delays and "too much" public scrutiny by determining that a project warrants only a negative declaration.

## THE THREE-STEP PROCESS

Under the state *CEQA Guidelines*, local governments must follow a three-step process in applying CEQA to a particular development project. Depending on the size and likely impact of the project, the result of this analysis can be anything from no further environmental review to a full-blown EIR. If more than one public agency is involved in the environmental review, the agency with the greatest responsibility for reviewing the project will be designated as "lead agency."

### STEP 1: IS THE ACTION IN QUESTION A "PROJECT" UNDER CEQA?

Generally speaking, any discretionary action involving the physical environment is a "project" subject to CEQA, ranging from the approval of a general plan to the issuance of grading permits for major projects. Ministerial actions, on the other hand, are not "projects" because their issuance does not involve any discretion. Similarly, many local ordinances not related to land uses (an increase in water rates, for example) don't qualify as "projects."

Traditionally, the classic example of a ministerial action exempt from CEQA was the issuance of a building permit. However, a 1987 Court of Appeal ruling suggests that even a building permit may not be ministerial if the city staff exercises some discretion in issuing it. The case* involved the proposed construction of a tall office building in the Westwood section of Los Angeles. The city did not subject the project to environmental review because the property was already zoned properly and no planning commission review was required; the only approval needed was the "ministerial" building permit. However, the Court of Appeal found that the city's "plan check" system for granting building permits on large projects did, in fact, involve discretion. For example, the city engineer was empowered to determine what dedications were required for ingress and egress. Thus, the court said, in Los Angeles even a building permit on a large project was subject to CEQA. The city subsequently established a discretionary review process for large buildings.

Even if an action is discretionary, sometimes it may be exempt from CEQA review anyway. Both the state legislature and the secretary of the state Resources Agency have identified specific types of projects that are exempt. Sometimes these exemptions reflect the fact that such projects are unlikely to create environmental damage; sometimes they merely attest to the lobbying power of a particular interest group. Statutory exemptions (those exemptions determined by the legislature) include demolition permits, adoption of coastal and timberland plans, and some mass transit projects. The legislature also exempted projects associated with the 1984 Olympic Games in Los Angeles. Categorical exemptions (those exemptions specified by the Resources Agency) are divided into some 19 categories, but they include building projects of under 10,000 square feet, projects of three homes or fewer, projects that will result in "minor alterations on the land," and the transfer of

* *Friends of Westwood v. City of Los Angeles*, 191 Cal.App.3d 259

land ownership in order to create parks. (A complete list of the exemptions is included in the *CEQA Guidelines*.)

## STEP 2: THE INITIAL STUDY

If a development proposal is found to be a "project" under CEQA and is not exempt, the local government then moves on to the next step: an assessment to determine if the project may produce significant environmental effects. Significant environmental effects include, for example, any project that would have a major impact on the aesthetic quality of an area; "substantially diminish" a habitat for fish, wildlife, or plant life; or displace a large number of people. Though the *CEQA Guidelines* include a list of significant effects, the state does not establish yardsticks or threshholds for these effects, leaving that determination up to the judgment of local communities. For their part, many local communities haven't adopted threshholds either, meaning that the determination of "significant" effects is made by an individual staff planner or planning consultant working on the project.

This determination is usually made with the assistance of a so-called initial study. In the initial study, a local planner or consultant uses a checklist to assess all the environmental factors and determine if the project may have significant environmental impacts. This checklist usually includes a long list of possible areas of environmental damage that government agencies should review — geology, air pollution, damage to plant and animal life, and so on. In the past, many cities have used such a checklist in stripped-down form, checking "yes," "no," or "maybe" with no further explanation. Though the "Naked Checklist" was widely used in the '70s and '80s, it is now illegal as the result of a Court of Appeal ruling in 1988.

If the initial study reveals that the project will have no significant environmental effects, then the local government prepares a document known as a "negative declaration," a simple declaration that no further environmental review is needed. Sometimes, if a developer can eliminate all significant environmental effects by changing his project or adopting mitigation measures, the local government will prepare what is known as a "mitigated negative declaration" — meaning certain steps must be taken but no further environmental review is necessary.

Though the mitigated negative declaration is permitted under the *CEQA Guidelines*, it is not explicitly mentioned in the CEQA law itself and environmental lawyers argue that it is often used a means of short-circuiting environmental review.

The case that outlawed the "Naked Checklist" involved both a checklist problem and problems created by a mitigated negative declaration. A private developer proposed building a sewage treatment plant for a small development project along the Mendocino County coast. In conducting the initial study, Mendocino County planners checked "no" for 38 of the checklist's 43 questions and provided a boilerplate answer for the other questions, where environmental problems had been identified. The permit was approved, with a mitigated negative declaration requiring approval from regional air pollution and water quality boards, as well as a plan for sludge disposal.

This skimpy environmental review up front led to problems later on. As it turned out, the Regional Water Quality Control Board found hydrological problems. The county then required the applicant, Harold K. Miller, to submit drainage studies. Miller then proposed a drainage solution, and the board of supervisors approved the project.

The county's environmental review did not hold up in court. In the *Sundstrom* case,* the Court of Appeal in San Francisco wrote: "The initial study ... displayed only a token observance of regulatory requirements. In the case of several questions marked — no, — evidence clearly disclosed that the project would disturb existing conditions, e.g., change present drainage characteristics and alter local plant conditions." The court went on to say that a "Naked Checklist" did not satisfy CEQA's goal of providing the public with detailed information about the environmental impact of a project.

Therefore, a "no" on the checklist now must be accompanied by a short explanation of why there will be no environmental impact. CEQA lawyer Dallas Holmes, who coined the term "Naked Checklist," likens the requirement to the 10th-grade math teacher's admonition that students show their work. Being required to show one's work may help to achieve the goal of discouraging cheating or guessing — a goal

---

* *Sunstrom v. County of Mendocino*, 248 Cal.Rptr. 352.

of both 10th-grade math teachers and California judges reviewing CEQA cases. (Incidentally, the Sundstrom case also ended the common practice of approving projects contingent on the results of subsequent environmental studies.)

### STEP 3: THE ENVIRONMENTAL IMPACT REPORT (EIR)

If the initial study reveals that the project may have a significant environmental impact, the local government must prepare an environmental impact report. EIRs are prepared for only the small minority of projects which, according to the initial study, "may" produce significant environmental effects. But, as many courts have pointed out, the EIR is the "heart" of CEQA — a broad-ranging document meant to provide lots of information to the public about the environmental effects of a big project.

In many ways, only the EIR can satisfy CEQA's requirement of informing the public. Even an annotated initial study will provide relatively little information about a project's environmental effects. That is why the courts, when presented with the question, usually have ruled that EIRs should be prepared on large projects.

Because of ever-broadening court directives about what it must contain, however, the EIR has become expensive and time-consuming. The typical EIR costs somewhere into five figures and takes several weeks (or months) to prepare; the team of consultants typically includes planners, geologists, biologists, even paleontologists. On very large projects, EIRs often go through several rounds, take several months (or years), and cost in the hundreds of thousands of dollars.

Developers often fight the preparation of an EIR for several reasons. The most obvious reason is the cost, which they must bear. In many cities, developers hire environmental consultants directly to prepare the EIR, though environmentalists have challenged this practice as a conflict of interest. In a growing number of cities, the city selects the EIR consultant and payment is funneled through the city to ensure greater objectivity.

The direct cost of the EIR may be the least of the developer's concerns however. Far more important is the time that preparing and debating an EIR takes. If a large EIR takes six months and $100,000 to prepare, the cost to the developer is far more than $100,000, because in all likelihood the developer is "carrying" the property — making option or interest payments each month that will amount to several hundred thousand dollars on a large parcel of land. A lengthy environmental review process can kill a project if a developer does not have deep pockets. Furthermore, the EIR is likely to greatly increase the cost of building a project, because the developer will be responsible for "mitigating" (minimizing or eliminating) any likely environmental damage identified in the EIR.

## TYPES OF EIRS

EIRs come in all shapes and sizes, and the distinctions are important. Sometimes they are prepared for specific development projects, sometimes for larger planning processes. Sometimes a series of EIRs is prepared on large projects; other times EIRs are added to or supplemented as new information arises. Here is a rundown:

*General plan EIRs.* The most common EIR deals with a specific development project — an office building, a hotel, a subdivision, a road-building project. But individual development proposals are not the only "projects" subject to CEQA. A city's general plan is also a project, so extensive EIRs must be prepared in conjunction with the preparation or revision of a general plan and/or its elements. The general plan revision and its EIR are often prepared simultaneously, sometimes even as part of the same document.

*Program EIRs and tiering.* Program EIRs and tiering are used to encourage efficiency in environmental review. The *CEQA Guidelines* encourage local governments to use "program" EIRs to deal with a series of related actions that may occur under one program. But program EIRs do not necessarily eliminate the need for more detailed environmental review on each specific action.

Tiering is a similar concept used in dealing with very large projects that will be reviewed and built over a long period of time, as with an extensive road-building program. Perhaps the best recent example of tiering involves the three proposed toll highways in Orange County. Initially, a broad EIR was prepared to examine the environmental impact of various proposed corridors. When the alternative corridors

were narrowed to a few, a more detailed EIR on the specific environmental impact of those three alternatives were prepared. Finally, when
a route corridor was selected — when, in the words of one lawyer who
worked on the project, the decision boiled down to "which trees to
fell" — a project-style EIR was produced.

On the one hand, tiering provides more environmental information
earlier in the process than a standard EIR produced after the planning
work has been done; on the other hand, if the entire process takes several years, the initial EIR's information may be out of date.

*Additions, supplements, etc.* Over time, the project in question
might change or new information may come to light about its environmental consequences. If so, further review under CEQA may be necessary. The ex-
tent of that
review, how-
ever, depends
on the scale
and signifi-
cance of these
changes.

Technical
corrections
that do not in-
volve substan-
tive changes

can be included in an *addendum*. If only small changes are required, a
*supplemental EIR* will suffice. If the project has been substantially
changed, however, a *subsequent EIR* may be necessary. Unlike a supplemental EIR, which need deal only with the changes in the project, a
subsequent EIR is really an entirely new EIR, subject to the same noti-
fication and review requirements of the original EIR.

In practice, local governments often prepare a supplemental EIR
when a subsequent EIR is called for — especially if there is political
pressure to push the project through. The reasons for doing so are obvious. A supplemental EIR is far less costly and time-consuming, and it
does not open up the entire environmental review process for discus-

sion. Also, in many cases, city approvals may be based on the certification of a previous EIR and neither city officials nor applicants want to jeopardize that approval.

*Draft and final EIRs.* The last important distinction must be made between the draft EIR and the final EIR. The draft EIR is the original document, including all environmental analysis, prepared by the local government staff or consultant. The draft is circulated to a vast array of individuals and organizations, including citizen groups, lobbying organizations, public utilities, and state and federal agencies. These people then comment on the draft and the staff or planning consultant must respond to all the comments. The comments and responses are then incorporated into the final EIR. If additional environmental information is revealed after the draft EIR is circulated, that information must also be circulated for comment.

## CONTENTS AND PREPARATION OF EIRS

Both the CEQA law and the *Guidelines* contain a vast array of requirements governing the organization and content of an environmental impact report. In keeping with CEQA's reputation as a complicated, procedurally oriented law, however, any one of these requirements can be used (or abused) to shape the scope of environmental review.

For example, the EIR must contain a project description which includes, among other things, a statement of the project's objectives. At first this requirement may sound straightforward and innocuous. But its wording can vastly alter the entire CEQA process regarding the project — especially the discussion of alternatives to the project, which is becoming a significant part of environmental review. Take, for example, a proposed highway. If the description states that the project's objective is to improve the flow of vehicle traffic, then the alternatives are likely to include a narrow range of alternative routes, configurations, and sizes. If, on the other hand, the project's objective is stated to be the fast and efficient transportation of people, then the alternatives will be much broader: buses, light rail, high-occupancy-vehicle lanes, perhaps even a monorail. A highway is almost certain to be more environmentally significant than the transit alternatives, but if the transit alternatives do not meet the project's objectives they will not even be considered under CEQA.

The EIR also must contain two elements designed to make it easy to read and understand. First is a table of contents or index. Second is a summary of its contents, written in understandable language, that does not exceed 15 pages. As EIRs become longer and more technical, these provisions become more important in achieving CEQA's goal of public information and debate.

The EIR also must contain discussion of separate important items relating to the environmental impact of a project. They are:

1. *Significant* environmental effects.

2. *Unavoidable* environmental effects.

3. Significant *irreversible* environmental change.

4. *Alternatives* to the proposed project.

5. *Cumulative impact* that the project might have in combination with other projects.

6. *Growth-inducing impact* of the project.

7. *Mitigation measures* that will minimize the environmental effects.

The first three items (significant, unavoidable, and irreversible effects) have traditionally been the guts of an EIR, as they may be determined by relatively straightforward and objective scientific inquiry. The next three items (alternatives, cumulative impact, and growth-inducing impact) have traditionally been called "back-of-the-book" items and given only the most cursory treatment in EIRs. As we shall see, however, these three items are receiving greater scrutiny from the courts, and are the subject of great debate. Mitigation measures have always received considerable attention in the CEQA process, but until recently little attention has been paid to whether they are actually carried out.

Typically, an EIR will be divided into sections derived from the initial study's checklist. Any item on the checklist checked "yes" or "maybe" will receive its own detailed discussion: air quality, water supply, traffic, plant and animal life, and so forth. Each section usually follows the same format. A typical format is to divide the section into four parts: the current environmental "setting" (which is required by law), an "impact analysis" that will describe the changes, a list of mitigation measures, and a final description of the environmental setting after the project has been built and the mitigation measures have been implemented.

These sections are typically written by specialists, such as traffic consultants, biologists, archaeologists, and so on. (Sometimes these specialists are on the staffs of the planning consultants that do EIRs, and sometimes they are subconsultants.) Some of this specialized material is gathered specifically for the project in question, but most EIRs rely heavily on databases in common use.

Traffic consultants, for example, may make counts of current traffic near the site. But to forecast the impact, they will almost certainly use the "trip tables" from the Institute of Transportation Engineers to determine how many vehicle trips are likely to be generated from the construction of a certain number of houses or a certain amount of office space. Similarly, biologists will walk the site to survey plant and animal life. But they will also use a state database of plants and animal life, and compile their own databases if they do many environmental surveys in the same area. At its best, this material can be insightful and useful. At its worst, it is true boilerplate. In fact, some of the information is so easily transferrable from one document to another that occasionally EIRs or their technical background reports will contain accidental references to another city or another project.

The adequacy of these scientific inquiries may, of course, always be challenged in court. And if something important is  overlooked by a technical expert, or by a planning consultant summarizing the technical expert's work for the EIR, the EIR may become legally vulnerable and the project may be in jeopardy. The last-minute discovery of an endangered species on the property, for example, is almost certain to kill or delay a project. In recent years, however, the scentific analysis in the EIR has not been the source of legal challenge and controversy. Most of the attention has been focused on the so-called "back of the book" items and on the effectiveness of mitigation measures.

## THE 'BACK OF THE BOOK' ITEMS

Traditionally, the "back of the book" items — cumulative impacts, growth-inducing impacts, and alternatives — have received very little attention, often as little as a page or two in an EIR. Partly this is because the methods of analysis required have not been well developed. But in part this cursory review of back of the book items has come from a desire to keep EIRs short and inexpensive. These items were simply not considered as valuable as the objective scientific information gathered by specialists. However, as growth and growth control have loomed larger as political and legal issues in California, agencies have been under considerable pressure — from courts and citizen groups — to give these sections equal time.

## CUMULATIVE IMPACT

The main purpose of the cumulative impact requirement is to make sure that a community does not approve a series of small projects without considering the overall effect of these actions on the environment. (Similarly, the cumulative impact requirement should make it harder for developers to slice large projects up into smaller pieces in order to avoid a CEQA review.)

Cumulative impact was given little attention until 1984, when the Court of Appeal in San Francisco forced the city of San Francisco to rewrite EIRs on four downtown skyscrapers because cumulative impact had not been considered adequately.* Specifically, the court said the San Francisco Planning Commission should have taken into account the likely construction of several additional office projects. (Some had already been approved, some were "in the pipeline," and others, while they had not yet been formally proposed, were the subject of wide discussion.) "The only reason we can infer for the commission's failure to consider and analyze this group of projects was that it was more expedient to ignore them," the court said.

The San Francisco case was a good example of both the weaknesses and the strengths of CEQA. The EIRs were routinely redrafted and recertified with hardly any fanfare, so the opinion had no effect on the construction project. Moreover, the buildings were almost finished by the time the court handed down its ruling. Yet the slow-growthers who

---

* *San Franciscans for Reasonable Growth v. City and County of San Francisco,* 151 Cal.App.3d 61.

brought the suit used the court ruling as another piece of evidence in their frankly political (and ultimately successful) struggle to curb office construction in downtown San Francisco. And, of course, once the Court of Appeal ruling was on the books, planners in San Francisco and elsewhere in the state had to pay attention to it.

The cumulative-impact requirement got another boost four years later in the California Supreme Court's ruling in the *Laurel Heights* case.* Though this case has received more publicity for its discussion of alternatives under CEQA (which will be explained in detail below), it also discouraged developers from cutting a project up into phases in order to avoid a tough cumulative-impact analysis. The University of California, San Francisco, had proposed moving its medical laboratories to the Laurel Heights neighborhood. Though UCSF clearly planned to move all its labs to Laurel Heights eventually, the EIR dealt only with the initial phase of the move. The Supreme Court struck down this approach, saying an EIR must deal with all "reasonably forseeable future uses" associated with the project.

## GROWTH-INDUCING IMPACT

Unlike cumulative impact, the question of growth-inducing impact has not been the subject of landmark court rulings in the last few years. And the analytical methods available for a growth-inducement study have been weak. Typically, a growth-inducement section will include a page or less of general information about the relationship of the project to the region's growth generally. For example, a draft EIR prepared in 1988 for a 1.5-million-square-foot office building in downtown Los Angeles was only three paragraphs long. It described the number of jobs that would be created by the construction of the project, stated in vague terms that in-migration to the region might result, and concluded by saying that the project was consistent with L.A.'s policy objective that the downtown area serves as a "regional center."

As "growth control" and "growth management" have become the main buzzwords of planning in California, however, the concept of

---

* *Laurel Heights Improvement District v. Regents of the University of California,* 47 Cal.App.3d 276.

"growth inducement" has become more important as well. In Orange County, for example, the growth-inducing impact of the new toll highways became a major issue. Supporters said the highways would simply relieve current traffic congestion. Opponents said the highways had the backing of developers because they would open up new areas for development.

Making such distinctions is not easy. It is not hard to understand that the construction of a new road is likely to induce growth in a localized fashion — encouraging the construction of gas stations, motels, and convenience stores at critical interchanges. But regional growth depends on a whole range of economic forces that are local, national, and international in scope. Furthermore, it is hard to assess the growth-inducing impact of new facilities in an already urbanized area. If the growth-control movement remains strong in California, it is likely that the growth-inducement analysis contained in EIRs will be subject to more legal challenge and stricter requirements.

## ALTERNATIVE SITES

The *CEQA Guidelines* state that an agency should not approve a project "if there are feasible alternatives ... available that would substantially lessen any significant effects." For this reason, EIRs must discuss a range of "reasonable" alternatives. An environmentally preferable alternative must be selected unless it is "infeasible." In recent years, the courts have greatly broadened the required alternatives analysis.

Traditionally, an EIR's alternatives analysis discussed only variations on the proposed project. For example, turning once again to the proposed office tower in downtown Los Angeles, the alternatives included: a smaller project; concentrating development on one part of the site or another; using the site for public facilities instead of private offices (because the site was publicly owned); and constructing no project at all. (The "no project" alternative is required under California case law.) Alternative sites have usually not been considered, because landowners typically own only one site.

In 1988, however, the California Supreme Court ruled in the *Laurel Heights* case that alternative sites must be extensively examined in an

EIR, at least when public projects are involved. The UC Regents had argued that little discussion of alternatives was necessary because the university had concluded that all alternatives were infeasible. But the Supreme Court said that the purpose of alternatives analysis is not just to inform decision-makers but also the public: "Without meaningful analysis of alternatives, neither the courts nor the public can fulfill their proper roles in the CEQA process."

But two years later, the Supreme Court declined to extend the alternative site requirements to all private projects. Ruling in a case commonly known as *Citizens of Goleta Valley*,* the court said that alternative sites need not be considered if the private landowners involved don't have a feasible chance of purchasing the land. The case involved a proposal to build a large Hyatt Hotel on a beachfront property near Santa Barbara. The Court of Appeal had ruled that many alternative sites should have been seriously analyzed — even those that did not lie within Santa Barbara County's jurisdiction — because CEQA is designed to serve the public, not the landowner. But the Supreme Court concluded that there is no point in analyzing alternative sites if the landowner in question won't be able to use them for the proposed project. However, the court did say that when feasible alternative sites are available, an EIR should consider them even if the project is private.

## GOVERNMENTAL ACTION AND MITIGATION

If an environmental impact report prepared under CEQA does identify "significant environmental effects," then the governmental agency reviewing the project has four options:

1. *Deny the project.* The discovery of significant environmental effects is, in and of itself, sufficient legal grounds to turn down a development project altogether.

2. *Approve an environmentally preferable alternative* to the project, as identified in the EIR.

3. *Approve the project, but only if mitigation measures are adopted* to lessen the environmental impact.

* *Citizens of Goleta Valley v. Board of Supervisors,* 52 Cal.3d 553 (1990).

4. *Approve the project in spite of environmental effects* and adopt a statement of overriding considerations, usually outlining the project's economic benefit.

In practice, the first two actions (denial and approval of alternatives) rarely occur, while the third and fourth (mitigation and overriding considerations) are used in most instances. The statement of overriding considerations is the "escape valve" which permits a local government to approve a project in spite of environmental damage.

It is this provision which places the final environmental decision in the hands of local officials, instead of making it an inevitable outcome of environmental investigation and review. As one CEQA lawyer once put it: "The EIR could show the most horrendous environmental consequences of a particular activity. And a planning commission or city council could approve the project by saying, 'Yes, we know about all these horrendous environmental effects; however, there are overriding considerations which permit us to approve the project anyway.'"

In theory, a statement of overriding considerations may be adopted only if is it supported by information on the record; findings are required to explain how this conclusion is drawn. In practice, overriding considerations are often used when a project's environmental damage is significant but local officials have other reasons (usually tax benefits but sometimes political reasons as well) for wanting to see the project approved. In many cases, the required findings are skimpy because the environmental damage is well documented but the supposed benefits of the project are not.

Perhaps the most common route is to approve a project, but require the developer to implement mitigation measures to lessen the environmental impact. In fact, without a statement of overriding considerations, a project with significant environmental effects can be approved only if the developer agrees to perform feasible mitigation measures.

"Mitigation" can mean anything from replacing destroyed trees to a mandatory carpooling program. If a project is subject to discretionary approval, CEQA-identified mitigation measures often form the basis for the conditions of approval; in cities with an active environmental community, these conditions can sometimes number 50 or more. No matter how many mitigation measures are required, however, local governments are faced with the difficult question of figuring out how to make sure the measures are actually carried out.

Historically, local planning and building departments have not had a strong record of enforcing even basic building codes. Code enforcement is considered a low priority in many cities, and the planners who oversee a project's approval usually do not follow up to see whether conditions are met. As conditions of approval have grown because of CEQA's mitigation requirements, this lack of follow-up has become a more significant problem. And as these conditions have become more performance- or service-oriented, their implementation has become harder to check. It is not difficult to determine whether trucks are loading and unloading only at certain hours during construction. It is much more difficult to determine whether an ambitious carpooling program is still working five years after the project is built.

A study by the University of California, Davis revealed that only 27 percent of the state's cities always make site visits to monitor mitigation measures. (For counties the figure was 54 percent.) The same study revealed that more than half of all local agencies never even receive a follow-up letter from developers regarding mitigation measures, though in this case the cities did better than the counties. Other surveys have found widespread lack of compliance with requirements for conservation easements and ride-sharing programs.

In fact, the problem of monitoring mitigation measures has become so significant that in 1988 the legislature took the rare step of amending CEQA to deal with the negligence. The law, AB 3180, requires local governments to establish a program to monitor the mitigation measures they require of developers.* The law is very short and not very specific, and different local governments have implemented it in different ways. Some are calling on building inspectors and zoning administrators to add environmental monitoring to their duties. Others have hired environmental experts in the planning department to run monitoring programs. Many have asked their regular EIR consultants to fold mitigation monitoring programs into their other work. (This has led to concern that AB 3180 might become just another paper require-

* Public Resources Code §21081.6.

ment, under which cities have a monitoring plan on the shelf but not in the field.)

Mitigation monitoring programs might be modest or expensive, depending on the project. Sometimes a code enforcement officer or planner may simply observe the grading of a site to ensure that trees or wetlands are not destroyed. On the other hand, the mitigation monitoring program for the $300-million expansion of the Orange County airport cost $750,000 in consulting fees over five years.

## ASSESSING CEQA'S EFFECTIVENESS

CEQA can be such an emotional issue to participants in the land-use planning process that it is often difficult to determine how effective a tool it has been in protecting the environment. There is no question that CEQA has achieved its goal of informing the public and generating public debate on the environmental consequences of building projects. Reams of environmental information are now available on virtually every large project, and the debate among citizens and local elected officials usually takes place on a sophisticated and informed level.

On the other hand, CEQA can easily be viewed as a "paper tiger," which generates a tremendous amount of material — at tremendous cost — but doesn't necessarily safeguard the environment. CEQA calls on local governments to establish many processes designed to make developers (and public agencies) accountable for the environmental impact of their projects. Frequently, however, those processes are reduced to rote exercises. The analysis in an environmental impact report becomes cut-and-paste boilerplate material, for example, or the checklist in an initial study becomes automatic and unthinking. So then the courts or the legislature will impose a new requirement meant to make up for the emptiness of these processes: requiring annotations in the checklist, for example, or a plan to monitor otherwise meaningless mitigation measures. Soon enough, however, these new requirements become empty exercises as well, as EIR consultants develop boilerplate material for checklist annotations, and prepare monitoring plans that are no more likely to be implemented than the mitigation measures they're supposed to be monitoring.

The roteness of the CEQA process makes meaningful public debate more difficult to achieve. But because the courts continually impose new requirements, CEQA is a moving target that local governments have a hard time dealing with. CEQA's unanswerable question is, inevitably, how much analysis is enough? The question of assessing alternative sites provides a good example. Consultants now acknowledge that, when an alternative sites analysis is required, they must prepare "mini-EIRs" on all the alternatives. But how long will it be before the courts fault these alternatives analyses as inadequate, forcing consultants to prepare ever-thicker EIRs for the alternatives, to say nothing of the proposed project itself? This question was clearly on the minds of the California Supreme Court justices when they ruled against the expansion of alternative sites analysis in the Goleta case.

These problems are perhaps inherent in a process-oriented state law such as CEQA, which does not impose environmental values on local decision-makers. A community's values remain the same, CEQA or not. If political forces drive a city or county in a certain direction — whether it's an overall pro-development policy or the approval of a specific project — CEQA is not going to change that direction. That is why local governments all over the state are constantly approving, for example, land-consuming, auto- oriented real estate projects in spite of the undeniable environmental degradation involved.

On the other hand, one of CEQA's overarching goals was to foster an environmental consciousness in California, and clearly the law has succeeded in this respect. CEQA inevitably provides a lot of environmental information to anyone who cares to pay attention, and the sum total of CEQA's processes over 20 years — empty and rote as any individual process may be — has encouraged many people to pay attention. CEQA is expensive and time- consuming and its inefficiencies undoubtedly drive up the cost of development in California. But the robust public debate over a project's environmental effects is exactly what the legislators who drafted the bill more than 20 years ago had in mind.

# CHAPTER 10

# OTHER ENVIRONMENTAL LAWS

CEQA may be the most pervasive environmental law that affects planning in California, but it is far from the only one. A whole series of state and federal laws, mostly dating from the '60s and '70s, also play a significant role in how communities are shaped. Most of these laws are designed to protect a particular environmental resource: air, water, wildlife, the coastline.

Many of the state environmental laws, such as the Coastal Act, the law establishing the bistate Tahoe Regional Planning Agency, and the Alquist-Priolo seismic safety act, seek to integrate environmental protection with the broad process of comprehensive planning. However, some of the laws — especially on the federal level — are narrowly focused on a particular aspect of environmental protection, and give no consideration to the broader context of planning which they so often affect. And while, at their best, these laws force local planning officials to consider environmental factors they might otherwise ignore, they can also take over the planning process and hold it hostage to one narrow set of considerations. It should not be surprising that the federal environmental laws have such a narrow focus; there are no comprehensive planning laws on the federal level, as there are on the state level, and so there is no broader planning context in which to place federal environmental protection.

When a threat to air quality or the preservation of rare wildlife or wetlands is identified, state or federal officials may stop or block development projects — even if those projects are consistent with local plans and have already received local approval. Sometimes this problem can be avoided by proper use of CEQA, since a good environmental impact report is likely to identify problems that may trigger these other laws. But it is not always possible for local officials and developers to get ahead of the environmental curve.

For one thing, a legal problem may not arise until a project is part of the way through the approval process. This problem often occurs under the Endangered Species Act. The federal government does not have the legal power to protect species until they are listed as endangered, and so projects can be stopped in mid-stream if a species in the area is suddenly placed on the list. Furthermore, there is no guarantee that state and federal agencies will apply the law consistently in all situations. With wetlands, for example, the U.S. Army Corps of Engineers may initially choose not to get involved in a local development dispute — but environmentalists or the Environmental Protection Agency may be able to force the Corps to take action later on, halting an approved project.

In recent years, as the environmental movement has gained new prominence, many of these laws have been strengthened and/or applied more aggressively. At the same time, attempts have been made to integrate these laws into the overall planning fabric. For example, local governments are working with regional agencies in figuring out how to implement the imposing requirements of the Los Angeles area's air-quality plan; in all likelihood, this effort will lead more local governments to include an air-quality element in their general plans. Similarly, officials in Riverside County — prime habitat for both rare wildlife and developers — are working with federal agencies in hopes of planning ahead on endangered species, so they do not get caught short again in the future. Despite these efforts, single-purpose environmental laws often remain "five-thousand-pound gorillas" that can dominate planning and development debates.

## PROTECTION OF 'CRITICAL AREAS':
## THE BAY, THE COAST, LAKE TAHOE

The first generation of specialized environmental laws dealt with fragile environmental resources that were not widespread but, rather, confined to specific geographic areas: the California coastline, the San Francisco Bay, and the Lake Tahoe area. And these laws — which were state laws, not federal laws — tried to integrate protection of these environmental resources with comprehensive planning processes. Although they have had significant ups and downs over the past 20 years, they have survived, and, by and large, they have succeeded in combining environmental protection with comprehensive planning.

The first such law, passed in 1965, created the Bay Conservation and Development Commission, or BCDC.* BCDC's goal is to protect the environmental resources of (and public access to) the San Francisco Bay and adjoining estuaries such as the San Pablo Bay and Suisun Bay. BCDC has total control over the dredging or filling of the bay — a widespread practice in the 100 years before the agency's creation. BCDC is responsible for drawing up a plan for the bay's conservation, and also has permit authority over all projects that would require dredging and filling of the bay. The agency's permitting decisions, of course, must conform with the overall conservation plan.

BCDC proved to be the model for the California Coastal Commission. Unlike BCDC, however, the Coastal Commission was not created by the legislature. After failing to get the Coastal Act out of Sacramento for several years, environmentalists placed the idea on the ballot as an initiative in 1972. Two decades later, Proposition 20 still represents a high point for the environmental movement in California.

The Coastal Act** created the California Coastal Commission — and, temporarily, a regional commission for each part of the state. Just as important, the Coastal Act created a planning process for coastal areas that was revolutionary at the time and still remains remarkable, given the resistance of local governments to state intrusion. Simply put, the law took coastal planning out of the hands of the local govern-

* Government Code §66600-66661.
** Public Resources Code §30000.

ments and gave it to the state.

Under the Coastal Act, each local government could no longer issue development permits in the coastal zone, as it always had done in the past. Instead, it was to work — with help of the Coastal Commission staff — on "local coastal plans." These LCPs, as they are often referred to, would usually be included as an element in the general plan. They would be designed to incorporate the state's coastal policies, as defined by the Coastal Commission itself, into local planning efforts. When the local coastal plan was completed and "certified" by the Coastal Commission, development permit authority, for the most part, would be returned to the city or county in question.

In the meantime, development permits along the coast would be subject to approval by the regional coastal commission for that area. Particularly during the years of Governor Jerry Brown's administration, the Coastal Commission was aggressive in asserting its jurisdiction, and this aggressiveness did not sit well with the state's developers. The leading state Supreme Court ruling on vested rights, *Avco Community Builders v. South Coast Regional Commission*, arose from Avco's attempt to block the Coastal Commission from reviewing a project that had already been approved by local officials. (A more detailed discussion of vested rights and the *Avco* case is contained in Chapter 11.) But this was just one of hundreds of cases between the Coastal Commission and developers over the years.

The Coastal Commission was equally aggressive in pursuing the policy goals set forth in the Coastal Act. In particular, the commission placed a great deal of emphasis on public access to the beach, affordable housing, and scaled-down development in the coastal zone. Especially during the '70s, environmental activists were able to use the Coastal Commission as a friendly forum to fight beachfront development projects. As a matter of course, the Coastal Commission demanded some sort of public access to the beach in return for any kind of building permit along the coast. (This practice eventually led to the famous *Nollan* decision, described in Chapter 6.) The commission also expressed a preference for beachfront hotels over private condominiums on the theory that hotels, with their transient occupancy, were more accessible to the public — even if they were expensive.

   The local coastal plans were all supposed to be completed by 1976. However, most of them dragged on for years afterward. For this reason, the legislature passed a second version of the Coastal Act in 1976. The regional coastal commissions, which were necessary when the workload of specific development permits was  high (before LCPs were approved), were disbanded in 1981.

   During the 1980s, the Coastal Commission's impact over local planning decisions waned somewhat — for two reasons. First, most of the LCPs were approved, so most development permits did not require Coastal Commission approval. And second, Gov. George Deukmejian adopted an openly hostile posture toward the commission. He tried to eliminate the commission's budget completely several times, and once signed the budget only on the condition that the commission shut down some of its offices. (The commission defied the order, choosing instead to reallocate other funds to keep the offices open.) Nevertheless, the Coastal Commission remains a powerful body with tremendous impact. For example, all amendments to local coastal plans still must be approved by the commission — and an LCP amendment is often required for a large project to be constructed. Moreover, some local land-use decisions may be appealed to the Coastal Commission and overruled by the commission if they are found to be contrary to the LCP or the Coastal Act.

   The Lake Tahoe area has had, if anything, a more tumultuous history of environmental planning than the Coastal Act. The area's fragile environment led to a political consensus more than 20 years ago that Lake Tahoe deserved special protection. But this consensus has often fallen apart in the face of conflicting interests. The first bistate compact between California and Nevada failed because the two states had dramatically different attitudes about development and environmental protection. Subsequently, the two states formed a new Tahoe Regional Planning Agency, or TRPA.* This agency almost failed as well, but was rescued by a complicated set of negotiations in the late '80s.

   The overriding environmental issue at Lake Tahoe is the remarkable clarity of the lake's water. That clarity has been disrupted by construc-

---

* Government Code §66807.

tion around the lake, which created soil runoff into the lake itself. In the mid-'80s, environmental groups sued the Tahoe Regional Planning Agency, claiming that the agency was permitting too much construction. A federal judge imposed a building moratorium in the area and,

as a result, served as the *de facto* planning director, making decisions about which projects should go forward and which should not. This led to countersuits from property owners who wanted to build.

Eventually, TRPA organized a massive negotiation that included some 20 different parties involved in the lawsuits. Over a one-year period, these negotiators agreed to a set of development guidelines that restricted the overall amount of construction in the Tahoe area but permitted certain property owners to proceed. The agreement was not perfect. In particular, commercial property owners complained that it did not permit enough commercial construction. Nevertheless, the resulting Tahoe plan provides a good example of how complicated environmental and development issues can be resolved within the context of comprehensive planning. (For more information on this negotiation, see Chapter 16.)

## SEISMIC SAFETY

In addition to environmental laws dealing with specific critical areas, the state has also passed several laws dealing with specific environmental hazards. Under state law, for example, all counties must adopt hazardous-waste plans subject to the approval of the California Department of Health Services. Perhaps the most important of these laws, from the point of view of local planning, is the Alquist-Priolo

Act, which is designed to ensure that development patterns do not create seismic hazards. Like other state environmental laws, Alquist-Priolo is designed to work within the context of the general plan process. However, the law also specifies planning standards local governments should follow in areas of significant earthquake hazard — standards that communities do not always enforce with equal vigor.

Under the Alquist-Priolo Act,* the state Division of Mines and Geology must identify areas where the risk of earthquakes is high and designate these areas as "special study zones." Upon further study, the agency determines whether the fault is "active" or not. If the study zone does not contain an active fault, then development may proceed. However, if active faults are found, then no buildings may be constructed within fifty feet of the fault. If the area on top of an active fault is already developed, the local government is encouraged to adopt policies that will lead to the removal of the buildings in question.

In one sense, the Alquist-Priolo Act is a top-down state mandate: Cities and counties must abide by the geological findings of the Division of Mines and Geology. However, the law is also designed to interact with local planning processes. State general plan law specifies that seismic safety information should be contained in the safety element, one of the seven required elements of a general plan. If the Division of Mines and Geology has identified study zones or active faults, the safety element should specify those areas, and the other elements of the general plan should not permit development of those areas.

After a series of large earthquakes in the '80s (Coalinga '83, Whittier '87, Santa Cruz '89), the Division of Mines and Geology has become more active in dealing with local planning issues. For instance, the agency is taking a closer look at environmental impact reports around the state and warning about seismic dangers if they are present. And some communities are taking earthquake problems more seriously as well. For example, the unincorporated community of Adelanto, in San Bernardino County, has banned new construction along some major streets because of seismic problems.

* Public Resources Code §2621-2630.

Generally speaking, however, communities do not give great weight to the provision of the Alquist-Priolo Act, and the legal authority of the Division of Mines and Geology is still somewhat questionable. Few communities have risked the political unpopularity and inevitable lawsuits that would result from a strict enforcement of the law — especially the parts calling for existing structures to be razed. And, in at least one recent court case,* a government agency — in this case the University of California — beat back a challenge from the Division of Mines and Geology by hiring its own engineers, who found the fault in question to be inactive.

Clearly, as the spectre of "The Big One" looms larger over California, concern about earthquakes will grow. But it remains to be seen whether cities and counties throughout the state will make a serious effort to address seismic concerns and integrate them into the planning process.

## AIR-QUALITY LAWS

The air quality issue in California is perhaps the leading example of how the comprehensive planning process can be subordinated to the interests of a single area of environmental concern. Because air pollution is such a significant environmental problem in California, both state and federal laws are strong.** These laws, in turn, vest great power in county and regional air-pollution-control districts. Indeed, in the Los Angeles area, the South Coast Air Quality Management District (AQMD) probably has more regulatory power over that entire region than any other single agency. And, as air-quality efforts have focused more on the pollution created by cars and trucks, AQMD and other air-quality agencies have focused more and more on the planning and development patterns that created auto-oriented communities.

To understand the impact of these laws, it is important to understand why California is so vulnerable to air pollution. Most of the state's metropolitan areas are located in valleys or basins surrounded

---

* *Better Alternatives for Neighborhoods v. University of California*, 212 Cal.App.3d. 663 (1989).

** 42 United States Code 7401 and (California) Health & Safety Code §39000 *et seq.*

by mountains. During the long, dry summer, pollutants become trapped in these valleys. They interact with each other, and with the heat, until photochemical smog is created. (Other forms of air pollution, such as acid rain and particulates, are not as important in California as they are in heavy industrial areas elsewhere in the country.)

The technicalities of state and federal clean-air legislation are intimidating. More than one expert has called the federal Clean Air Act "the single most complicated law ever passed by Congress." Most of the complexities of the law are (thankfully) beyond the scope of this book. Suffice it to say that, beginning in the late '60s, the state Air Resources Board began enforcing emissions standards for cars and trucks, while local air-pollution control districts began regulating the pollution emitted by heavy industrial facilities such as oil refineries and steel mills. These regulations had only a limited impact on the state's development patterns — discouraging construction of new oil refineries and similar facilities (especially in the Los Angeles basin), and, perhaps, hastening the decline of heavy industry in the state. They certainly didn't change the typical automobile-oriented pattern of new development.

During the 1980s, however, a resurgence of concern about air quality led to more direct pressure on local governments and their planning policies. When various areas in the state missed cleanup deadlines under the federal Clean Air Act, environmentalists were able to sue in order to force a tougher round of regulations. Growing traffic congestion dove-tailed with air quality as a political issue, leading to a series of tougher state air-quality laws.

So far the impact of these lawsuits and laws has been felt mostly in the Los Angeles region. Under pressure from the federal government, the South Coast Air Quality Management District, a state-established agency that covers most of four counties around L.A., passed a new air-quality plan in 1989 that was hailed as the toughest in the nation. This plan includes provisions that will crack down on many sources of pollution that were not previously regulated — everything from charcoal barbecues to dry cleaners.

But the plan also paid unprecedented attention to local land-use planning processes and development patterns. For example, AQMD began requiring all large employers to undertake programs that will encourage ridesharing and other efforts to reduce vehicle trips. The agency also generated a whole slew of proposals about local land-use planning, began analyzing large development proposals throughout Southern California for their effects on air quality, and also encouraged local governments to add an air-quality element to their general plans.

Though South Coast AQMD was the first air-quality agency to undertake these steps, by 1990 it was clear that most other agencies in the state would follow suit. Pressured by environmentalists' lawsuits, air-quality officials in the Bay Area, Ventura County, Bakersfield, Fresno, and Sacramento were all moving in the same direction. It is questionable how much legal authority these agencies have over local governments. South Coast AQMD argues that, under state and federal laws, local governments must take steps to comply with the regional air-quality plan.

The exact reach of AQMD's legal power, however, does not matter so much as the agency's high profile and political clout. AQMD has 1,000 employees and considerable legal power over a politically controversial issue, while the region's comprehensive planning agency, the Southern California Association of Governments, has less than 200 employees and virtually no legal power. Therefore, an agency like AQMD is able to dominate the political debate over planning and development based on a single issue.

In many respects, the power of a "single-issue" agency works to the benefit of regional planning. AQMD's clout will almost certainly force cities and developers to create communities that are more sensitive to the environment. At the same time, however, actions that help one issue may hinder another. Some air-quality experts, for example, have encouraged development of Southern California's "high desert" areas because they are not as susceptible to smog as the Los Angeles basin and Southern California's inland valleys. But because weather patterns in the high desert are far more extreme, new developments there will likely consume far more energy for both air conditioning and heating. At the same time, more intense development in temperate coastal areas would minimize energy consumption, but might endanger fragile coastal resources protected under the Coastal Act. Comprehensive planning is a balancing act, and that balance can be upset by undue attention to a single environmental issue.

## WETLANDS PROTECTION

Under the Clean Air Act, the federal government has been only indirectly involved in local planning and development issues. Under the Clean Water Act,* however, the federal government can become directly involved in local issues when wetlands are involved.

Though the definition varies, the term "wetlands" generally refers to swamps and other lands where water is often present. Once considered unhealthy, wetlands are now regarded as essential components of a viable ecosystem because they provide habitat for wildlife, prevent floods, and help flush pollution out of water supplies.

Section 404 of the federal Clean Water Act prohibits anyone from draining or filling a wetland without a permit from the Army Corps of Engineers. Historically, this process was not a concern for developers, because the Army Corps was a development-oriented agency. Sometimes the Corps issued the permit without much fuss; on other occasions, the agency chose not to intervene, because the staff did not have time to deal with every wetlands matter.

As the environment has emerged as a front-page issue, however, wetlands have become a focus of environmental concern. This has been especially true along the Southern California coast and in the Central Valley, two areas where the once-plentiful supply of wetlands has dwindled dramatically. The wetlands issue has held up some of the largest development projects in California, such as the huge Playa Vista development near Los Angeles International Airport and the Bolsa Chica project along the coastline in Huntington Beach. After years of litigation, both of these disputes have been resolved, because developers are now more willing to negotiate with environmentalists than they used to be in order to get their projects off the ground.

Generally speaking, however, environmental groups and state agencies such as the Coastal Commission have played a much greater role in pressuring developers to deal with wetlands issues. The Coastal

* 33 U.S.C. 125.

Commission has pursued a "no net loss" policy along the coast. In some cases, the commission has permitted long-distance mitigation of wetlands, as when the Port of Los Angeles was permitted to restore a lagoon in San Diego County. (Some developers have created new wetlands artificially, but there is controversy among environmentalists as to whether artificial wetlands can operate as successfully as restored natural wetlands.)

Under the Clean Water Act, the Army Corps does not have exclusive jurisdiction over wetlands issues. The federal Environmental Protection Agency has veto power over Corps decisions. Even during the latter years of the Reagan administration, the EPA began to use that power more aggressively. In one celebrated case, EPA denied a wetlands permit to a shopping-center developer because that developer could have bought a non-wetlands site instead.* Then, in 1988, George Bush promised to pursue a federal "no net loss" policy. As EPA administrator, Bush chose William Reilly, one of the nation's leading advocates of a "no net loss" policy. Although Bush subsequently softened his stand, his position — and his appointment of Reilly — brought the wetlands issue national attention.

In the '90s, the state is likely to tighten wetlands regulations as well. Maryland led the way in 1989 by becoming the first state to adopt a "no net loss" policy. Maryland also used provisions of the Clean Water Act to regain control over wetlands regulation from the federal government. Environmentalists used the Maryland example to try to encourage similar action in California. In particular, many bills were introduced in the legislature to salvage the few remaining wetlands in the Central Valley, an area that once had millions of acres of wetlands.

However, a "no net loss" policy creates cumbersome problems for developers, who must search high and low for other sites where wetlands can be created or restored in order to obtain project approvals. One emerging technique that may simplify the process is the "mitigation bank." Under this concept, a government agency or environmental group will purchase and/or restore a large wetlands area in order to

* *Bersani v. Robichaud,* 850 F.Reporter 36 (1988).

create a "bank." Then developers who want to dredge and fill wetlands elsewhere may "buy" into the bank — in essence, fulfilling their "no net loss" responsibility by helping to pay off a wetlands purchase already made. The first wetlands mitigation bank in the state was created in Humbolt County by the California Coastal Conservancy, a state conservation agency. In 1981, the Coastal Conservancy purchased the Bracut Marsh, and now developers who intrude on wetlands by building within the City of Eureka may mitigate the loss by helping to pay for Bracut restoration. A mitigation bank can be a sensible solution to a complicated problem, especially when the wetlands being lost constitute a small area.

## ENDANGERED SPECIES PROTECTION

Like wetlands, endangered species are entitled to special protection under federal law. And these protections, too, have come to play an important role in local planning and development in California in recent years.

The federal Endangered Species Act* prohibits any private party from killing (actually called "taking" under federal law) a federally listed endangered species without first obtaining a permit from the U.S. Fish & Wildlife Service. Since California is blessed with both rapid growth and a unique biological diversity, it should not be surprising that local governments and developers run into the endangered species problem on a regular basis.

Indeed, virtually every innovative approach to dealing with endangered species in this country has emerged from conflict between developers and biological diversity in California. But the peculiar inflexibility of the Endangered Species Act makes it difficult for local planners and developers to deal with the issue ahead of time. As with the wetlands issue, projects are often stopped by environmental concerns after they have already received local approval.

The law spells out procedures by which the Fish & Wildlife Service may designate species that are in danger of extinction. Once a species is placed on the endangered list, the agency has the power to halt all

* 16 U.S.C. 1531.

development that might place that species' future existence in jeopardy. Thus, for example, when Fish & Wildlife concluded that rapid home construction in western Riverside County would place the Stephens' kangaroo rat in jeopardy, the agency was able to threaten local officials with criminal prosecution if they permitted those developments to proceed.

California also has an endangered species law. The state law* parallels the federal act, and appears to serve two purposes. First, it permits the state to take action on species that are threatened statewide, but not nationally. And second, it permits the California Department of Fish & Game to work in conjunction with the federal Fish & Wildlife Service in protecting federally endangered species.

Biologists usually have a good idea of which species are likely to be placed on the U.S. Fish & Wildlife Service's endangered list in the near future. But until that listing actually takes place, Fish & Wildlife cannot take action, nor can it make any guarantees that current preservation efforts will be sufficient in the future. This inflexibility causes

development interests great frustration. In 1989, for example, Fish & Wildlife issued an emergency listing classifying the desert tortoise as endangered. The listing halted hundreds of millions of dollars of construction projects in the Las Vegas area.

Fish & Wildlife is not completely inflexible, however. Under the

* Fish & Game Code §2050-2098.

law, the agency has the power to reach negotiated solutions and permit "incidental taking" of endangered species if it is part of an overall plan to preserve that species in the long run. The idea of a "habitat conservation plan" emerged out of a dispute over proposed development of San Bruno Mountain, south of San Francisco.

Home construction threatened the habitat of the Mission Blue butterfly, as did an invasion of gorse, a shrub. Under the San Bruno agreement, some home construction on the mountain was permitted. But most of the mountain was preserved, and either sold or donated to the county and the state. The result was that, in spite of the development, 87 percent of the butterfly habitat was preserved. Furthermore, as part of the deal, the developers agreed to fund a maintenance program for the habitat that would help protect it from the encroaching gorse — so that the development actually helped preserve the habitat rather than destroy it.

The resulting "habitat conservation plan" was the first of its kind in the nation, and formed the basis of important 1982 amendments to the Endangered Species Act permitting similar agreements. Since that time, Fish & Wildlife has approved more than two dozen habitat conservation plans, or HCPs, dealing with endangered species; virtually all of them involve situations in California. The next logical step in this progression is to set aside habitats before species become endangered. But because of the the inflexibility of the Endangered Species Act, this is not as easy as it sounds.

In the kangaroo rat controversy, Riverside County, Fish & Wildlife, and developers agreed on a plan to create a preserve and permit home construction to proceed elsewhere in the county. Developers are paying $1,950 per acre developed in order to provide the funds to buy the preserve. But Riverside County has more than 20 other endangered species, and a dozen more than are likely to be listed as endangered in the future. After the kangaroo rat controversy was settled, county officials went to work on a plan to create a multi-species habitat for all the endangered and threatened species. The idea, of course, was to avoid future surprises from the Endangered Species Act. The cost was huge: $500 million, to be paid for with a combination of public and private funds. And, because the idea was not met with great enthusiasm by the

public, county officials tried to broaden its political popularity by combining it with a scheme to create additional county parks. But even this
effort was not enough to  guarantee that further efforts would not be
required in the future. Under existing law, all the U.S. Fish & Wildlife
Service could do was give some assurance that these efforts would
probably suffice. If the multi-species habitat failed and some species
had trouble surviving, Riverside County's public officials and developers would have to go back to the drawing board.

CHAPTER 11

# THE CONSEQUENCES OF REGULATION:
# LAND-USE REGULATION AND PROPERTY RIGHTS

Over the past 20 years, all the rules and regulations discussed in the preceding chapters have made life much more difficult for landowners and developers all over California. The easy permit approvals that developers once counted on have disappeared. The planning and pre-development costs they must figure into their pro formas have escalated dramatically. Because of vague and/or ever-shifting general plan, zoning, and subdivision policies, many developers have found it difficult to figure out just exactly what they are permitted to build. Many have designed projects that comply with existing land-use regulations, only to be confronted with lengthy hearings under discretionary review ordinances or CEQA — and then asked to scale down their projects and carry a heavy infrastructure burden as the price of approval. Many more have made it all the way to project approval — even obtained building permits — only to be thwarted by a new slow-growth initiative, a less sympathetic city council, or some other change in local political attitudes.

And all developers, whether they have confronted such problems or not, have watched public opinion turn against them. Building huge neighborhoods for the returning war veterans and young families of the late '40s and '50s, they were seen as heroes. Today, these same developers are often the objects of public scorn.

Since the late '70s, California landowners and developers — and, especially, the well-organized and politically powerful homebuilders — have been fighting back. They have fought back, mostly without success, in the arena of public opinion. They have tried to fight back, with limited success, in the legislature, And most important, they have fought back in the courts, where they have scored the first significant legal victories for "property rights" advocates since *Euclid v. Ambler* gave land-use regulations constitutional legitimacy more than 60 years ago.

These legal victories, culminating with the U.S. Supreme Court's ruling in the so-called *First English* case in 1987, have forced many local governments to rein in their most far-reaching land-use restrictions and, in many cases, re-orient their planning policies. Instead of simply restricting the rights of property owners to achieve public goals, local governments now  must use land purchases, transfers of development rights, and other techniques that will protect private property rights as well as further the public interest.

## THE ROAD TO *FIRST ENGLISH*

Forging an alliance with conservative ideologues, the building industry has succeeded in turning the tide by reviving a legal concept that had lain dormant for more than 50 years: the regulatory "taking." This concept was ratified by the U.S. Supreme Court in 1922. In a case involving coal-mining restrictions in Pennsylvania, Justice Oliver Wendell Holmes wrote that if a land regulation was so restrictive that the landowner was robbed of all economically viable use of his land, the regulation constituted a "taking" under the Fifth Amendment.* The government was required to pay just compensation to the landowner, just as if the landowner's property had been taken by eminent domain. Relying on due process and equal protection grounds instead, property lawyers did not rely heavily on the takings concept in *Euclid v. Ambler* and subsequent challenges to zoning.

---

* *Pennsylvania Coal Co. v. McMahon,* 260 U.S. 393 (1922).

However, in the 1970s, when land-use regulations in California first became burdensome to developers, the concept was revived. Many builders began to claim that a regulatory taking had occurred, and they filed what became known as "inverse condemnation" suits. In one sense, these suits were identical to traditional eminent domain suits because they sought to establish the "just compensation" due to the landowner by the government under the Fifth Amendment. In another sense, however, these lawsuits were the opposite — the "inverse" — of a traditional condemnation suit because they were filed by the landowner, not the government. The most important court ruling on inverse condemnation in the 1970s — and, indeed, the ruling that California homebuilders spent most of the 1980s trying to overturn — involved a five-acre parcel of land in Tiburon owned by Donald Agins and his family.

Agins had bought the undeveloped parcel in the late '60s, drawn by its spectacular views of San Francisco Bay. At the time, the Agins' zoning called for one-acre lots, meaning Agins could build five houses. In the early '70s, however, the town of Tiburon downzoned the property to permit only one house on the entire five acres. (Tiburon's action took place at about the same time that the nearby city of Petaluma enacted its famous growth management ordinance. The Bay Area was growing rapidly and suburban citizens, for the first time, were flexing their political muscles to restrict growth.)

The Agins family filed an inverse condemnation suit, claiming that their property had been taken by the downzoning and demanding $2 million in damages as just compensation. The California Supreme Court disagreed, however. In the Agins decision,* the court essentially outlawed inverse condemnation suits in California. The justices said that because a regulation can be changed easily, then, by definition, no regulation can create a taking for which the landowner must be compensated. If a regulation is so restrictive that it might create a taking, the court ruled, then the legal remedy is not to pay compensation to the landowner, but merely to invalidate the regulation so the landowner can build.

* *Agins v. City of Tiburon,* 24 Ca.3d 266 (1979).

The Agins ruling was merely one of several "anti-landowner" rulings handed down by the California Supreme Court in the late '70s and early '80s. It was issued only three years after the Avco case, which made vested rights very difficult to obtain, and just a year before the court opened the floodgates for ballot-box zoning in the Arnel case. Anxious to see the Agins case overturned, the building industry quickly appealed it to the U.S. Supreme Court. But the court ran into the difficult question of when a legal challenge to any regulation is "ripe" for review by the courts.

Courts are not supposed to review a plaintiff's complaint unless that plaintiff has "exhausted" all administrative procedures — that is, until the plaintiff has done everything he or she can do outside of court to resolve the issue. Because regulations can be changed at any time, the question of when administrative procedures are exhausted is a very tricky one. If a developer tries, and fails, to get the city council to change a regulation, has he exhausted all administrative remedies? If the developer has applied for a zone change and been rejected, does that satisfy the question of ripeness?

In Tiburon, the Agins family had never formally applied to the city to rezone the property back to the one-house-per-acre zoning that had been in place when the land was purchased. Thus, the U.S. Supreme Court ruled in 1980, the *Agins* case was not "ripe" for judicial review.*

Between 1980 and 1986, the U.S. Supreme Court heard three more cases on the question of regulatory takings. Two of the cases, like the *Agins* case, were from California, because California was one of the few states in the country where the state courts had ruled that a landowner could not obtain compensation for a regulatory taking. Each time, the U.S. Supreme Court found some similar reason that the case was not ripe for review. In a 1986 case from the Davis area, for example, the Supreme Court ruled that a constitutional challenge to a land-use regulation is ripe only after the local government has rejected a specific development plan and also denied a variance.**

At the time, many land-use lawyers — and even the justices them-

* *Agins v. City of Tiburon*, 444 U.S. 255 (1980).
** *McDonald, Sommer & Frates v. Yolo County*, 477 U.S. 340.

selves — were frustrated by the court's inability to get past this question. There appeared to be enough votes on the court to overturn the *Agins* rule on constitutional grounds. In the context of the ripeness issue, however, the *Agins* rule did make a certain amount of sense. Clearly, there is a difference between a landowner whose land is subject to severe restrictions, which can be changed, and a landowner whose land has been taken for construction of a freeway. The first landowner may not be able to use his property now, but he may be able to use it in the future. Thus, it is hard to argue that a "permanent" taking has occurred.

## THE *FIRST ENGLISH* CASE

Finally, in 1987, the U.S. Supreme Court — by this time bearing the imprint of Ronald Reagan, who had appointed three justices — found a case that permitted the Agins rule to be overturned.

Once again the case was from California. Specifically, it involved Los Angeles County's decision to prohibit reconstruction of a church camp in Tujunga Canyon after a fire and a flood. In 1977, a fire had denuded the canyon; the following winter, partly because the trees were gone, a flood washed away the retreat owned by the First English Evangelical Lutheran Church of Glendale. The Board of Supervisors then passed an ordinance prohibiting reconstruction of most buildings in the flood zone, including the church retreat. At first the prohibition was temporary, but later the county made it permanent.

Claiming its property had been taken, the church filed an inverse condemnation suit against the county, seeking damages under the Fifth Amendment. Not surprisingly, the church didn't get very far in the California courts because the *Agins* rule essentially prohibited such lawsuits. The Court of Appeal in Los Angeles ruled that such a case could not be filed in California, and the California Supreme Court declined to hear the case.

At this point, however, property rights advocates saw the opportunity to make the *First English* case into the test case they had been seeking. The facts of the case were strong, and the  circumstances surrounding this incident had good publicity value. (The retreat was not merely a church camp, but a camp for handicapped children.)

Represented by a top property-rights lawyer, the church appealed to the U.S. Supreme Court, which agreed to hear the case. The court's intent was not to decide whether a taking had occurred at the First English camp. (Such a determination is typically made only after a trial.) Rather, the Supreme Court simply wanted to address the question of whether a landowner who claims a taking has occurred is entitled to just compensation, instead of simple invalidation of the ordinance in question.

By a 6-3 vote, the Supreme Court overturned the *Agins* rule and decided that a landowner whose property has been taken by regulation is, indeed, entitled to money damages.* As for the vexing question of

how takings can occur if a regulation can be changed, the court introduced the concept of a "temporary" taking. Even if a confiscatory regulation is overturned or changed, the court said, the government still must compensate the landowner for the loss of his property during that interim period of time. Noting that the future of the First English camp had been in litigation for almost a decade, Chief Justice William Rehnquist said: "The United States has been required to pay compensation for leasehold interests of shorter duration than this." Therefore, he added, "(i)nvalidation of the ordinance or its successor ordinance after (a) period of time, though converting the taking

---

* *First English Evangelical Lutheran Church of Glendale v. County of Los Angeles,* 482 U.S. 304 (1987).

into a 'temporary' one, is not a sufficient remedy to meet the demands of the just compensation clause."

Sixty-one years after *Euclid v. Ambler*, the building industry had finally managed to reverse the trend toward giving local governments greater leeway in land-use regulation. Property owners have rights, the Supreme Court was saying, and while land-use regulations protect the public welfare (and sometimes even public health and safety, as in *First English*), they must protect the private property owner's rights as well.

That *First English* represented a turning point in history became even more clear only 17 days later, when the Supreme Court issued its ruling on exactions in the Nollan case, which was discussed in Chapter 6. In that case, the courts said that exactions levied by government agencies must be directly linked to the project on which they are imposed — and if they are not, the government has created a taking of property for which, under *First English*, compensation is due.

The *First English* ruling is important not only for what it did, but also for what it did not do. The Supreme Court did not decide (and never intended to decide) whether a taking had occurred with regard to the church camp. That job, the court said, is more appropriately left up to lower courts examining the specific facts of the *First English* case. (In a controversial decision, the Court of Appeal subsequently ruled that the facts of the *First English* case, taken on their face, showed that no taking had occurred and therefore no trial was needed.)* The Supreme Court ruling in *First English* also laid down no rule establishing exactly when a regulatory taking occurs. In its decision, the court merely stated that when a taking has occurred, compensation is due.

Thus, even today, land-use law experts are unsure whether Tiburon's downzoning of Donald Agins' property more than 20 years ago constituted a taking of property. Perhaps a taking occurs when a downzoning removes half of a property's value. Perhaps it only occurs when 80% of the value is removed by downzoning. Perhaps it depends

---

* *First English Evangelical Lutheran Church of Glendale v. County of Los Angeles*, 210. Cal.App.3d 1353 (1989).

on the situation — how much the landowner originally invested, how much profit he has realized, and so on. Because this is an undecided constitutional question, the answer will come only from future court rulings.

The *First English* case also did not lead to an "explosion" of litigation, as Justice John Paul Stevens, a one-time city attorney, predicted in his dissent. There is no question that more inverse condemnation suits have been filed and that many more have been threatened. But the courts are not clogged with them.

## LAND-USE RESTRICTIONS AFTER *FIRST ENGLISH*

What has changed, somewhat, is the balance of power between governments and developers. No longer may local governments look to the regulatory restriction of land uses as the answer to all their planning problems. Today they must be more creative in establishing a well-rounded planning program. To be sure, a local government may place considerable restrictions on private land in order to protect it from over-development and to achieve other city goals. But *First English* has made clear, in most cases, that regulation cannot be used to stop all development on a piece of private land. It's true that a complete ban on all development may hold up in court if public health or safety is at risk. In order to preserve private land for scenic or environmental purposes, however, the government is going to have to compensate the landowner in some fashion.

Thus, in the post-*First English* world, this compensation takes one of two forms: either outright acquisition of the land or the purchase or transfer of development rights. Alternatively, cities and developers work out the compensation issue by negotiating "development agreements," which give both sides assurance that their goals will be met.

### LAND ACQUISITION

Many governmental agencies originally adopted strict regulations on land development because they could not afford to buy the land. Beginning in the 1970s, land prices throughout California began to escalate rapidly, and they continued to do so in the 1980s. At the same time, Proposition 13 slashed local government revenue so severely that purchasing land for scenic, open space, or environmental purposes was simply out of the question. Strict regulation was often the only way for government agencies to protect land from development.

Since the *First English* case was handed down, California has seen a renewed interest in preserving land by purchasing it. Up until the late '80s, the after-effects of the tax revolt made voters reluctant to support any public program that cost money. However, the state's rapid growth — and, especially, the rate at which land on the suburban fringe was converted to development — led to a shift in public attitudes. As environmental issues came to the fore in the late '80s, support for land acquisition grew, even though public resources were scarce and land prices were high.

The first dramatic evidence of this political shift was the passage of Proposition 70, a statewide ballot initiative in 1988 that authorized a $770 million bond issue to establish a state land acquisition program. The brainchild of California environmentalists, Proposition 70 was the first bond issue in more than 70 years to reach the ballot via the initiative process.

Proposition 70 was sometimes called the "park barrel" initiative — a play on the legislative slang phrase "pork barrel" — because of the way the signatures were gathered. Local environmental groups helped to gather signatures to place the measure on the ballot; in return, their "pet" land acquisition projects were specifically included in the initiative. But the initiative led to some crucial land conservation efforts, including the purchase of 2,700 acres of land near South Lake Tahoe and a 700-acre tract that connected the City of Glendale's park system with Angeles National Forest.

The success of Proposition 70 spurred local environmentalists and local governments around the state to consider similar bond programs. The first major local initiative came in the East Bay, where Alameda and Contra Costa counties joined together for passage of a $225 million bond issue to acquire both open space and new parklands. Many other local bond issues, large and small, followed. By 1990, political support for land acquisition programs was so well established that the drafters of Riverside County's habitat conservation plan, which was described in Chapter 10, never even considered a regulatory scheme to restrict development. Instead, developers agreed to pay a fee that would help create a habitat for endangered species, but a large percentage of the funds was expected to come from a bond issue similar to the East Bay bond issue. As in the East Bay, acquisition of land for the Riverside habitat was linked to acquisition of land for parks in order to increase public support for the concept.

### DEVELOPMENT RIGHTS

Just as important as land acquisition, however, is the purchase or transfer of "development rights" in order to preserve sensitive land. The concept of development rights is based on the idea that a landowner's property rights, which are protected under *First English*, can be separated from the property itself.

Say, for example, that a developer owns a piece of farmland, zoned for residential use at six houses per acre, with a market value of $100,000 per acre. In economic terms, the developer has two separate property rights. First is the farmland itself, which is worth perhaps $10,000 an acre as farmland. And second is the right to build six houses per acre, which adds the other $90,000 per acre to the value of the land. A government agency can preserve the land as farmland by paying the developer $90,000 an acre for the development rights, or by allowing the developer to transfer the development rights somewhere else.

The purchase of development rights has been popular in other parts of the country for many years. For example, Suffolk County, on New York's Long Island, has used bond proceeds to buy development rights from farmers in order to protect its strong agricultural base. Although more than 1 million people now live in Suffolk, the county still has 35,000 acres of farmland. Between 1980 and 1990, the county purchased development rights for 6,000 acres and has plans to acquire rights for about 10,000 more, permanently preserving the area's agricultural economy.

No governmental entity in California has gotten as heavily involved in the acquisition of development rights. Instead, private land trusts have performed the same function in many parts of the state — especially coastal farming areas such as Marin County. (Such purchases are sometimes called the acquisition of "conservation easements.") But some of the funds in Proposition 70 were earmarked for acquisition of development rights, so the practice may become more popular in the future.

But most government agencies cannot afford to purchase development rights, just as they cannot afford to purchase land outright. Therefore, many agencies are attracted to the concept of "transferrable" development rights, or TDRs, which permit landowners to move their development rights from one location to another, thereby protecting sensitive land without costing the government any money.

The TDR concept is simple. A landowner may have the right, under zoning, to build six houses per acre on a parcel of land. But the government agency may want to preserve the property as undeveloped. So

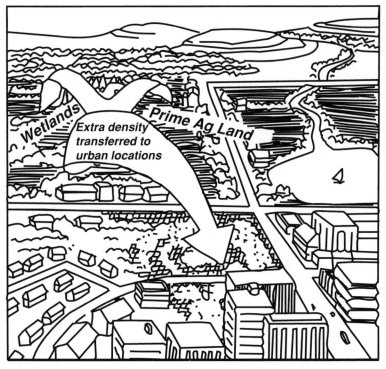

**Transferrable development rights**

the government grants the landowner permission to transfer his right to build those six houses to another nearby parcel — allowing the construction of 12 houses per acre on the new parcel, rather than only six. Most of the time, the "receiving" parcel will be owned by a different landowner, and the owner of the "sending" parcel will recoup his land investment by selling his development rights to the other property owner.

TDR programs have been implemented in such diverse locations as the urban core of downtown Los Angeles and the rural canyons of the Santa Monica Mountains. They provide perhaps the best hope for a successful balance between property rights and preservation of sensitive land. But TDR programs are very difficult to implement successfully. Sending and receiving zones must be separate enough to achieve public policy goals, but close enough to assure the process is not abused. There must be an ample supply of buyers and sellers, so that no one can "corner the market" on development rights in the area and drive the price up or down significantly. And the government agency must be able to assure that TDR buyers will be able to gain approval for their projects quickly and without unnecessary hassle. (This means that residents of the "receiving" zone must accept the idea of higher densities in their area — never an easy political task in California.)

Planning consultant Madelyn Glickfeld, who has drawn up several TDR programs in California, has written that a successful program "requires planning conditions and a level of political commitment to implementation that does not exist in many localities." A TDR program only works if conditions are right, and even then functions best "not as the sole strategy to mitigate the effects of harsh regulations, but as one of several different positive strategies to avoid takings."

In other words, despite its seductive appeal, a TDR program by itself can't solve all planning programs any more than restrictive regulation can. In the post-*First English* world, regulation, forward-looking plans, acquisition of land, and the manipulation of development rights must work together to serve the public interest and still protect private property rights.

\* \* \*

## DEVELOPMENT AGREEMENTS
## AND OTHER NEGOTIATED SOLUTIONS

All the strategies discussed above assume that land is held in small parcels by many different landowners. But in California — and, especially, in Southern California and the Central Valley — most undeveloped land is held in the form of huge ranches, usually several thousand acres in size. (This form of ownership dates back to the large "ranchos" granted to influential families at statehood in 1850.) When the large development companies that own this property seek to develop it, they usually seek approval for the entire tract at once, though they may develop it in phases. This is one of the reasons development agreements (which will be discussed in detail shortly) are so popular, and also accounts for the financial ability of California developers to provide huge up-front exactions. In the post-*First English* world, this pattern of land ownership and development also provides an opportunity for negotiated solutions encompassing many of the strategies discussed above.

Many landowners agree to "cluster" their developments on certain portions of their property in order to preserve sensitive lands — a kind of internal transfer of density. Some landowners also agree to dedicate some land to public agencies for preservation as parks or wild land. If the tract is big enough, and the balance of power between government (or environmentalists) and the developer is roughly equivalent, it is possible to negotiate a large solution that includes preservation of both property rights and sensitive lands using regulation, land dedication, clustering, and other techniques.

The best example of this kind of agreement is the Irvine Coast development plan in Orange County. This agreement involved a prize piece of the Irvine Company's land: a 9,400-acre tract between Laguna Beach and Corona del Mar that constituted the largest undeveloped area along the Southern California coast.

The company had been trying to develop the property since the 1960s, and in 1982 had received Coastal Commission approval. Although the project included considerable open space, it also included low-density "estate" housing and office development along Pacific Coast Highway. However, Friends of the Irvine Coast sued to stop the development on environmental grounds, and the Irvine Company began to reconsider its plans.

After several years of negotiation, the company and environmentalists finally agreed on a dramatically revised plan. The company would be permitted to build 2,600 houses, four hotels, and two golf courses, but the development would be clustered on the property. About 6,500 acres of land would be deeded to various public agencies in the form of open space, and the company would be required to build a $40 million road at the beginning of the project.

Just as important as the terms, however, was the timing. Land dedication would occur in four steps during the life of the project, so that the company would be permitted to build each phase of the project only after turning over certain open-space lands to the public. The company also agreed to dedicate some of the land in a wilderness state and provide protection for some wildlife habitats.

## DEVELOPMENT AGREEMENTS

In recent years, most large-scale negotiated solutions have been incorporated into "development agreements," or DAs.* The development agreement is a contract between a city or county and a developer. The intent of the DA is to provide security for both sides. The local government gets a legally binding promise that the developer will provide infrastructure and/or pay fees required by a new project. In return, the developer gets a legally binding promise that he will be able to build the project, even if the locality passes a growth-control initiative later on. More than 500 development agreements have been used in California, ranging from 10,000-unit subdivisions with 20-year build-outs down to single buildings that will cover only a few acres.

The concept of a development agreement came in response to a property-rights issue that emerged from California case law of the 1970s. A 1976 California Supreme Court case, usually known as the *Avco* case,** made it very difficult for a developer to obtain a "vested right" to build — that is, a guaranteed right to build, even in the face of future growth restrictions or political reversals.

* Government Code §65864-65869.5.
** *Avco Community Builders v. South Coast Reg'l Commission,* 17 Cal.3d 785 (1976).

The case arose out of the passage of Proposition 20, the coastal initiative, in 1972. At the time, Avco Community Developers, a large homebuilder, had spent more than $2 million planning and grading a subdivision site in Orange County that had already been approved by local officials. Even though grading had already begun, the brand-new Coastal Commission claimed it had the power to review the project because Avco hadn't yet established a "vested right" to build. When the case went to court, the state Supreme Court agreed: California developers could obtain vested rights only after getting building permits and investing "substantial expenditure." And Avco's $2 million investment wasn't enough, the court said.

Horrified, the building industry went to the legislature, seeking a law that would overturn the *Avco* ruling. At first, Governor Jerry Brown vetoed the bill. Shortly thereafter, however, Proposition 13 cut property taxes dramatically. Suddenly, local governments were searching for any scheme that might provide them with new revenue sources — and, especially, with money for the sewers, roads, schools, and other pieces of infrastructure required to support new development. Thus, in the legislative arena, the builders' desire for vested rights was married to the local governments' desire for capital funds.

The development agreement law that passed in 1979 envisioned that developers would be willing to make huge up-front infrastructure investments in exchange for vested rights to build, especially on a long-term, multi-phase project. But, as written, the law permits virtually open-ended bargaining between developers and local governments. Theoretically, DAs must conform with local general plans. But in practice, everything is thrown open for discussion — especially since DAs are often processed concurrently with general plan amendments. The law specifically classifies DAs as legislative in nature, meaning they are subject to initiative and referendum. (And they have, on occasion, been turned down by the voters.)

Given the controversy surrounding the Avco case and the subsequent legislation, it was surprising that they were used only sporadically for several years after the bill passed. The most notorious early example came in Santa Monica, where a slow-growth city council used the development agreement process to force Welton Becket, a large architectural/development firm, to cough up affordable housing, a child-care center, and a host of other concessions on the Colorado Place office project.

But as real estate development in California boomed during the Reagan-era economic recovery, so did the use of development agreements. In 1986, a team of researchers at the University of California, Berkeley, was astonished to discover more than 400 DAs either in place or in the works throughout California, rather than the 50 or 100 they had expected to find.

Just as astonishing was the range of projects and jurisdictions involved in development agreements. The UC Berkeley study found that 30 percent of California's cities and 37 percent of the state's counties had used DAs. The size of mixed-use projects varied from 54,000 square feet and nine residential units on one DA in Santa Monica up to a deal between the Irvine Co. and the City of Irvine which involved 6 million square feet of office and retail space. Residential projects involved in DAs ranged from a 3,800-unit project in Fremont, near Oakland, down to a 14-unit deal in Vista, a small city near San Diego.

## USES OF DEVELOPMENT AGREEMENTS

Many of the provisions included in development agreements could be dealt with through other regulatory agreements such as the specific plan. But developers find the vested rights available through development agreements to be very attractive, especially if they are expected to make large front-end investments in infrastructure. The risk on a multi-phase project without such vested rights is too great. One good example came in the small Ventura County city of Moorpark, where Urban West Communities, a homebuilder, negotiated a 10-year DA for a 2,500-home subdivision called Mountain Meadows. Relying on the agreement, Urban West made infrastructure investments it valued at $28 million. But in a controversial election, voters rejected the DA, while imposing a growth cap of 250 homes per year for the entire city. Claiming it had a vested right to build, Urban West went to court. The company eventually won the vested rights case on other grounds, but the project was held up for years in the process and easily could have lost in court.

In recent years, development agreements have been most popular in rapidly growing counties such as Orange and Riverside, where large developers own huge tracts of land on which they are planning subdivisions with several thousand houses. These DAs have truly represented the institutionalization of development fees — with counties extracting far more in fees and/or infrastructure than they would have obtained under traditional processes. (Although untested in court, these agreements are presumably exempt from the post-*Nollan* nexus requirement. They are specifically exempted from the provisions of AB 1600.)

In Orange County, for example, development agreements have been the cornerstone of the Foothill Circulation Phasing Program. Large landowners such as the Irvine Co., Mission Viejo Co., and Rancho Santa Margarita Co. have plans to build some 60,000 units in the area. But traditional sources of funds were inadequate to pay for the arterial roads required by the new developments. So 19 Orange County developers agreed to provide more than $200 million in exchange for a vested right to build their projects. The vast majority of the funds came from bond issues, and the DAs — guaranteeing that the houses will receive governmental approval — were vital in marketing the Orange County bonds on Wall Street.

Similarly, in Riverside County, developers have agreed to pay more than $4,300 per unit in fees as part of DA deals, compared with development fees of $2,700 per unit for more conventional permit approvals.

Increasingly, cities and counties are using these agreements to deal with tricky problems involved with timing and sequencing, to lock in assurance that a particular mix of development will occur, and to bring together small developers in order to fund large public improvements. In one of the first high-profile development agreements, the City of Irvine and the Irvine Co. used a development agreement to work out a problem over the timing of a mixed commercial/residential development. Company officials wanted to build the residential portion of the project first, but city officials wanted to get the sales tax flowing from the commercial portion. In a development agreement, the company agreed to make payments to the city if residential construction ran ahead of commercial development. The Irvine Co. has paid the city an average of $1 million per year as a result of this agreement.

## PROBLEMS WITH DEVELOPMENT AGREEMENTS

Despite the popularity of development agreements throughout California, however, they do pose three significant problems for cities. First, their constitutionality is open to question and so far no appellate court in California has ruled on the issue. Second, the negotiations between city and developer may unfairly lock out citizen groups — or, indeed, may constitute an attempt to circumvent their efforts. And third, re-negotiation may be necessary in many cases, but both developers and local officials are often afraid to try it for fear that they will lose more than they gain.

The development agreements in Orange and Riverside counties raised questions about citizen participation. In both counties, slow-growthers placed growth-control initiatives on the ballot in 1988, causing the Board of Supervisors to rush through DAs prior to the election. The result was quick approval — and vested rights — for 60,000 units in Orange County and about 100,000 units in Riverside County. Many of these projects had already received all other governmental approvals. Some were partially built. On other projects, the counties were able to exact additional concessions from developers in exchange for the DAs. Nevertheless, the projects protected by DAs are immune from any future growth measure or change in political sentiment.

Some jurisdictions have specifically refused to bargain away this kind of power. The City of San Diego, for example, won't approve a DA if it permits protection from either a future growth-control ordinance or a future increase in development fees. Yet developers in San Diego have sought DAs anyway, partly because they lock in exactions at current rates, even if the city raises fees and exaction requirements in the future.

Now that the development agreement law has been in place for a decade, a second-generation problem has cropped up: re-negotiation. The law's drafters didn't really contemplate re-negotiation, though they did specify that DA amendments should go through the same notice-and-public-hearing process as the original agreement.

But re-negotiation, which is common in long-term private real estate contracts, seems inevitable in the case of 15- to 30-year development agreements as well. For developers, market and financial circumstances change; for cities and counties, the political climate might change, as might the cost of public facilities required to service a project. And, recognizing a DA's vested rights as "currency" of a sort, many developers sell the projects before they are built — bringing in new owners who may want to change things around. A few cities have responded by building a process for re-negotiation into the original agreement. In Santa Monica, for example, the community development director can sign off on small changes herself, but larger changes go to the planning commission and big amendments must go through to the city council.

The biggest threat that looms over development agreements, however, is the prospect that they are unconstitutional. Many legal scholars have argued that development agreements violate the constitutional provision that prohibits a governmental agency from contracting away its police power. Because developers are so highly motivated to make DAs work, however, few have bothered to sue. Since the law was passed in 1979, not a single appellate case has been handed down dealing with the constitutionality of development agreements.

Until such a court ruling does appear, development agreements are likely to play an important role in shaping the future of California's land development patterns. The development agreement is a good example of the kind of governmental policy that takes into account not just environmental protection and community character, but property rights as well.

CHAPTER 12

# INTRODUCTION TO FINANCIAL AND IMPLEMENTATION TOOLS: THE FISCALIZATION OF LAND USE

U p until now, we have discussed planning mostly from the perspective of governmental regulation. Regulation deserves a great deal of attention, because it is the most common tool for carrying out governmental planning policies, and because California's, planning laws and regulations are voluminous and complicated. But regulation is reactive. It depends entirely on the private market to turn the planning concepts into on-the-ground reality. Despite this obvious fact of life, government planners don't always understand that private investment and development does not automatically occur when a new publicly adopted plan or regulatory scheme is put into place. Trained to deal with physical designs and policies, professional planners rarely recognize that developers also require favorable market and economic conditions in order to act. Thus, planners are often disappointed and/or confused when developers move slowly to take advantage of planning opportunities because of a weak market and high interest rates.

Traditionally, plans sat on the shelf until market conditions changed and developers became interested in building. Since the passage of Proposition 13,* however, cities and counties throughout California have become far more impatient about new development. No longer are they content to draw up plans and then wait until the market changes in their favor. Instead, cities and counties are taking all sorts of pro-active steps to implement their plans. They are using redevelopment powers to jump-start development projects. They are fighting with each other over incorporations and annexations involving desirable territory — i.e., territory that has the potential to produce lots of revenue and/or jobs. And they are entering into innovative financing schemes to get large development projects under way in emerging areas. In short, they are using their own financial resources and legal powers to subsidize, cajole, and otherwise lure developers who can implement their plans on a fast-track schedule.

The reason is money — or, more specifically, tax revenue. The tax revolt of the late '70s and early '80s forced local governments to reassess the financial implications of plans, and led to what many experts have come to call the "fiscalization" of land use in California. Since 1978, virtually all the traditional sources of local revenue — ad valorem property tax revenue,** state funds, and federal funds — have been drastically reduced or even cut out completely. Many of these funding sources, including general obligation bonds and state and federal grant programs, provided most of the money for public works pro-

* Proposition 13 was a constitutional amendment passed by initiative in 1978. (It is now contained in Article XIIIA of the state constitution). Written in response to rapidly rising property taxes (which were partly the result of rapidly rising real estate values), Proposition 13 rolled back property tax assessments to 1975 levels, permitted an annual increase in assessment of only 2 percent except in the event of a sale, and, for all practical purposes, capped property-tax rates at 1 percent per year. (A higher rate requires a two-thirds votes, which is very difficult to obtain.) Since property tax rates at the time were approaching 2 percent in many parts of the state, Proposition 13 cut local government revenues dramatically.

** Commonly, property tax is levied *ad valorem,* or by value. The county assessor "assesses" the value of each piece of property; each jurisdiction sets a local tax rate; and then the tax bill is computed by multiplying the assessment times the tax rate. For example, the county's property tax rate might be $1 per $100 of assessed value. If a house is assessed at $100,000, the annual property tax bill would be $1,000.

Prior to Proposition 13, county assessors reassessed all properties periodically, so that a house might be assessed at $100,000 even if the current owner bought it 30 years ago for only $10,000. Under Proposition 13, however, properties may be reassessed only when they are sold. If the properties are not sold, the assessment may rise a maximum of 2 percent per year.

jects made necessary by new development. Left without these general sources of funds, local governments have been forced to take a hard-headed look at the entire financial situation — assets, liabilities, costs, opportunities for more revenue.

By their very nature, local governments are territorial in outlook. And traditionally, land has been their leading resource and their preoccupation. Land defines a locality's boundaries. Land development is virtually the only business over which local governments can exercise broad regulatory control. The way land is used determines a community's character, as well as the cost of its services. And, traditionally, the value of land formed the basis for a local government's revenue stream, in the form of *ad valorem* property taxes. So when city managers, finance directors, and economic development specialists began to chart how their cities and counties would survive financially in a limited-tax world, they naturally paid close attention to the land in their communities, how that land is used, and the amount of tax revenue those land uses generate.

Thus, the relationship between land use and public finance, once tenuous, became much stronger. At a minimum, localities would not permit new development projects to occur unless those projects "paid for themselves" — that is, produced sufficient revenue to maintain roads, build parks, support police and fire protection, and cover all the other costs the project creates for the local government. This argument is part of the rationale for fees and exactions. Beyond that, however, land-use planning was transformed from a physical design process into an exercise in financial planning. In their general plans, local governments must now set aside at least some land for big tax producers. Very often, local leaders believe they cannot afford to approve new projects — or even continue to tolerate existing real estate developments — that are financial losers for the city treasury.

## HOW THE LOCAL TAX SYSTEM WORKS

Local governments in California receive the vast majority of their tax revenue from two sources: property tax and sales tax. Prior to Proposition 13, of course, property tax was by far the more important of the two. But since Prop. 13 placed restrictions on property-tax rates, sales-tax revenue has become the key source of revenue for local government. In many communities, sales tax revenue actually exceeds property tax revenue.

Under Proposition 13, property tax rates are limited to 1 percent of the assessed value of a property. (Property tax revenues are typically divided among city, county, school district, and special districts, though they are collected by counties.) Generally speaking, the rate cannot be increased except when approved by a two-thirds vote of local residents — a nearly impossible task. Furthermore, property may not be reassessed except when it is sold. If it is not sold, assessed value may rise by no more than 2% per year, no matter how rapidly the market value is rising.

The stated purpose of these provisions was to protect longtime homeowners who had bought houses at inexpensive prices but could not afford rapidly escalating property tax. (Another motive was to constrain local governments from "liberal" spending practices.) In practice, Proposition 13 has led to the well- publicized inequity in property taxes paid by homeowners. A longtime homeowner may pay $500 a year in property tax, while his next-door neighbor, living in a virtually identical house purchased after the passage of Proposition 13, may pay $5,000.

But Proposition 13 has also created a stratified real estate market from the point of view of the city treasury. Many commercial properties have risen greatly in value, but are undertaxed because they have not changed hands lately. For example, if a major corporation built an office building in downtown Los Angeles in 1980 for $100 million, the property-tax revenue today would still be a little over $1 million — about the same as it was when the building was built. However, if a Japanese investment company purchased the office building today for the current market value — say, approximately $400 million — then the property tax revenue would suddenly increase from $1 million to $4 million per year. That's a windfall for local government by any definition of the word.

Furthermore, because property-tax revenue after Proposition 13 bears little relationship to the cost of providing a property with public services, some developments are clearly winners and some are clearly losers. An office building or shopping center pays a lot of property tax, but it takes up relatively little land compared to a subdivision, requires minimal police and fire protection, and produces no children who must be educated by the local schools. A subdivision of single-family homes sprawls across the landscape, requires extensive police and fire protection, and generates a vast number of children who must be educated. But it produces relatively little property-tax revenue and no sales-tax revenue.

The sales-tax structure permits even more blatant manipulation. The permanent state sales tax is 6 cents for every dollar of retail sales. Of that 6 cents, the state government keeps 5 cents and gives 1 cent to local government. Furthermore, that 1 cent is returned to the local governments based on the location where the retail sale occurred. Thus, if a resident of Walnut Creek buys a watch at Macy's in San Francisco for $100, then San Francisco gets $1 in sales-tax revenue and Walnut Creek gets nothing. Furthermore, if an unincorporated community incorporates into a city, all the future sales-tax revenue in that community is transferred from the county treasury to the city treasury. (Each county may also adopt — with voter approval — up to 1 percent in additional sales tax if it is earmarked for a specific purpose, such as jail construction or transportation. That is why the sales tax rate in some areas is 6 1/2˙ or 7 percent.)

## IMPACT ON PLANNING

It is not too difficult to see that this tax structure leads many financially strapped local governments to "fiscalize" their land-use policies. Many localities use both their legal powers and their financial resources to clear out the losers and replace them with projects that will jack up tax revenue. In many cases, the traditional concern with a balanced community that will provide its citizens with everything they need — a variety of housing types, jobs, shops, culture — has been replaced with an overriding desire to increase the local tax base.

Perhaps the most obvious problem is the impact that the sales-tax system has on planning. The sales-tax split encourages localities to compete with each other in order to lure projects that generate lots of retail sales, principally shopping centers and auto dealerships.

But there are more subtle implications as well. For example, because they are unable to increase property tax rates (at least for general fund purposes), local governments can realize higher property tax revenue only when property changes hands, or when new, more valuable development is constructed. Thus, many cities and counties use their powers to encourage the sale or redevelopment of valuable property. And many communities zone vast tracts of land for tax-rich commercial and industrial development even though those same communities are in dire need of more housing. The tax issue gives many cities — and especially suburban cities — yet another reason not to pursue housing policies that will provide units for below-market buyers and renters.

The fiscalization of land use is not the dominant factor in every land-use planning decision in the state. Often, for example, local politicians will support low-density housing over commercial development because of slow-growth sentiment. And in fast-growing communities, local leaders bridge the tax "deficit" on housing projects by imposing hefty fees on new residential subdivisions. Nevertheless, financial considerations have gone a long way toward destroying the goal of thoughtful and well-balanced community plans in California. And, ironically, the financial and boundary tools associated with land-use planning — redevelopment, annexation, bond financing — have been used not to reinforce good planning, but to exploit planning for financial gain. The next several chapters will examine exactly how this occurs.

# CHAPTER 13

# CAPITAL AND INFRASTRUCTURE

Imagine a situation where two virtually identical pieces of farmland, the Jones tract and the Smith tract, lie several miles apart. Let's say both consist of several hundred acres that are still being actively farmed. Let's also say that both lie just beyond the urban fringe and might be ripe for development or, at least, land speculation. The county government, as part of a program to preserve farmland, has placed both pieces of land in a restrictive agricultural zone and perhaps even entered into Williamson Act* contracts with both landowners.

Now imagine that there is one difference between the two tracts: access. Let's say the Jones tract is several miles from any major road, while the Smith tract has a four-lane freeway running down the middle of it.

It's not to hard to imagine how this planning scenario is likely to play out. Because it is located far from any existing freeway, the Jones

---

* The Williamson Act (Government Code §51200 *et seq.*) permits counties to provide tax breaks to farmers who agree to keep their land in agricultural production. It is meant to serve as a way of discouraging farmers from selling out to land speculators or developers. Some 15 million acres of land in California is held in Williamson Act contracts, but farmland is dropping out of the program quickly on the suburban fringe.

tract will probably remain viable farmland for many years to come. But preserving the Smith tract as agricultural land — which is the county's public policy goal — will be much harder. Tempted by the Smith tract's proximity to the freeway, developers will probably start making offers on the land even though it's in a farmland preserve, and they will begin applying political pressure on the local government to open the tract up for development. Once this speculation and political pressure begins, the tract will almost certainly be developed sooner or later.

This little scenario illustrates the overwhelming power of capital improvements to control the development process and shape communities. Plans and regulations may reflect a community's vision of its own future. But major pieces of infrastructure, such as highways, water and sewer lines, and airports, are far more powerful in actually determining patterns of development. Plans and regulations can be changed with a simple majority vote of a planning commission and city council. But development cannot occur without proximity to vital pieces of infrastructure such as freeways. This infrastructure cannot be moved once it is built. And hooking onto existing infrastructure is so much easier and cheaper than building new public works projects that development will almost always follow the infrastructure that's already there. Building a freeway interchange on the Smith tract, for example, would require only a tiny fraction of the time and money needed to build a new freeway to the Jones tract.

Thus, the building of infrastructure — sometimes known as "capital improvements" or "public works projects" — is just as important to a community's future as all the lengthy and complicated planning processes covered earlier in this book. The plans are not likely to become reality if the infrastructure is not in place to permit crucial development projects. And if infrastructure is placed in the "wrong" location — in conflict with what plans call for — then there is little hope a community will realize the vision of the future it has laid out for itself in its plans.

Historically, one of the great weaknesses of planning in California has been a lack of coordination between the agencies that build infrastructure and the agencies that do local planning. Probably no public agency that has had a greater influence on California's current development patterns than Caltrans, the state Department of Transportation. Caltrans almost singlehandedly constructed the statewide California freeway system, which is one of the great public works projects of the century and an important element in the state's continuing prosperity. Yet during the construction of this massive system, Caltrans rarely interacted with the local governments that regulate land development around the freeways, nor did the agency give much consideration to the growth-inducing effects of the freeways. No local planning vision could have withstood the power of Caltrans to alter and shape a community's character.

The same was true with regard to many other pieces of a community's needed infrastructure. Water was provided by large "wholesalers" like Southern California's Metropolitan Water District, which responded to market demand even when those actions contradicted local attempts to shape or restrict growth. In the '60s and '70s, sewage systems were paid for largely by the federal government, which was concerned with water quality under the Clean Water Act, not the impact of sewer lines on a community's growth. Many airports are owned and operated by cities but located far beyond their borders, adjacent to small communities. Most large pieces of infrastructure were built by regional or state agencies that had little understanding of, or concern for, the impact their projects had on local communities.

Even in their own infrastructure planning, communities did not always fit their plans together with their capital improvement programs. Planning departments and public works departments were not always in close contact, so a new housing tract might be constructed in one part of town while new traffic lights were installed somewhere else.

In recent years, the entire system of planning for and building infrastructure in California has changed dramatically. On the local level, capital improvement plans must, by law, be consistent with the general plan. More significantly, however, the traditional sources of funding for infrastructure have disappeared. This has presented local governments in California with both opportunity and risk.

In the future, the planning and financing of major public works projects, even freeways, will occur largely at the local level, not at the state or federal level. This situation provides local governments with an unprecedented opportunity to use infrastructure planning to reinforce overall planning efforts. At the same time, the financial squeeze almost inevitably forces local governments into a financial partnership with individual developers in order to pay for new infrastructure. Sometimes this partnership involves having developers pay for new infrastructure, but more often it requires the local government to risk its own financial reputation in order to provide infrastructure for a large private development. This road is fraught with peril if it is not approached carefully, because it intertwines private and public interests and leads to a further fiscalization of land use.

## THE CAPITAL IMPROVEMENT PROGRAM

Each city and county in the state is supposed to draw up a "capital improvement program," or CIP, usually for the upcoming five-year period, that identifies the capital projects to be undertaken and the source of funds for those projects.

Theoretically, the CIP should be closely tied to the general plan, so that private development projects are coordinated with the construction of public infrastructure projects needed to support them. In fact, state general plan law requires consistency between the capital improvement plan and the general plan, and a discussion of capital facilities must be included in several general-plan elements.*

In practice, of course, the relationship is not always close. Coordination between the CIP and the general plan requires a good working relationship between the local planning department and the public works department — a relationship that does not always exist. Very often, the public works department pursues its own construction agenda with little regard for likely future development patterns. However, as private developers shoulder the cost for more and more capital improvements, this relationship is likely to draw closer. A few cities have already combined their CIP with their growth management system, because impact fees from new development provide the funds for the capital improvements.

* For a more specific discussion of these requirements, see page 176 of the state's *General Plan Guidelines.*

## How Capital Improvements Are Financed

Just as most houses are too expensive for the average person to buy with cash (especially in California!), most infrastructure improvements are too expensive for local governments to pay for "up front" out of the current year's budget. Throughout the postwar period, infrastructure has been paid for either by grant money or by the issuance of bonds. To be more precise, infrastructure finance came from one of four sources: federal grants, state grants, general obligation bonds, and revenue bonds. A decade ago all four of these funding sources were flourishing. Today all have been sharply curtailed.

### Federal Grants

Between the '50s and the '80s, the federal government poured an enormous amount of money into infrastructure for community development around the country. This trend began in the 1950s, when the federal government agreed to fund the lion's share (87 1/2 percent) of the cost of constructing interstate highways. (Federal funding for the interstate highway system was based on the presumption that the interstate system was needed for national defense purposes, although the interstate trucking industry also benefited.)

Beginning in the 1960s, the federal government also paid for many local sewer systems and sewage treatment plants in order to improve water quality under the Clean Water Act. In the Nixon Administration, many of these infrastructure grants, along with some housing funds, were wrapped up into "community development block grants," the so-called CDBG program. CDBG money was distributed to communities around the country, rather than concentrated in large cities, and the funds came with few strings attached, permitting local governments to pay for a wide array of infrastructure investments.

Local governments never saw the highway money — it was funneled to the states to build the interstate system — but obviously the program had a profound impact on shaping the development of postwar communities. As for the sewer grants and, later, the block grants, localities regarded these funds as "free money," permitting them to invest in infrastructure at no cost to the local taxpayer. What was actually happening, of course, was that taxpayers all over the country were

subsidizing specific local infrastructure projects. Sometimes this process permitted the federal government to encourage private investment
in depressed areas by building projects that the local or state government could not afford. More often, however, there was pressure in
Congress to distribute these funds in a politically equitable manner, so
that even prosperous communities received ample funds. But because
these funds were regarded as "free," localities often spent them with
little regard for cost-effectiveness.

In the '60s and '70s, a vast array of other federal grant programs
were established to assist local governments. For example, the
Economic Development Administration provided grants that permitted
both infrastructure investment and subsidies to businesses that provided local jobs. The Urban Development Action Grant (UDAG) program
provided "gap" financing for commercial revitalization projects, often
in downtown areas.

Needless to say, during the federal budget cutbacks of the 1980s, all
these programs either vanished or were reduced to a fraction of their
peak funding. For example, Community Development Block Grant
funds, a longtime staple of local planning budgets, were cut from $5.7
billion in 1981 to $2.7 billion in 1991. Sewer-treatment construction
grants under the Clean Water Act during the same period were cut
from $5.4 billion to $1.6 billion. The UDAG program was eliminated
by the Reagan administration. Thus, local governments had to wean
themselves off of a lucrative and politically attractive source of funds
for infrastructure construction and community development.

## STATE GRANTS

Like the federal government, the California state government also
spent generously on infrastructure between the '50s and the '80s. The
peak period came during the Pat Brown's gubernatorial administration
(1958-1966), when the state made a conscious effort to use infrastructure as the foundation for future prosperity.

The Pat Brown era is perhaps best remembered today for large public works projects at the state level — specifically, the state water project, which transported water from Northern California to Southern
California; the freeway system, which was largely completed during

this period (and funded with both state and federal money); and the higher education system, which greatly expanded the University of California, the California State University system, and the community colleges.

Obviously, this state-level infrastructure shaped California's postwar development to a considerable degree. But in the '50s and '60s, California also established several programs for funding local infrastructure projects. For example, public schools were constructed as needed with state bond proceeds, with local school districts repaying the state later. Such programs have been underfunded ever since Proposition 13 passed in 1978.

## BOND ISSUES

When federal and state funds are not available, local governments often pay for capital improvements by issuing tax-exempt bonds.

A bond is similar to a home mortgage. It is a way for a government entity to borrow a large sum of money and pay it back, with interest, over a long period of time — usually 20 to 30 years. Of course, bond issues, like mortgages, are very expensive when compared with cash purchases; in each case, the homeowner or governmental entity can expect to pay approximately three times the actual cost of the home or facility over the 30-year period. But, like mortgages, bonds have the advantage of requiring little up-front cash on the part of the governmental entity issuing them. When financing facilities that will last 20 to 30 years, such as buildings, sewers, and other public facilities, bonding is considered a prudent method of financing.

And, just as a homeowner seeking a mortgage goes to the bank, a governmental entity seeking to issue bonds goes to another type of financial institution, a bond underwriter. Bond underwriters, like banks, are really "middlemen" between people who want to lend money and people who want to borrow it. In the case of a "traditional" savings-and-loan, the bank is the middleman between depositors, who in effect loan money to the bank in return for a pre-determined interest rate, and borrowers, who pay a higher interest rate to gain access to that same money. In the case of a bond issue, the underwriter is the middleman between Wall Street investors, who want to purchase tax-exempt government bonds as an investment, and the government agencies that want to issue bonds to raise capital funds. In fact, the primary buyer of municipal bonds is the wealthy individual, who has considerable funds to invest and is attracted by the stability of municipal bonds and the fact that the interest income he or she receives is not taxable.

Local governments issue several types of tax-exempt bonds, and — as with federal and state grants — most of these bonds used to be more abundantly available than they are today. The three most common types of bonds, historically, are general-obligation bonds, revenue bonds, and special assessment bonds. Between the '50s and the '80s, the first two types of bonds were most common — but recent events have made both of them very difficult to use today.

*General-obligation bonds* are probably the bonds most people think of when they think of a governmental bond issue. Simply stated, these bonds must be repaid out of general tax revenue. For this reason, they are considered by investors to be the safest type of tax-exempt municipal bond to buy.

General-obligation bond issues always must be approved by the voters in advance. In recent years, the California state government has issued several billion dollars in general-obligation bonds each year because the state's voters have approved them. These bond issues have provided funds for all sorts of purposes, including school and prison construction, home mortgages for veterans, and protection of wildlife habitat. Statewide bond issues, however, may be placed on the ballot without raising taxes (though they must be repaid out of state tax revenues). Local general-obligation bond issues are different, however. These bonds are typically paid off by an increase in the local property tax rate — meaning that if a general-obligation bond is issued, each property owner's taxes will go up.

Prior to Proposition 13, general-obligation bonds were typically used to build such facilities as city halls, police stations, local jails, libraries, and schools. Proposition 13, however, virtually prohibited local property-tax increases to pay for new bond issues. Thus, the use of general-obligation bonds at the local level has been greatly reduced.

Prior to the Tax Reform Act of 1986, *revenue bonds* were also commonly used by local governments. Unlike general-obligation bonds,

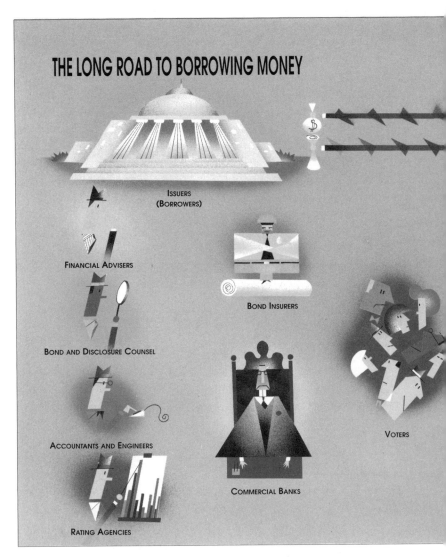

revenue bonds are not backed by the governmental entity's pledge to use tax revenue to pay them off. Rather, revenue bonds are usually paid off by some stream of income from a specific project being constructed with the bond proceeds. For example, a city might issue revenue bonds to build a parking garage, and then pay back the bonds

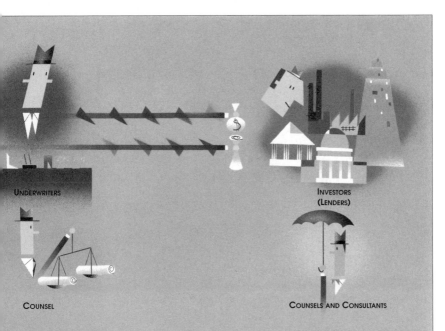

UNDERWRITERS

INVESTORS
(LENDERS)

COUNSEL

COUNSELS AND CONSULTANTS

ssuing a municipal bond is a complicated undertaking. Initially, the government officials who will issue the bond must consult with their **financial advisers** on the viability of the issue and with **bond and disclosure counsels** (attorneys) to ensure that the bonds meet all legal requirements.

**Accountants and engineers** provide audited financial and feasibility studies of the project to be funded by the bond. These are particularly essentially for revenue bonds, which must be paid back with revenue from the projects they are used to build.

**Rating agencies**—Standard & Poor's Corp., Moody's Investors Service, and occasionally tch Investors Service—provide a letter ranking for the bond, indicating its safety as an investment. The ranking may be upgraded if the bond is insured through a **bond insurer** or with a letter of credit from a bank. **Banks** also serve as agents for registering the bond and paying interest to investors, and as trustees for the issue. Most original long-term bond issues must also receive the approval of the **voters** before they are sold.

**Underwriters** get the bonds to market. The services they provide differ according to the type of bond and whether they won the right to handle it through competitive bidding or a negotiated deal. Theoretically, underwriters must carry any unsold bonds, which is why they usually consult with both the issuer's and their own counsel about the viability of the bonds.

**The investors—individuals, banks, and companies**—can turn to several sources for information. These include the opinions from the bond and disclosure counsels, the audited financial and feasibility studies, and the basic bond ratings. Source: Public Securities Association

with revenue derived from parking fees.

Revenue bonds were used for a wide variety of purposes. Some were used to construct facilities for specific businesses a locality wanted to lure or retain; these bonds were known as "industrial development bonds." Many others, known as "mortgage revenue bonds," were used to provide low-interest mortgages for apartments or single-family houses, especially in high-cost areas. The chief attraction of these bonds was the fact that they were tax-exempt. Since interest income was exempt from taxes, the bonds could command a lower interest rate on Wall Street, thus allowing local government to provide below-market financing to the homebuyers, developers, and businesses they wanted to favor.

The federal Tax Reform Act of 1986, however, dramatically restricted the use of tax-exempt revenue bonds. Now, California is allotted only a limited dollar amount of tax-exempt revenue bonding power each year. Local governments seeking to issue industrial development bonds and mortgage revenue bonds must compete with each other, and with a variety of state agencies, for "allocation." Of course, governmental entities may issue taxable revenue bonds, but such bonds inevitably carry a higher interest rate. In short, revenue bonds, like general obligation bonds and state and federal grants, have ceased to play a significant role in financing California's growth.

### ASSESSMENT DISTRICTS AND MELLO-ROOS BONDS

The result of all these financial changes has been to shift the cost of new growth from taxpayers at large (federal, state, and local) to the consumers of that new growth (developers, homebuyers, new businesses). As with so many other things in society, there has been a shift from general tax subsidies to "user fees." We have already seen how impact fees and exactions now play a much larger role in providing funds for the infrastructure required by new growth. But these fees alone do not provide all the funds necessary — and, especially, they do not provide the large sums required up-front for roads, sewers, schools, and so forth. Thus, impact fees are used together with (and sometimes supplemented by) a type of bonding oriented around "user fees": assessment districts.

Assessment districts are not new in California; in fact, they were first authorized by the state in 1911.* The concept is simple. Everyone who benefits from a particular public improvement is included in a special district established to pay for that public improvement. Furthermore, not all property owners pay the same assessment. Each pays according to the benefit their property receives from the public improvement. For example, in a street-lighting district that covers a residential subdivision, all property owners may pay the same amount, because all are perceived to benefit equally from the presence of street-lights. In contrast, if an assessment district were created to build a free-way interchange, those properties closest to the interchange would pay more, because their property values are likely to rise higher as a result of the interchange.

From the '50s to the '80s, assessment districts were not used very often, mostly because so many alternatives were available. Since the early '80s, the use of assessment districts has been on the rise. But the most popular type of financing in recent years has been an offshoot of the assessment district, the so-called Mello-Roos district.

Mello-Roos "community facilities districts"** are special districts that raise funds from property owners within a given area in order to provide public improvements in that area. Unlike assessment districts, however, Mello-Roos districts (named for the two legislators who sponsored the bill authorizing them) are designed in direct response to the problems created by the passage of Proposition 13.

Proposition 13 requires virtually all tax increases to be approved by a two-thirds vote. However, certain "special" taxes, whose revenue is earmarked for specific purposes, still may be approved by a simple majority vote. Thus, Mello-Roos districts are authorized to levy "spe-cial" taxes on all property owners within a given area in order to pay for specific projects — usually public facilities required by a new development project. Large new subdivisions in places such as Riverside or Orange counties often use Mello-Roos tax levies to finance construction of schools, roads, and sewers by creation of a Mello-Roos district. The Mello-Roos district floats tax-exempt bonds, and the Mello-Roos taxes received from property owners in the subdi-vision are used to pay back the bonds.

---

* The provisions of state law most often used in creating assessment districts are Streets and Highways Code Section 5000 *et seq.* (the Improvement Act of 1911); Streets and Highways Code Sections 1000 *et seq.* (the Improvement Act of 1913); and Streets and Highways Code Sections 8500 *et seq.* (the Improvement Act of 1915).
** Government Code §55311 *et seq.*

Mello-Roos districts have several other popular characteristics as well. Most important, in contrast to assessment districts, property owners do not pay the Mello-Roos tax based on benefit. Every parcel owner within the Mello-Roos district pays the same amount of tax. This can be very important when financing schools, for example — because it permits the Mello-Roos district to levy taxes on all property owners, even if they don't have any children in school.

Also unlike conventional assessment districts, Mello-Roos funds may be used for the operation and maintenance of facilities, not just the capital cost of their construction. And finally, while new Mello-Roos districts must be approved by the district's voters, the law makes it very easy for the developer of a new project to set up such a district. Under the law, if there are fewer than 12 voters in a district, only property owners may vote on the district's creation and its initial tax levy.

In practice, this means that a large land developer completely controls the creation of Mello-Roos districts. Typically, a developer and a county create the Mello-Roos district together (it may be called, for example, "Orange County Community Facilities District #5") as part of the initial development approval. Oftentimes, the Mello-Roos district is part of a package of approvals that includes a specific plan (which lays out the infrastructure requirements to be financed with Mello-Roos bond proceeds) and a development agreement (which guarantees that the developer will be able to build the houses necessary to pay off the bonds). The new district will be administered by the county, which will float the bonds, construct the roads and schools, and then add the Mello-Roos tax to a new homeowner's property tax bill. Indeed, many new homeowners in California have received a stunning surprise when their first bill arrives, because it is far higher than the 1% of assessed property value permitted under Proposition 13.

## HOW BOND FINANCING CAN AFFECT PLANNING

The widespread use of assessment districts and Mello-Roos districts to finance infrastructure has changed the relationship between infrastructure finance and land-use planning.

Up until the last decade, virtually all common financing tools required the commitment of general tax money, whether local, state, or federal. Thus, if a specific development project failed, that failure might be embarrassing — but it probably would not create financial problems for the city or county where the project was located. Now, however, the raising of capital has become a far more integral part of the land-use process. It creates a stronger link between the local government and the developer, making it harder than ever for the local government to act dispassionately in land-use matters.

When a development agreement, a specific plan, and a Mello-Roos district are all processed together, then the demands of infrastructure finance are sure to help shape the land-use patterns a new development project will contain. This is good in many ways, because it may encourage clustering and other efficiencies in the use of land in order to keep the infrastructure cost low. At the same time, however, the imperatives of infrastructure finance can also work against good planning.

If Mello-Roos bonds are issued by a city or county, then that city or county has a financial stake in the project. While the local government may not actually have to pay off the bonds if problems arise, nevertheless a default would look embarrassing on Wall Street and harm the locality's financial reputation. (And, in all likelihood, some clever lawyer for the bond's purchasers would tangle the locality up in litigation for years.) In essence, the local government has made the same kind of commitment to this project that it would make to a redevelopment project or an industrial park financed with industrial development bonds. Thus, a city or county is likely to place very high priority on making sure that such a development project is successful.

But imagine how this commitment could come into conflict with the planning process. Infrastructure guru Dean Misczynski, of the Senate Office of Research, offers this nightmarish scenario for planners: Suppose that shortly after a large residential project in County X has been financed with Mello-Roos bonds, a competing land developer comes to the county and asks for permission to build another huge residential project on adjoining property. In all likelihood, the adjoining property is also designated for residential development in the general plan. And the construction of housing is a state priority. But the second project will compete with the first project — and, therefore, could threaten its success in the marketplace. With so much riding on the financial success of the first project, how could the county's planners review the second project impartially?

The problem is compounded by the fact that only a few people involved in the land development process do not have a financial interest in the approval of a project. This is especially true when large bond issues are involved. Under common practice, both the bond underwriter and the bond counsel — both of which work, theoretically, for the city or county involved — receive a percentage of the bond issue's proceeds. Thus, even consultants who are supposed to be working for the public have an interest in seeking a project go forward, whether or not its prospects for success are good. This situation often exerts tremendous pressure on staff planners, who usually don't have the technical skill to spot a project that is financially shaky.

Given the anti-tax attitude of the last 15 years, it's understandable that the burden of infrastructure finance has shifted from taxpayers to the final purchasers of developed real estate. At the same time, however, infrastructure finance has not been completely "privatized." The money is still funneled through public coffers via assessment and Mello-Roos districts. This mixture of public and private funds and goals has created a delicate situation. Fortunately, at this writing, California has seen no major Mello-Roos bond defaults. But if rising land and home prices slow down in the 1990s, as they are expected to do, then trouble may lie ahead.

# CHAPTER 14

# DRAWING BOUNDARIES

Communities are defined by the way they draw boundary lines around themselves. The planning power of any local government only extends as far as its boundaries. And so, of course, does its taxing power.

Communities have always used boundaries as weapons — to keep out poor people or noxious industries, to maximize tax revenue, and to gain control over newly emerging areas. Since the passage of Proposition 13, however, this warfare has increased. By virtually prohibiting tax increases, Proposition 13 turned local government finance into a "zero-sum" game. Cities constantly battle counties, and each other, over territory that holds the potential for a valuable tax base. Often, it is virtually the only way to increase their tax revenue.

But cities can also capture additional tax revenue by incorporating, annexing new land, and adjusting their boundaries in other ways. In this regard, boundary-drawing is simply an extension of the fiscalization of land use discussed in the other chapters. Cities and counties covet particular pieces of land for their revenue potential, and then create planning policies designed to exploit that potential.

## CITIES AND COUNTIES

To understand the competition for land among local governments in California, it is important to understand the position that different types of local governments find themselves in today.

Local government comes in many forms in California. By far the most numerous are school districts and special districts — single-purpose agencies that exist to provide specialized services. A Mello-Roos bond financing district, as described in the last chapter, is a special district.

But the most important local government entities in planning terms are cities and counties. These entities are general-purpose government agencies responsible for a wide range of subject and service areas, including land-use decisions and general taxation. But, as Chapter 1 explained, there is a significant difference in the purpose of cities and counties.

Counties are subdivisions of the state, designed to carry out state policy in a decentralized way. Cities are entities created by local citizens to provide urban services. Counties are concerned with such matters as social services and criminal justice, and they carry out land-use planning only in unincorporated areas — that is, only when a city government does not exist. (This does not mean that counties do not supervise development in urbanized areas; in many counties, unincorporated communities have several hundred thousand residents. And in such counties, land-use matters are prominent political issues.) For cities, on the other hand, planning and community development is a matter of leading concern, along with police and fire protection, trash pickup, and other matters that are difficult for counties, with their vast rural areas, to handle.

## THE ZERO-SUM GAME

Theoretically at least, counties are far more financially dependent on the state than cities are; after all, they are, in many ways, nothing more than mini-state agencies. On the other hand, cities have considerably more legal power to obtain tax revenue — which is only natural, since cities, at least theoretically, have to raise most of their revenue locally.

The most important sources of tax revenue for local governments are property taxes and sales taxes. Lots of other revenue sources are available, including user fees, special taxes, and some aid from state and federal agencies. But all those funds come with strings attached, while property and sales tax revenues can be used for any purpose. Therefore, much of the competition over tax-rich territory comes from the way tax revenues are divided among local governments.

General property tax revenues are divided among cities, counties, and school districts. The exact percentage varies from county to county, but, in general, the county gets the lion's share. In the City of Los Angeles, for example, L.A. County gets 45 percent of the property tax revenue, with 33 percent going to the L.A. city government, and most of the rest going to the L.A. Unified School District. This formula is

considered a favorable split for the City of L.A.

Of California's 6 percent general sales tax, 1 percent is returned to local governments — and the money is not returned to the community where the buyer lives, but, rather, to the jurisdiction where the sale took place. Thus, for example, if a person from Azusa buys a $15,000 Honda at a dealership in Duarte, then Duarte receives $150 in sales tax revenue and Azusa gets nothing.

Obviously, this system penalizes cities that do not have many retail sales outlets, but it also penalizes counties when cities incorporate. If, for example, the Honda dealership were located in an unincorporated area of L.A. County, then the county government would receive the $150 in sales tax. But if the area then incorporated as a city, the $150 would go to the new city's treasury. Newly incorporated cities also receive a share of the property tax formerly received by counties, but the transfer of funds is not as extreme.

Prior to the passage of Proposition 13 in 1978, this tax-split system worked reasonably well. Counties didn't lose tax revenue when cities incorporated or annexed, because the cities funded their operations by imposing additional property taxes. (This situation also discouraged the incorporation of new cities, because voters knew it would mean a tax increase; that is why some parts of California have many unincorporated areas that are fully developed as urban and suburban communities.) And because property tax revenues were so large prior to Proposition 13, sales taxes did not play such a significant role in local government budgeting.

But Proposition 13 disrupted this system by turning it into a zero-sum game. Because Proposition 13 made it virtually impossible to raise property-tax rates, cities and counties must share what little property tax is available. Because Proposition 13 dramatically reduced property tax rates, there is much less property tax to go around, so sales-tax revenue has become far more important than it was before. And because of the limitations on raising tax rates, the only way for a city or county to increase its tax revenue is either to permit the construction of new buildings, which will increase property taxes, or to generate more retail sales within their jurisdiction, which will, in turn, increase sales tax revenues.

Therefore, cities and counties throughout California are engaged in an intense competition for land that holds the potential for new development — and, especially, for new shopping centers, auto dealerships, and other businesses that generate a lot of retail sales. Cities will often try to reach out and grab nearby land if it has tax-producing development on it, or holds the potential for such development in the future. Adjoining cities will fight with each other over annexation. Residents of an unincorporated area with lots of retail shops will often seek to incorporate in order to keep their tax dollars "at home," rather than allow the money to be transferred to the county government. Counties fight back by trying to stop annexations and incorporations through political persuasion, lawsuits, and other hardball tactics. Needing new development for tax reasons, some counties have also begun to abandon their longstanding planning policies, which attempted to discourage urban sprawl by channeling new growth into existing cities.

For example, in 1986, the unincorporated Sacramento suburb of Citrus Heights decided to incorporate, largely because residents realized that a local mall generated $2 million a year in local sales tax revenue. Faced with such a large loss of funds, Sacramento County's supervisors — and the county's Deputy Sheriff's Association, which foresaw big layoffs — took a series of legal steps to block the incorporation election. Despite the support of the Local Agency Formation Commission (about which more will be explained a little later), Citrus Heights' incorporation has been postponed for years.

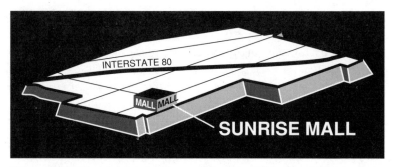

**Citrus Heights residents placed tax-rich Sunrise Mall just inside proposed city boundaries, much to county's dismay.**

In a somewhat similar fashion, Fresno County has used hardball tactics against Fresno and other cities in that area over the tax implications of annexation. After a series of annexations and redevelopment projects had eroded Fresno County's tax base, county supervisors simply terminated their standing tax-sharing agreements, first with Fresno and then with all other cities in the county. (These agreements specify how property and sales tax revenues will be divided after an annexation.) Without these agreements in place, no annexations could be approved. Little by little, the supply of readily developable land in the Fresno area dwindled, putting pressure on the cities to reach an agreement with the county. Eventually most of the cities agreed to give the county a percentage of sales tax revenue in annexed areas and tax-increment funds in redevelopment areas. The Fresno dispute was bitter, but illustrative of the kind of warfare that results from the zero-sum situation in local government finance.

## LAFCOs

These border battles are usually played out in front of a body called the Local Agency Formation Commission. LAFCOs have final authority over all boundary-setting actions (except redevelopment) and therefore have a profound impact on urban development patterns in the state.

Under state law,* each county must establish a LAFCO according to the state's rules. Typically a LAFCO consists of two county supervisors, two representatives of the county's cities, and one member of the public — though in some counties, special districts may be represented. LAFCOs are charged with setting boundaries that discourage urban sprawl and encourage efficiently serviced urban development. LAFCOs have no land-use power, but their decisions affect development patterns, because they determine which local jurisdiction will have responsibility for planning new areas. A newly incorporated city, for example, may plan the future of its undeveloped area far differently than a county government would have.

Theoretically, LAFCOs are state entities separate from all local

* Government Code §65000.

government jurisdictions. LAFCOs exist because boundary decisions — unlike local land-use planning — are considered matters of state concern. (Thus, boundary decisions are not subject to local initiative and referendum.) In point of fact, however, virtually every LAFCO is housed within the county government. In many cases, the LAFCO's executive officer is paid by the county government, and some even have other responsibilities in the county's chief administrative office. Given the contentious relationship between cities and counties over boundary issues, this close relationship with the county sometimes harms the LAFCO's credibility with city officials.

Indeed, the LAFCO process can often become very political, since a majority of the LAFCO members are elected local officials. Sometimes, LAFCOs have been accused of being controlled by city or county officials who want to accommodate developers that are big campaign contributors. In some instances, this accommodation may lead to the annexation of a key piece of property to a city that can provide water and sewer service to that property. At other times, it may mean voting to leave a particular piece of property out of a city or its sphere of influence, especially if the city is expected to pursue slow-growth planning policies.

LAFCO policies vary from county to county. In Ventura and Santa Clara counties, the LAFCO has a strong tradition of directing growth inside city boundaries, and as a result only 10- 15 percent of the population lives in unincorporated areas. Sacramento County, on the other hand, has formed no new cities since 1946, and as a result more than 60 percent of the population lives outside city limits.

LAFCOs deal with a broad range of boundary actions, including incorporations, annexations, dissolution (the opposite of incorporation), detachment (the opposite of annexation), and the creation of "spheres of influence" for cities. LAFCOs also adjust the boundaries of special districts. Dissolutions are very rare, but detachments are quite common, as cities are constantly making small adjustments in their boundaries. In some cases, LAFCOs have used detachment in conjunction with annexations in order to preserve open space and maintain compact cities. The Ventura County LAFCO, for example, has often sought to maintain farmland by requiring cities to detach agricultural property when they annex territory slated for urban development.

Though annexations are often contentious, probably the most controversial actions that LAFCOs consider are the approval of incorporations and the creation of spheres of influence.

## INCORPORATIONS

Communities usually seek to incorporate as cities for one of two reasons. The first is a desire to control local tax dollars, a feeling which often arises when a community is located far away from the county seat. The second is a desire to control a community's growth. Because counties must rely on new development to increase tax revenue, they often encourage growth in unincorporated areas, which leads to a backlash by local residents. In this context, incorporation becomes a slow-growth measure, whose purpose is to "draw a line" around the area and then elect a local city council that will change the planning policies.

Incorporation is often preceded by the creation of other governmental entities, such as special districts or a general-purpose Community Services District, which is not unlike a city in many respects. But incorporation itself cannot proceed without the LAFCO's approval.

Perhaps the most important step the LAFCO takes in reviewing a proposed incorporation is the fiscal review. Unless a new city is going to show a healthy budget surplus, the LAFCO is not supposed to approve it. But this fiscal review is not as simple or non-political as it might seem.

In several instances, incorporation proponents have engaged in bitter disputes with LAFCO fiscal consultants over the likely cost of city services. High-end assumptions can sink a cityhood movement; low-end assumptions can help it. Also, a city's likely policies after incorporation can enter into this equation. For example, suppose a new city is proposed by a group of citizens who have made it clear that they will pursue slow-growth policies if incorporation succeeds. Obviously, the slow-growth policies will affect the proposed city's fiscal health. A change in development plans might harm the city financially by slowing down new construction. This financial information may be used to support or oppose incorporation, depending on the political motivations of the city and county officials who sit on the LAFCO.

Pessimistic fiscal projections have killed more than one proposed city. But optimistic projections can lead to equally sad results. For example, the only city in recent California history that incorporated with a questionable financial future was East Palo Alto. The area is a minority ghetto in San Mateo County, just across the county line from affluent Palo Alto; it is afflicted with crime and poverty, and has little tax base. Nevertheless, East Palo Alto was permitted to incorporate in 1983 as an affirmation of racial justice. The city has tried to lure tax-producing development, but this effort has been opposed by residents of Palo Alto, who fear their quality of life will be damaged. The city can barely pay its bills, and talk of dissolving the city has increased.

Once the LAFCO has approved an incorporation, the issue often proceeds to a vote. Under state law, after approving an incorporation LAFCO must conduct a protest hearing and hold the comment period open for 30 days. If opposition is expressed by between 25 percent and 50 percent of the people who live in the area or the owners of between 25 percent and 50 percent of the property, then a vote must be held. (If more than 50 percent of either group complains, then the incorporation cannot occur.) In point of fact, a vote is almost always held — and, in the vast majority of cases, if cityhood makes it to the ballot, it will win. Since Proposition 13 eliminated the possibility of tax increases, voters have realized that incorporation is "free." Thus, since 1978, the number of new cities has been on the rise, accelerating the financial problems of counties.

### SPHERES OF INFLUENCE

Local LAFCOs establish spheres of influence, which will usually extend beyond a city's current boundaries into undeveloped areas beyond. By creating a sphere, the LAFCO defines the probable ultimate boundaries of the city. The sphere gives a city an indication of what property LAFCO will permit the city to annex; this assurance, in turn, allows the city to draw up a general plan that includes the sphere area.

As with incorporation, the creation of a sphere of influence might seem to be a technical, non-political decision that simply acknowledges likely future development patterns. In fact, sphere decisions are

highly political. Some landowners and developers will lobby the
LAFCO to be included in a city's sphere; others will lobby to be left
out. And because developers are major contributors to both city and
county election campaigns, the city and county officials who sit on the
LAFCO will often try to accommodate them.

The most celebrated sphere battles have occurred in Los Angeles
County, where the LAFCO has tried to limit the spheres of new cities
because developers prefer to deal with the county planning department.
When the City of Agoura Hills incorporated in 1982, for example, the
L.A. County LAFCO created a sphere of influence co-terminus with
the city's boundaries. Fearing rampant development in nearby unincorporated areas, Agoura Hills sued, claiming that a city's sphere must be
larger than its boundaries. But the Court of Appeal rejected the argument, saying LAFCO had acted properly.*

The City of Santa Clarita suffered a similar fate when it incorporated five years later. Consisting of unincorporated areas such as
Valencia, Newhall, and Saugus, the city had incorporated partly to stop
what it regarded as irresponsible development under L.A. County policies. Therefore, Santa Clarita asked the L.A. County LAFCO for a
sphere of influence of 90 square miles (compared to the city boundaries of 40 square miles). Under pressure from homebuilders in the
area, however, the LAFCO denied the request and, as with Agoura
Hills, established a sphere co-terminus with city boundaries.
Undaunted, Santa Clarita returned to the LAFCO two years later with a
request for a sphere covering 200 square miles! This request, at least,
motivated the LAFCO staff to recommend the 90-square-mile sphere
Santa Clarita had wanted originally, but again the LAFCO commissioners turned the request down.

## BOUNDARIES AND PLANNING

Even when cities and counties cooperate on boundary changes,
however, the financial pressures inherent in local planning can lead to
trouble.

In 1986, for example, Yolo County honored West Sacramento's

---

* *City of Agoura Hills v. LAFCO of Los Angeles County,* 198 Cal.App.3d 480 (1988).

request for incorporation, despite the fact that the port town was the county's most intensely developed commercial and industrial area. By permitting cityhood, Yolo lost $3 million a year, which put the mostly rural county into deep financial straits.

Not long afterward, however, a Sacramento developer came to the county supervisors and asked for permission to build an industrial-commercial park in the Interstate 80 corridor between Davis and Sacramento. The request contradicted the county's longstanding policy of channeling all new growth into cities, but the developer had already been rejected by the slow-growth City of Davis. Yolo County was loathe to abandon its longstanding planning policies, which were designed to protect agriculture, but financial problems forced the county to do so. The supervisors agreed to consider the developer's application, and their action led to strained relations with Davis for years afterward.

The Yolo County situation is not unusual. Many counties that have channeled urban development into cities now face financial strains because they have followed good planning practices. The supervisors in these counties face the unpleasant choice of either alienating agricultural and environmentalist constituencies by permitting more development or, alternatively, allowing their counties to drift toward bankruptcy.

At the same time, however, some cities and counties have begun working together to sort out the planning and financial issues associated with boundary-setting. A model of cooperation is the 22,000-acre Otay Ranch project outside San Diego, where officials from San Diego County and the City of Chula Vista are working together. Rather than compete for the most desirable chunks of the project, Chula Vista and the county established a joint planning office housed separately from the city and county governments. The planning team will sort out the planning and financial issues, then make recommendations about both annexation and financial responsibility. But such cooperative efforts are still all too rare, and they are not encouraged by state law.

* * *

## COUNTYHOOD MOVEMENTS

City boundaries are changed all the time, but county boundaries would seem to be inviolate. They have remained virtually unchanged since 1907, when Imperial County was carved from the eastern portion of San Diego County.

Since 1974, however, local citizens have been permitted to initiate countyhood movements in much the same way that they initiate city-hood movements.* No new counties have yet been formed, but close to a dozen countyhood votes have been held.

Under state law, if countyhood advocates gather enough signatures, the governor must appoint a County Formation Commission, similar to a LAFCO, to oversee the process of creating a new county. Like the LAFCO, the commission must review the proposed county's fiscal sit-uation and then schedule a vote. However, to succeed, a countyhood proposal must win a majority of votes, not just in the area seeking to become a new county, but also in the rest of the county. This require-ment has proved to be the undoing of most countyhood movements.

Shortly after the countyhood law was passed, several sections of Los Angeles County tried to secede — including the ever-disgruntled Santa Clarita area — but those efforts failed. Outside of L.A. County, most of the countyhood proposals have come from remote areas which are far removed from the county seat. The countyhood movement that came closest to success was a proposal to separate the City of South Lake Tahoe from El Dorado County. The most recent countyhood vote came in 1988, when San Bernardino County voters rejected a plan to carve Mojave County out of the vast desert areas north of the San Bernardino Mountains.

* Government Code §23300.

# CHAPTER 15

# REDEVELOPMENT

Redevelopment may be the single most powerful planning tool available to local governments in California. It is also perhaps the most widely abused and twisted tool available to local governments in California.

Redevelopment is designed to cure blight; yet "blight" can be legally defined as anything from low-tax properties to narrow lots. Redevelopment is meant to revive depressed slum areas; but it has been applied to farmland in the suburbs. Redevelopment is meant to permit cities to amass the financial wherewithal to deal with difficult social problems; yet governmental entities use it to protect or increase tax revenue with little regard to how those social problems are addressed.

Not all of California's 400-odd redevelopment projects involve abuse. More than a few have actually served the original purpose of helping distressed neighborhoods return from the brink. Redevelopment has provided jobs and housing for those who need them. Especially in poor neighborhoods of Los Angeles, redevelopment has created successful shopping centers where no private developer would dare to take the chance. Throughout the state,

redevelopment has been used in combination with "enterprise zones"*
to entice industry into run-down areas. And redevelopment has provided the vehicle for constructing cultural and entertainment complexes of
regional significance, where conventional methods might have failed.

But many redevelopment projects have served no greater purpose
than enhancing city treasuries. This is not a venal purpose *per se*, but it
is far from the original, noble purpose redevelopment was supposed to
serve. In the financially uncertain world in which local governments
must operate, the power of redevelopment is seductive indeed.

The roots of redevelopment lie in the old and now unfashionable
concept of "urban renewal." After World War II, the federal government embarked on a major program of slum clearance, giving cities
huge sums of money to raze slum neighborhoods. Such areas were
considered health and safety hazards — breeding grounds for disease
and social disorder. The federal urban renewal program encouraged
cities to bulldoze problem areas and start over again by building public housing projects, playgrounds, commercial areas, and the rest of a
community's infrastructure.

To complement the federal program, California adopted the
Community Redevelopment Act in the early 1950s.** To help achieve
a social restructuring of unprecedented scope, the redevelopment law
granted cities and counties two powers of immense importance. First,
they were granted the power to acquire property by eminent domain,
even if private development projects were planned for the site.
(Traditionally, eminent domain could be used only for a purely "public" use such as a park, school, freeway, or jail.) Second, cities and
counties were given the power to create "tax-increment financing" districts, which permitted them to issue bonds against the future property-

---

* The enterprise zone is a British idea to encourage development in depressed areas by
providing tax breaks and suspending cumbersome regulations. The California version of
this idea (Government Code §7070-7078 and §7080-7099) provides companies with
some state tax breaks, but it is necessarily limited in scope and value because (1) no regulations have been suspended, (2) companies still must pay full federal income tax no
matter where they are located, and (3) the California Constitution prohibits property-tax
abatements, a common technique in other states.

** Because its goal was to protect public health and safety, the law was placed in the
Health & Safety Code, where it remains today at §33000 *et seq.*

tax increases inside the redevelopment area. In short, the redevelopment law gives local governments (1) the power to rearrange private land ownership patterns, and (2) the financial resources to subsidize private development projects deemed to be in the public interest. There is simply no other planning tool in California that gives local governments such sweeping power to operate pro-actively.

In the '50s and '60s, many California cities used redevelopment to acquire and raze huge properties in depressed areas, usually near decaying downtowns. (Most of the land acquisition costs were paid for out of federal urban renewal funds, which dried up by the end of the 1970s.) Beginning in the '70s, however, redevelopment began to fall out of fashion, for two reasons. First, many of the most prominent redevelopment sites sat vacant for a decade or more, because private developers simply did not want to take them on. (Perhaps the most prominent examples were the Yerba Buena project in San Francisco, some of which is still vacant, and the Bunker Hill area in Los Angeles, which eventually — against all odds — became a prestigious business address.) Second, community organizers and anti-poverty activists began agitating against the use of redevelopment, which they claimed razed neighborhoods unnecessarily and displaced the very people redevelopment was supposed to help. When Proposition 13 passed in 1978, experts throughout the state predicted that redevelopment would become even less popular among local governments, because the drastic cut in property taxes would make it very difficult for tax-increment financing deals to "pencil out."

In fact, the opposite occurred. In the decade after the passage of Proposition 13, redevelopment became more popular than ever. And the reason was money. Within redevelopment's vague and flexible requirements lay an opportunity for cities to manipulate the use of land and the division of tax revenue for their own financial benefit.

In most cities, there is little difference between the city government and its redevelopment agency. Except in Los Angeles, San Francisco, and a few other large cities, the city council also serves as the board of directors of a redevelopment agency. The city manager often serves as executive director of the redevelopment agency (and often a portion of his salary is paid for by redevelopment funds). And once a redevelopment project area is created, all the subsequent increases in property-tax revenue within that area go to the redevelopment agency's treasury. The city does not have to share those funds with the county government, school districts, or special districts. Though the city council and city manager face many restrictions in actually using that money, they still gain control of it. This is often a covert but very powerful reason that cities pursue redevelopment aggressively.

In extreme cases, cities shield virtually all of their property tax revenue from other government agencies. The classic examples here are industrial cities around Los Angeles, such as Industry and Irwindale — communities that have few residents to please and a great deal of "blighted" property to redevelop. Such cities can use their redevelopment funds for an endless game of economic development. By using their tax-increment funds to provide land and infrastructure, they can induce new industries to locate in their redevelopment areas; and the new industries then provide huge amounts of tax-increment funds, which will be used to lure yet more industries into town.

But ordinary cities also manipulate redevelopment this way. This manipulation is not completely malevolent; cities justify it by saying that they are assuring themselves of a secure tax base and therefore assuring good services for their residents. There is some truth in this argument. But the financial manipulation also has harmful side effects. In any event, it is the most significant aspect of redevelopment in California today.

## HOW REDEVELOPMENT WORKS

Cities and counties that undertake redevelopment must follow a carefully prescribed set of procedures. Typically, the city council or county board of supervisors will select a large "survey area" and hire a consultant to examine which parts of the survey area can be classified as "blighted" and, therefore, may be included in a redevelopment project area. After this initial reconnaissance, the planning commission selects a proposed project area and a redevelopment plan is prepared.

By law, the redevelopment plan must contain certain pieces of information, such as a map of the project area, development standards within the project area, a financing scheme, and a plan to involve property owners in the redevelopment process. An environmental impact report is prepared; property owners are notified; public hearings are held. If the project includes residential areas, a "project area committee," made up of citizens within the project area, must be created. Finally, the city council must adopt the plan. The redevelopment plan must be found to be consistent with the city's general plan, but, of course, a general plan amendment can easily rectify any inconsistencies.

But plan adoption is not the end of the redevelopment process. Typically the redevelopment plan will cover between 20 and 35 years, laying out an ambitious series of projects about what new development will be attracted into the area, what inducements the city will provide to developers, and how needed infrastructure will be paid for. Once the plan is adopted, the city will try to find developers willing to build the specific projects called for in the redevelopment plan. The deal that is struck between the city and the developer depends on market conditions and each side's bargaining position, but generally speaking such a deal (called a "disposition and development agreement") will involve several elements. Often the city has already assembled a large parcel of land via eminent domain. Typically the city will agree to a "land write-down" — meaning the city will sell the property to the developer at a loss. This is a crucial inducement for private investors. (The loss is usually made up for with tax-increment funds.) The developer will agree to a specific program and very detailed development standards. The city may agree to build infrastructure, and both sides will agree on a schedule.

Stripped to the bare essentials, redevelopment consists of three elements — eminent domain, tax-increment finance, and the concept of blight. In recent years, two other factors have become important as well: the role of the project area committee and the responsibility of redevelopment to provide housing.

## THE FINDING OF BLIGHT

The whole purpose of the California Redevelopment Law is "to protect and promote the development and redevelopment of blighted areas." Thus, for a locality even to establish a "redevelopment project area," that locality must make a legal finding that the area is blighted.

Obviously, the original notion of a "blighted" area derived from the unsafe, unsanitary slum neighborhoods of the pre-war era, which led to so much white flight and disinvestment after World War II. The original definition of blight talked about buildings that were "conducive to ill health, transmission of disease, infant mortality, juvenile delinquency" and so on. But under California's redevelopment law, the term "blight" is expansive, opening the door for redevelopment lawyers to find blight where most people wouldn't expect it. Until recently, raw land could be declared blighted under certain circumstances — if it was prone to flooding, for example, or if it had been divided up into "paper subdivisions" with unusable lots. This provision explains how places like Indian Wells, a golf course resort town near Palm Springs, and Hidden Hills, a horsey gated community near the San Fernando Valley, could find "blighted" areas inside their city limits.

The legislature banned the practice of declaring raw land blighted in 1984. (Now any land inside a redevelopment project area must be 80 percent urbanized.) With that one exception, however, the definition of blight is very broad indeed. Under the law, areas can be declared blighted if they have characteristics like these:

• Economic dislocation or disuse.
• Lots of irregular form or shape.
• Lots laid out without regard for topography.
• Inadequate streets and open spaces.
• Stagnant and unproductive use of land.
• Loss of population.

It is not hard to see how these definitions can be applied broadly. If any area laid out without regard to topography is blighted, then a redevelopment lawyer would probably have no trouble declaring the entire city of San Francisco blighted. Similarly, the provisions involving inadequate streets and irregularly shaped lots would permit a city or county to declare any area developed before World War II blighted, since modern standards are different. In practice, redevelopment lawyers lean heavily on economic blight, permitting local governments to create redevelopment areas in commercial districts where businesses may be viable but tax receipts are not as high as the city would like them to be. And it is hard to challenge the finding of blight in court, because, legally speaking, a blight finding carries a "conclusive presumption" — meaning the courts will virtually always defer to the judgment of the city council.

In some cases, cities and counties actually use the blight definition responsibly, permitting them to place true slums in redevelopment areas. Generally speaking, however, the broad definition of blight permits these governmental entities — especially cities — to create a redevelopment project in virtually any older area where the city is not receiving maximum tax revenues possible. This is the first step in converting redevelopment from a social tool into a financial tool. Because once such an area is placed inside a redevelopment project area, all its properties are subject to the awesome power of eminent domain and tax-increment financing.

## EMINENT DOMAIN

As the chapter on the Subdivision Map Act explained, land is virtually impossible to piece back together once it has been subdivided. But the redevelopment of an older area will almost always require reassembling land into large parcels under single ownership. Thus, redevelopment agencies have unusual power to use eminent domain in assembling land, even if the ultimate property owner will be a private entity.

Typically, a redevelopment agency will use eminent domain to assemble land and then sell it at a much lower price — a "land write-down" — to a private developer who will build a project that fits the redevelopment plan. Thus, through redevelopment, a city might pay $30 million in an eminent domain proceeding to unwilling sellers in order to assemble a large parcel. But then the city will sell the property to a developer for $20 million, or $1 million — or even $1, depending on how badly the city wants a particular developer involved in a particular project, and what it can afford, both financially and politically.

Traditionally, local governments could exercise their eminent domain powers only for schools, roads, and other publicly owned projects. In recent years, however, the courts have stated that eminent domain may assist a public purpose even if the land ultimately ends up in private ownership. In a landmark case,* the U.S. Supreme Court ruled that "it is not essential that the entire community, nor even any considerable portion ... directly enjoy or participate in any improvement in order (for it) to constitute a public use."

But the notion that a city government can use power of eminent domain to reshape land ownership patterns has many opponents — especially small business owners and longtime homeowners of modest means.

The prospect of eminent domain can be frightening for a homeowner or a small merchant. Such people might eventually get a fair market value for their property, but only after months — or years — of court disputes and lawyers' fees in the eminent domain action. If they are strongly rooted in the neighborhood where they live or do business, they'll probably object to the idea that their property is "blighted," and that it should be part of a redevelopment effort in the first place.

The typical property owner first learns of a redevelopment project when he or she receives a small notice in the mail saying their property "may be subject to eminent domain." Understandably this often leads to an apoplectic response. The first public meeting on a proposed redevelopment project is often filled with  dozens or even hundreds of enraged property owners who fear that redevelopment means they will lose their homes.

In recent years, these local residents have combined with a group of anti-redevelopment activists in California to oppose — and occasionally kill — several redevelopment projects throughout the state. The activists, who have worked in many different communities, are motivated by a strong libertarian belief that a redevelopment project using eminent domain constitutes an unchecked alliance of "big government" and "big business" that will squeeze out the little guy. As one anti-redevelopment activist put it: "Redevelopment is a political tool to get rid of property owners you don't like."

Perhaps the most dramatic example of the power of anti- redevelopment activists came in Anaheim, where the city proposed a 4,000-acre redevelopment project that included Disneyland, the seedy commercial

---

* *Hawaii Housing Authority v. Midkiff,* 467 U.S. 229 (1984).

strips in the Disneyland area, and many modest residential neighbor-hoods nearby. Joining with the anti-redevelopment activists, residents of the proposed redevelopment area were incensed at the plan, which they believed was a ruse to use redevelopment to subsidize an expansion of Disneyland into nearby residential areas. Soon, community opposition coalesced around the rallying cry: "The Mouse Wants Your House." Faced with more than a thousand angry residents, the Anaheim City Council withdrew the plan.

As a result of the Anaheim failure and others like it, many redevelopment projects are now approved on the condition that they not use eminent domain. And anti-redevelopment activists have also used fear of eminent domain to mobilize opposition on "Project Area Committees," or PACs. (PACs, which are a required forum for citizen participation, will be discussed in more detail later on.)

## TAX-INCREMENT FINANCING

Eminent domain is only part of the reason that redevelopment is attractive to cities, however. Just as alluring is access to tax-increment financing, which permits a city to gain control of property tax revenues that otherwise would be split with other governmental entities.

The concept of tax-increment financing is to use the future growth in property-tax revenues generated within a redevelopment area to finance the redevelopment program itself. Once a redevelopment project area has been created, all future increases in property tax revenue within the area's boundaries — the tax "increment" — go directly to the redevelopment agency. (All redevelopment plans will predict vastly higher property-tax revenues as a result of the plan's implementation; obviously, it does not always work out that way in real life.)

The purpose of this practice is to give the redevelopment agency financial leverage to do land write-downs and infrastructure improvements. Although a redevelopment area won't be generating any tax increment at first, the typical redevelopment officials will issue bonds to be paid back by future tax-increment revenues. (Sometimes the redevelopment agency will also borrow money from the city treasury and pay it back later.)

Tax-increment financing is a dramatic shift away from normal taxation policy — which is why cities find it so attractive, and why other governmental entities, such as counties, often oppose redevelopment. Typically, in areas not subject to a redevelopment process, property taxes will be divided among cities, counties, school districts, and special districts. The financial formula varies from county to county, but typically the county gets the lion's share of the tax revenue. The formula for the City of Los Angeles, for example, calls for Los Angeles County to receive 45 percent of the property tax revenue (some is then distributed to special districts administered by the county), while the city gets 33 percent and the school district gets 18 percent. Inside redevelopment boundaries, however, the L.A.'s Community Redevelopment Agency receives 100% of the tax increment — a figure that has grown huge because many of the redevelopment areas have been in place for 20 years or more.

Tax-increment revenues grow when the assessed value of property within the redevelopment area grows. In California today, assessed value can grow only two ways: if a new project is constructed, and if a property is sold, which triggers a reassessment under Proposition 13.

For example, a dilapidated commercial building may be assessed for $100,000. Such a building would produce $1,000 per year in property tax revenue, divided among the city, the county, and the local school district. However, as part of a redevelopment plan, a city may build new roads or sewers, or it may subsidize the construction of a new building nearby. These efforts may improve the commercial market in the neighborhood, leading the building's owners to tear down the old building and replace it with a new building assessed at $1 million. Under Proposition 13, the new building will generate $10,000 a year in property tax revenue. But still only $1,000 would go into the fund divided among county, city, and school district. The other $9,000 would go into the coffers of the city's redevelopment agency. If all goes according to plan, the money will already be accounted for. The redevelopment agency will have anticipated this increase in value, and arranged to use the funds to help pay off the redevelopment bonds which were used to improve the area in the first place.

That's the way tax-increment financing is supposed to work. But the system provides a number of loopholes that permit cities to use tax-

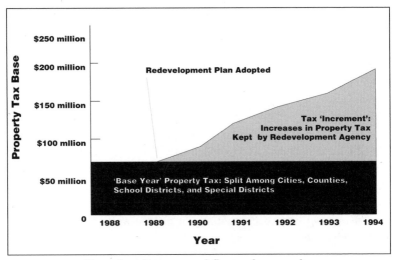

**How tax-increment financing works**

increment financing as a tool of financial manipulation.

The most obvious loophole has to do with the sale of property. Under Proposition 13, property is reassessed only when it is sold. Thus, the assessed value of almost any property is artificially depressed until a sale occurs, and a property-tax "windfall" occurs after the sale. Ordinarily, all the governmental entities share in this tax windfall. But inside the boundaries of a redevelopment area, the only beneficiary of such a windfall is the city's redevelopment agency.

Take, for example, a downtown-type skyscraper that sold in the 1970s for $50 million. The annual property tax revenue on that property would be about $500,000. But suppose that sometime during the 1980s, the property was included in a redevelopment area. And then suppose that the property was sold to Japanese investors in 1990 for $400 million. The tax revenue on the property would now rise to $4 million. But the city's redevelopment agency would receive receive all the tax increment — which, in this case, would total $3.5 million. The county, school district, and city general fund would divide only the original $500,000.

It is hard to answer the question of whether a city redevelopment agency is "entitled" to such a windfall. On the one hand, redevelopment officials will usually argue that, without their efforts the property would never have become so valuable. On the other hand, California property values rose so fast during the 1980s that the sums involved are far greater than any redevelopment official ever could have forecast. In downtown Los Angeles, where this phenomenon has been most prevalent, stratospheric property prices have brought the L.A. Community Redevelopment Agency hundreds of millions of dollars more than anyone ever expected it to have. And CRA does not have to share these funds with any other taxing entity.

The prospect of such a large potential windfall leads many cities toward a very obvious piece of manipulation: gerrymandering redevelopment boundaries to include a piece of property that is already likely to be sold or redeveloped privately in the near future.

For a city undertaking a new redevelopment effort, the most important task is finding sources of tax increment in the early years of the project. Without a big tax-increment generator inside the project area, the city will have a hard time selling its redevelopment bonds, because Wall Street investors won't have much confidence that the project is financially feasible. And if the project does fall on its face in the first few years, the city treasury will have to make up the financial deficit. Thus, the soundest financial move a city can make for a fledgling redevelopment area is to include a significant property that's about to be sold or redeveloped privately — even though that sale or private redevelopment has nothing to do with the city's own pending redevelopment efforts.

The second important financial loophole in redevelopment has to do not only with property tax, but also with sales tax. Because Proposition 13 cut property tax rates so dramatically, sales tax is now more important than ever as a source of revenue for local government. Also, cities, if they are incorporated, receive a 1 percent cut of the 6 percent state sales tax on retail sales occurring inside the city limits, and they do not have to share that revenue with counties or any other governmental entities. The temptation of sales tax leads cities to a second rather obvious piece of manipulation: using property tax funds under a tax-increment financing scheme to bring in businesses that produce a lot of sales tax revenues.

Say, for example, that a city creates a redevelopment project area that includes a 30-year-old shopping center. The shopping center may be assessed at $10 million, which means it generates $100,000 a year in property-tax revenue that is split among city, county, and school district. And the shopping center may produce $20 million a year in retail sales — bringing the city $200,000 a year in sales tax revenue.

The city probably recognizes the redevelopment potential of the shopping center — and, especially, the likelihood that a new or renovated shopping center could really boost the city's sales tax revenue. A typical redevelopment deal would probably go something like this: The city would buy the shopping center for $20 million and then sell it to a private developer for perhaps $12 million, taking an $8 million "hit" on the land write-down. The developer then invests $20 million to rebuild the shopping center, which is now expected to produce $40 million a year in retail sales.

Now take a look at the resulting tax situation. The shopping center will now be assessed at $32 million instead of $10 million, meaning it is producing $320,000 a year in property tax revenue instead of $100,000. All of the additional $220,000, however, goes to the city redevelopment agency — presumably to help pay off redevelopment bonds used to cover the $8 million land write-down. But now take a look at the resulting sales-tax situation. Instead of $200,000 a year, the city is getting $400,000 into the general fund.

The city has used the redevelopment process to invest property-tax funds, which are restricted in use and would otherwise have to be shared with other governmental entities, in a venture that has led to a $200,000-a-year increase in sales-tax revenue, which can be used for any purpose and does not have to be shared with the county or the school district. When written, the redevelopment law simply did not anticipate that sales tax would be such an important revenue source. (Tax-increment financing schemes may be set up with sales tax revenues, but this technique is rarely used.)

Cities often manipulate the redevelopment law to generate hotel "bed tax" in the same fashion. A tax-increment financing scheme may be created to finance the construction of a new hotel inside a redevelopment project area. But the hotel will throw off huge amounts of local bed tax revenue — and unlike sales and property taxes, the bed tax rate is determined by the local government, not by Sacramento.

Needless to say, the financial manipulation of redevelopment is not popular with other governmental entities — especially counties, which have few revenue sources of their own and usually take the biggest financial hit. Schools are not seriously affected; partly because of their powerful Sacramento lobby, school districts are reimbursed by the state for funds lost as a result of redevelopment projects.

But counties (and special districts, which counties often administer) are not reimbursed by the state. Thus, counties fight a constant battle against cities to stop or curtail redevelopment activities. Typically, a county will review all the new redevelopment projects being proposed by cities within the county by forming a "fiscal review committee," composed of all the government entities that would lose tax money to the redevelopment project. Sometimes cities and counties go to court over redevelopment. More often, however, they negotiate a solution, with the city agreeing to "pass through" a percentage of the tax-increment funds to the county. The pass-through can range from 10 percent to 60 percent of the resulting property tax, depending on factors like the city's redevelopment debt service and the county's cost of providing services to the redevelopment area.

Clearly, these financial games are far removed from slum clearance and the revival of blighted areas. But they take place in the redevelopment arena because of the financial pressure that local governments feel — and also because cities and their redevelopment officials have effective lobbies in Sacramento. Occasionally, one state legislator or another introduces a bill that would permit cities to set up tax-increment financing districts outside the redevelopment process — relieving the city of creating the fiction that an area is blighted in order to improve its own revenue situation. Also in Sacramento, county lobbyists often try to chip away at redevelopment powers in hopes of reducing the financial leverage that cities gain in the  redevelopment process. By and large, however, the financial games continue unabated.

* * *

## THE ROLE OF THE PROJECT AREA COMMITTEE

Ordinary citizens have traditionally played only a small role in shaping redevelopment plans, even if their own homes or businesses are affected by the plans. As the section on eminent domain explained, disgruntled citizens have often organized around opposition to a redevelopment agency's eminent domain powers. In recent years, however, a powerful vehicle for citizen participation has emerged: the project area committee, or PAC. In some cases, the PAC has been used by cities to rubber-stamp city redevelopment decisions. In other cases, it has served as a forum for redevelopment opponents. In a few cases, it has been used as intended — as a forum for constructive discussion between redevelopment officials and affected citizens.

Under the state redevelopment law, the city must create a PAC if a redevelopment project is likely to displace a substantial number of low- and moderate-income residents. In practice, virtually all cities in California create PACs in their redevelopment areas, for fear of getting hammered by citizen criticism otherwise.

PACs must be made up of people who have an interest in the redevelopment area — people such as tenants, homeowners, merchants, business owners. Traditionally, cities have created PACs simply by appointing members. But many cities have run into legal trouble by forming PACs this way, because it's not what the redevelopment law calls for. The language of the law says that PACs should be created by "calling upon the residents and existing community organizations." Some courts have suggested that this means PACs must be organized in a kind of "town meeting" atmosphere. The city may call the meeting, but those attending the meeting select their own PAC representatives and city officials can't participate. It's not uncommon for the resulting PAC to be somewhat hostile to the city's redevelopment plans, since the most vocal people at the town meeting are likely to be people who don't like the project.

Once the PACs are set up, they have — at least theoretically — surprising power. Most important, they may request a budget to hire consultants and lawyers. Over the past several years, this mechanism has given California's anti- redevelopment activists the opportunity to step into local disputes by representing PACs. Occasionally, property owners who oppose redevelopment can afford to pay for their own legal and expert advice. (For example, the Anaheim anti-redevelopment battle was funded by KOA Kampground, which has a lucrative operation near Disneyland.)

But when they can't, the PAC — if it's sufficiently hostile to redevelopment — can sometimes squeeze the money out of the city. A prominent example here occurred in Huntington Beach, where a hostile PAC hired two anti-redevelopment activists, one as a consultant and the other as a lawyer. The consultant and lawyer helped the PAC kill the project. (Among other consequences, the city manager resigned.) And in the end, the consultant and the lawyer were paid out of city funds.

It's not inevitable, however, that organized citizens and a city redevelopment agency should wind up at odds. Occasionally, cities have permitted their PACs to hold true power. One good example is the PAC for the Lincoln Avenue redevelopment corridor in Pasadena, which has emerged as a powerful committee, thanks to the city's neighborhood-oriented political scene — and some 20 years of contention over redevelopment. The Lincoln Avenue PAC has the power to review virtually all development proposals in the area and commands a budget of about $50,000 a year for office space, a staff member, and an outside lawyer. Understandably, redevelopment planners are not always pleased when PACs try to assert power over projects. There is no question that PACs are narrowly focused and often force cities to scale down grand redevelopment plans. On the other hand, PACs are one of the few forces capable of introducing citizen participation and accountability into the redevelopment process, where both are sorely needed.

## REDEVELOPMENT AND HOUSING

Throughout the '70s and '80s, cities (and counties) have used redevelopment powers mostly for economic development purposes. These localities have concentrated on fostering the construction of hotels, office buildings, auto malls, shopping centers, industrial parks, and other development that would either improve the tax base or create job opportunities.

Lurking underneath this rush to economic development, however, are the California redevelopment law's requirements regarding housing. These requirements have been in the law since the 1970s, but historically there have been so many loopholes and escape clauses that most cities have been able to avoid them. As California's affordable housing situation has become more and more bleak, however, the legislature has closed more and more loopholes. The result is that in the 1990s, redevelopment agencies will have to focus much more closely on housing, rather than commercial and industrial development.

The redevelopment law's basic requirement is the "20-percent set-aside." According to this requirement, every redevelopment agency must set aside 20 percent of its tax-increment revenue for low-and moderate-income housing. (As with most housing programs, low-income housing is defined as housing affordable to households with less than 80 percent of the county's median income, while moderate-income housing means housing affordable to households with an income of between 80 and 120 percent of the median.)

But "affordable" housing — especially low-income housing — is politically unpopular in cities all around the state. In many cases, local politicians have supported redevelopment projects for the purposes of economic development or revenue enhancement, only to run into the politically sticky problem of "public" housing. So cities around the state have taken advantage of the redevelopment law's many loopholes regarding the housing set-aside.

For example, when the housing set-aside requirement was first passed in 1977, it applied only to new redevelopment projects, and it exempted projects already in existence. Needless to say, the older projects generate the most tax increment, so the exemption substantially reduced the funds available. Furthermore, if more than 80 percent of a redevelopment project's tax increment is set aside to pay off bonds, then the city does not have to set aside the whole 20 percent for housing. This loophole has encouraged many cities to float more bonds in order to get their bond debt up above 80 percent. Finally, any city may choose not to set aside any funds for housing if the city makes a finding that the funds are not needed. Many cities, for example, make findings that other efforts, such as community development block grant programs, are sufficient to meet the city's affordable housing needs.

The biggest loophole of all, however, concerns the set-aside money itself. Although redevelopment agencies are required to set aside 20 percent of the tax-increment money for housing, until recently no state law actually required them to spend that money. Faced with the question of building politically unpopular low-income housing or simply letting the housing money sit in the bank, many cities chose to put the money in the bank. The state Department of Housing and Community Development has estimated that California cities are sitting on about $200 million in redevelopment housing money.

In recent years, however, the state legislature has passed several bills attempting to close these loopholes. Two in particular are expected to have a considerable impact. The first was AB 1735, passed in 1987, which forces cities that don't set aside 20 percent of their funds for housing to make up the difference eventually.* This bill was aimed especially at older redevelopment projects, which sometimes have more than 80 percent of their tax increment earmarked for debt service. These cities must carry the difference between 20 percent and the amount they actually set aside as debt on their books, and eventually they must pay the money back, probably on the back end of the project.

The second new law was AB 4567, also passed in 1987, which forces cities to actually spend the housing money they set aside.** Under this bill, any city that accumulates more than $500,000 in its redevelopment housing fund has to spend the money within five years or turn it over to the county housing authority. (The money may also be turned over to another housing agency, or the county may use the money for housing within the city's limits under contract to the city.)

If the intent of these two laws (and others passed since then) is achieved, then by the middle '90s redevelopment agencies around the state should have refocused their efforts on housing. Some redevelopment agencies may actually become housing developers — a return to the past, in a way, because in the '50s and '60s big-city redevelopment

---

* Chapter 1111, Statutes of 1987.
** Chapter 1564, Statutes of 1987.

agencies built thousands of units of public housing. Others may simply serve as financial conduits. For example, in response to AB 4567, the City of San Jose, which collects more than $12 million a year in housing set-aside money, simply transferred the funds from the redevelopment agency to the city housing department to fund city construction and rehabilitation programs.

Problems remain with redevelopment and housing. Many cities will continue to resist constructing housing within their borders. Perhaps the most striking recent example was the case of Indian Wells, an affluent desert community near Palm Springs which was working with a private developer to build a large resort, partly inside a redevelopment area. Indian Wells had made little provision for housing the low-wage workers who would be employed at the resort, and so poverty lawyers sued the city. Eventually, the city and the poverty lawyers agreed on a settlement to construct low-income housing that would be subsidized by Indian Wells redevelopment money but located outside the Indian Wells city limits.

Governor George Deukmejian eventually vetoed a bill that would have made the deal legal, but the story points out just how hard it is to get redevelopment agencies to build housing. Many aggressive redevelopment agencies are located in cities that are not balanced — cities that have a preponderance of industry or high-income housing. Providing affordable housing inside the boundaries of such cities is politically difficult and, sometimes, physically impossible. Yet the alternative has been to let the housing set-aside money sit in the bank. Though AB 4567 will help, loopholes remain, and undoubtedly most of these cities will continue to avoid the construction of low- and moderate-income housing inside their borders.

The dilemma about redevelopment and housing seems to reflect the chronic difficulties involved in getting California's local governments to use redevelopment for the original purposes for which it was intended. Redevelopment is a powerful tool because it is meant to deal with powerful social problems. Yet cities — and, to a lesser extent, counties — have been able to manipulate the powerful tool to their own financial advantage without applying them to the social problems redevelopment was meant to address. Citizen opposition and tougher housing set-aside requirements should make it more difficult for cities to abuse redevelopment in the future. But accountability in redevelopment remains one of the biggest planning and municipal finance problems in the state.

# CHAPTER 16

# MAKING PLANNING WORK IN CALIFORNIA

C alifornia has more planners than any other state in the country, and it's likely that Californians spend more time debating the future of their communities than anyone else. But all this does not mean that planning "works" in California.

The goal of planning is, or should be, to shape the built environment for the benefit of society — to meet the needs of all people and accommodate a growing economy, while at the same time conserving natural resources and protecting the environment. To put it another way, planning's job should be to assure that people and activities are arranged on the landscape in a rational, efficient, and equitable manner.

To be sure, in selected communities and selected circumstances, planning in California has taken long strides toward achieving this goal. But from the broad perspective — as this book has tried to point out — the state and its communities have fallen far short. Indeed, every planning "success" in California seems to carry with it some kind of long-term failure.

Thanks to the planning process, the disarray in road and traffic patterns that predominated 20 years ago has disappeared. For example, few new developments suffer from the plethora of curb cuts that plagued drivers in the past. Yet partly as a result of this efficient system, which has encouraged auto travel, the state is now infested with cars, traffic congestion, and the resulting air pollution.

California's preference for "home rule" has given small cities throughout the state a remarkable degree of freedom in shaping their communities — even when those small cities lie in the middle of huge metropolitan areas. Yet California — the most diverse state in the country — remains highly segregated by race, ethnicity, and income, partly because local control of land use has been wielded in the interests of such segregation.

And California has been a leader in opening the planning process to participation by all citizens and all interest groups. Yet citizen unrest about growth and development is more intense here than anywhere else in the country, and citizen groups can often hold the entire planning process "hostage" in order to pursue a narrow agenda that includes little regard for the overall public interest.

These are but a few examples of the broader trend. In short, although the process is extensive and inclusive — and while planners can justifiably point to many successes — planning in California suffers from systemic failure. The planning process simply doesn't work anymore. The assumptions on which that process was based — well-balanced cities, limited citizen participation, free-flowing highways, ample property-tax revenue, affordable housing — are outdated. At best, this fact means that planning is unable to address the problems California faces today. At worst, it means that the planning process is subject to the easy manipulation by interest groups that this book has often described.

To break through this logjam, then, it is necessary to question many of the assumptions on which current planning law and practice in California are based. By doing so, it will be possible to craft a new vision of what planning in California should be and who it should serve.

This is not an easy task, because the state's entire planning "infrastructure" — planners, consultants, lawyers, developers, designers, economists — has been built up around these assumptions, and will feel threatened by the challenge. Indeed, many of the likely compo-

nents of a reformist agenda in planning
have been kicking around for years, but
they've been batted down by lobbyists
for local government, the development
industry, and others who prefer the status quo. Yet an effort at reform must be
made. California has already fallen
behind as a leader in planning, and if
the state continues to grow as fast as it
did in the 1980s, it simply won't be
equipped to handle the future.

A program to reform California's
planning system must address the
broad range of outdated assumptions
and other problems that this book has
identified. Such a reformist agenda
must include at least five important
components.

### 1. CALIFORNIA MUST BREAK THE PATTERN OF AUTO-ORIENTED, SUBURBAN-STYLE GROWTH, AT LEAST IN METROPOLITAN AREAS.

The auto-oriented subdivision-and-
shopping-center lifestyle that emerged
after World War II was a logical
response to the conditions of the time.
Central cities were overcrowded; the
burgeoning middle class was able to
afford automobiles and a more bucolic
way of life. And, of course, even
before World War II, an auto-oriented
lifestyle was part of the supposedly
carefree California dream.

Yet California's population has more
than tripled since the end of World War

## NEO-TRADITIONAL PLANNING

Re-orienting
communities away from
the automobile would
have been unthinkable
even a decade ago. But
today it is not, because,
for the first time since
World War II, some plan-
ners and architects have
begun designing proto-
type alternatives to the
conventional suburban
community. Rejecting
many of the supposedly
"modern" concepts
about how developments
are laid out, advocates of
so-called "neo-traditional
planning" have advocat-
ed a return to traditional
grid street patterns,
mixed-used develop-
ments, and neighbor-
hoods oriented around
walking distances. In particular, they point to the
potential for neo-tradi-
tional development pat-
terns to reduce (or at
least disperse) vehicle
trips, reducing traffic congestion and smog.

Not surprisingly, devel-
opers were the first to
catch on to the power of
neo-traditional planning.
Beset by citizen opposi-
tion to projects, required
by many localities to

reduce the number of vehicle trips, and always looking for ways to stand out in the marketplace, developers were ahead of their counterparts in planning in advocating neo-traditional planning. However, many urban planners — and citizens as well — find that neo-traditional planning conforms to their natural sense of what communities should be.

The leading advocates of neo-traditional planning in California have been two developers' architects, Peter Calthorpe of San Francisco and Andres Duany, a Miami designer who has done considerable work in California. In 1988, Calthorpe unveiled the "pedestrian pocket" idea — a proposed method of organizing a well-balanced neighborhood around a town center or transit station. Each of Calthorpe's "pockets" constitute 50 to 100 acres and include 2,000 housing units as well as a full complement of service and retail businesses and some office space. Calthorpe's idea was that the pockets could be replicated on a large

II, and auto-oriented, suburban-style development has become the root of many of our most highly visible planning problems. Today cars are necessities rather than luxuries — not only for commuters, but also for homemakers, high school students, the elderly, and the poor. The number of registered vehicles, licensed drivers, and miles traveled is growing far faster than the population as a whole. Traffic congestion and air pollution, much of it created by auto emissions, have become intolerable in the state's metropolitan areas. The search for a bucolic suburban lifestyle has sent auto-dependent commuters up to 70 miles away from their jobs — chewing up important farmland and/or environmentally sensitive areas formerly unaffected by the pressures of urbanization.

On one level, many Californians have, in recent years, recognized the need to wean themselves off the automobile. Both statewide and in major metropolitan areas, voters have approved plans to spend several billion dollars to construct and operate rail transit lines — perhaps the largest non-federal commitment to rail transit in American history. By the end of the 1990s, the BART (Bay Area Rapid Transit) system will stretch deeper into the Bay Area's suburbs, while a variety of rail lines will crisscross the auto-oriented Southern California megalopolis.

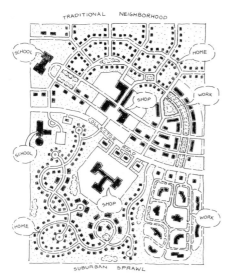

**Andres Duany's conception
of new and old neighborhoods.**

Rail-transit systems are already operating in San Diego, San Jose, and Sacramento — though, admittedly, with mixed success.

Yet this commitment is not reflected in the planning efforts of California's communities, as the pitiful ridership figures in most areas will attest. Most general plans envision an auto-oriented future not unlike the present, filled with subdivisions, shopping centers, and business parks that are, for all practical purposes, accessible only by car. Virtually everyone involved in the growth debate accepts that the suburban style of site planning, with its rigid separation of land uses, its cul-de-sacs and curvilinear streets, and its almost

scale or squeezed in between traditional suburban subdivisions.

Shortly after Calthorpe unveiled his idea, he got an unusual opportunity to try it out. Sacramento developer Phil Angelides scrapped a traditional suburban subdivision he had planned and hired Calthorpe to redesign it — even though Angelides already had all necessary governmental approvals for the project. The resulting 800-acre project is not exactly a "pocket." It contains some elements of a traditional subdivision, including a preponderance of single-family homes, that Calthorpe did not include in his original idea. Nevertheless, the Angelides project received a tremendous amount of publicity, stimulating widespread interest in neo-traditional planning.

Duany's approach is more closely drawn from "traditional" towns. In particular, Duany has criticized traffic engineers for encouraging developers to build single-purpose streets that isolate land uses from each other and force virtually all traffic onto arterial highways.

For example, a typical suburban development will include homes, apartments, office buildings, schools, and shopping centers in close proximity to each other. But most of these buildings are located in isolation on their own separate streets. This pattern forces people into their cars, and also creates traffic congestion on arterial highways because people have few choices in driving from one place to another.

Duany's approach revolves around a traditional grid street system, in which a series of straight streets intersect with each other at regular intervals. Under Duany's pattern, people have many more choices in traveling from one place to another. Walking and bicycling short distances is not hard. And even if people choose to drive, traffic congestion on arterials is reduced because drivers can take other routes in traveling short distances. In California, Duany has worked for developers on several huge projects, including the innovative Playa Vista development in Los Angeles.

total dependence on the car, is inevitable. One of the reasons the slow-growth movement is so strong in California is that most citizens simply do not believe that new development can be made up of anything other than traditional suburban tracts, consuming tremendous amounts of land and generating tremendous amounts of traffic.

Because this "world view" is so solidly entrenched, local governments are still pursuing land-use policies that reduce the potential for transit ridership. Influenced by slow-growth sentiment and frustration with traffic congestion, local politicians and planners continue to create spread-out communities that seek to solve growth problems by minimizing the number of new residents — thereby maximizing dependence on the automobile. The idea of linking new subdivisions to potential transit lines usually doesn't even come up.

For years, planners have tried to deal with auto-oriented problems through "demand management" — encouraging carpools, shorter work weeks, off-peak commuting, and other efforts designed to get cars off the road at rush hour. But these solutions attack the symptom, not the cause. By and large, California's built environment is designed to be traversed by a driver alone in his or her car. For this reason, demand management techniques —

carpooling in particular — will always involve a level of inconvenience that most people simply won't accept.

To break the grip of auto-oriented, suburban-style development, the physical orientation of California's communities must change. The rigid segregation of land uses must be broken down, and urban design efforts must encourage people to walk short distances — say, from their office to a nearby store. Most important, for the state's massive rail effort to succeed, communities must be oriented around transit stations, so that rail travel is located within easy walking distance of many jobs, stores, and, especially, homes.

This will not be an easy task, especially given the fact that automobiles have been a part of California's mythology for so many decades. But it must be done. To continue California's historical dependence on auto-oriented, suburban style development is not only destructive to the environment; it will also ensure the failure of the state's massive investment in rail transit.

## 2. CITIZEN PARTICIPATION MUST BE CHANNELED INTO USEFUL AND CONSTRUCTIVE FORUMS.

For the past 20 years, California's planning system has operated under the assumption that more citizen participation is always better. This impulse is

Perhaps the biggest obstacle to neo-traditional planning ideas, however, is the existing zoning and development codes. Even if developers and planners want to lay out communities differently — indeed, even if the broad objectives of a city's general plan encourage neo-traditional planning — the specific requirements of a city's codes often force the creation of suburban-style projects. Sometimes these codes speak overtly about suburban-style projects by requiring huge building setbacks and minimal lot coverage, even for office buildings. In other instances, the codes force developers into a suburban site plan unwittingly; for example, massive parking requirements leave developers and planners little leeway for anything other than an auto-oriented development.

For neo-traditional planning to work, its concepts must be supported not only in the broad policy documents, but also in the bowels of the zoning and development codes around California.

understandable, given the fact that, historically, ordinary citizens were shut out of the planning process.

Yet the involvement of all these citizens has strained the process. As this book has observed over and over again, the typical city or county official today is confronted with a stupifying array of groups claiming to represent the public interest: historic preservationists, environmentalists, merchants, homeowner groups, non-profit housing boosters, and so on. And, of course, developers will suggest that they represent the public interest as well, because they represent the homebuyers and businesses who constitute their market.

Given all these conflicting agendas, the public interest has become much harder to discern. And the traditional two-sided planning process — in which public officials and staff planners presume to represent the public interest against the private interests of the developer — has given way to a different type of environment. Like public policy in Washington or Sacramento, local planning is now a form of "interest-group politics." There are many more organized groups interested in planning issues than there used to be. Any of these groups can exert enough pressure on the political system — or, failing that, on the legal system — to prevent a plan or project from going forward. Thus, for the local government to take action on a planning issue, all these groups must be dealt with in one way or another.

Yet traditional planning processes are not designed to deal with multiple interests. The public hearing is, in a sense, a courtroom, with a planning commission or city council sitting in judgement of a plan or a development project. Citizen groups are given limited time to speak. Melding all these different interests in such an adversarial process can be awkward and difficult. Each group's position may become so hardened by distrust for the other parties that no one will budge, even if an alternative is proposed that would achieve these goals. Issues are dealt with in an either/or manner.

Typically, in this kind of situation, one of two things happens. Either the project or plan proceeds without all these objections being dealt with, or it is killed by litigation (or the threat of litigation) on the part of a citizen group. In either case, someone is unhappy.

In recent years, we have seen a surge of interest in negotiation and dispute resolution techniques generally, as evidenced by the success of such books as *Getting to Yes* and the increasing use of negotiation in the environmental field. This interest has led many people to adopt those techniques for use on planning and development issues.

Explaining these methods can sometimes be difficult because they are abstract processes. Typically, these negotiations begin by convening all interested parties and hiring a trained, neutral "facilitator" to run the meetings.

In describing such a negotiation, it is not enough merely to state that, as a result of using one of these methods, a development project was agreed upon that contained 50,000 square feet of space with a 14-foot wall separating the commercial area from an adjoining residential neighborhood. More important are the techniques used to get people who don't like each other — in fact, who usually won't listen to each other — to reach agreements that both satisfy their needs and uphold a community's planning principles. The idea is to move beyond "half-a-loaf"- style solutions by understanding each party's true, underlying interest.

The "currency" of these negotiations is not the simple compromise but, rather, the "trade-off" among a vast majority of concerns and issues. For example, instead of demanding a

## THE LAKE TAHOE NEGOTIATIONS

Perhaps the most successful set of negotiations in recent California history occurred in Lake Tahoe from 1985 to 1987, where a group of some 20 different parties with a long history of friction reached consensus on a new plan for the Tahoe area.

Environmentalists have sought to preserve the pristine nature of the area and, in particular, the remarkable clarity and quality of Lake Tahoe's waters, which were being damaged by soil erosion caused by construction. However, many private landowners purchased subdivided lots in the Tahoe area expecting to build, only to be stymied by environmental regulations later on. The bistate Tahoe Regional Planning Agency adopted a regional plan in 1983, but environmentalists and the state Attorney General's Office sued. A federal judge in Sacramento issued an injunction against new development. At this point, TRPA proposed a large multi-party negotiation with an outside facilitator. Half the cost was borne by TRPA, the other half by a foundation.

The facilitator organized the parties into five interest groups: developers and property rights advocates; environmental protection and limited development advocates; local environmental agencies and commissions; local governments; and state and federal agencies. In the first stage, in July and August of 1985, the group laid down ground rules. In the second stage, in September and October of 1985, the group members agreed to break down into small groups to "brainstorm" on moderately difficult issues, such as how to evaluate the environmental sensitivity of lots already subdivided. During the third phase, at the end of 1985, the group tackled the most controversial issues, particularly the question of how much commercial development to allow — which, by itself, was the focus of 14 consecutive meetings. By April of 1986, however, almost all the members of the group had agreed on a wide range of issues.

smaller building, a group of citizens might agree to a building that is the same size, but reconfigured so that its shadow does not fall on their neighborhood.

The need for innovative methods of dispute resolution has also given rise to more interest in an old-fashioned way to accommodate many interests: financial payment.

In recent years, some economists have recognized the fact that zoning and permit approvals are commodities of value that may be traded from one party to another. Most planners don't think this way, but developers do; many developers specialize in obtaining permit approvals and then selling the permitted land to someone else at a higher price. In critiquing land-use regulations, economists have suggested that the economic aspects of land-use regulation could be harnessed in ways that will deal with planning disputes more effectively than regulation and litigation.

Say, for example, a single-family neighborhood is feeling pressure from developers who want to build dense apartment complexes and office buildings. The neighborhood could choose to resist — or the neighbors could get together and sell out to the developer, essentially granting to the highest bidder permission to change the neighborhood's character. Alternatively, the developer could build a large new office complex or shopping center and indemnify neighboring homeowners, in order to guarantee them a certain property value after the new project is completed.

Developers and neighborhood groups have negotiated for wholesale buyouts in Atlanta, Dallas, and the Washington, D.C., area. Though no buy-outs (or sell-outs, depending on your point of view) have been consummated, the idea appears well suited for older, postwar suburbs where single-family neighborhoods are gradually being surrounded by high-rise apartments and office buildings. In Los Angeles, for example, certain areas of the Westside and the San Fernando Valley — especially those close to major arterials such as Ventura and Wilshire boulevards — might be well positioned for buy-outs. Not coincidentally, these areas have been the scene of L.A.'s most vicious development battles.

Financial solutions may sometimes be only part of the answer — or no answer at all. People often have a sentimental or emotional attachment to their neighborhoods that exerts a far stronger pull than money; their main goal is not to protect their investment, but to protect their quality of life. And, indeed, for older people, some handicapped people, and people with mental illness-

The group's agreement included:

• A limit on the amount of commercial development that could be approved in the Tahoe area.

• A transferrable development rights system.

• A system of reviewing lots to see which ones were environmentally sensitive and which ones were not.

• A commitment to permit construction by lot-owners who were partway through the process when the injunction was issued.

• A commitment by the federal government to purchase environmentally sensitive building lots on which construction would not be permitted.

Some members of the group, principally the commercial property owners, did not endorse some aspects of the agreement. Nevertheless, the federal judge dismissed the lawsuit and the TRPA approved the new regional plan.

es, a geographical move can be so disruptive and disorienting that it does not lend itself to a monetary solution.

Nevertheless, financial pay-outs and indemnifications may have special application to California because home prices are so high. With the average cost of a house more than double the national average, most of the wealth of California's middle-class residents is wrapped up in home equity. This financial dependence on one's home is one of the major sources of friction between developers and citizens; the typical homeowner believes his or her home represents his or her financial future, and, as a result, is simply scared of any community change.

However odious they may seem to some, cash transactions may alleviate some of those fears and, therefore, defuse some of the tension inherent in many planning disputes. And whether cash transactions are involved or not, multi-party negotiations and other methods of alternative dispute resolution may prove far more useful than the traditional public hearing process in reaching consensus on local land-use policy.

### 3. THE PAROCHIAL NATURE OF LOCAL LAND-USE DECISIONMAKING MUST BE REFORMED.

One of the most cherished privileges of Californians is the privilege of non-partisan, decentralized, "home rule" local government. Though California has a few very large cities — Los Angeles, San Diego, San Jose, San Francisco — most people live in smaller cities (between 30,000 and 200,000 people) where the city government can be held immediately accountable to the concerns of the local residents. This system of local government — which was quite deliberately created by the state's Progressive-era leaders some 80 years ago — has created a fragmentation unmatched anywhere else in the country. The state has 450 different cities; Los Angeles County alone has almost 90, and if it were not for signs at the city limits it would be difficult to tell where one ends and another begins. Orange County, with a population greater than Philadelphia's, has a half-dozen cities with a population of more than 100,000, but none with more than 300,000; there is no dominant "central" city.

This fragmentation has succeeded in keeping local government "close to the people," and — along with non-partisanship — it may have helped to keep the state relatively free of political corruption. But there is no question that it has prevented the state from truly coming to grips with its planning problems.

One small but illustrative example comes from San Luis Obispo County on the Central Coast. When slow-growth sentiment first arose in the 1970s, the city of San Luis Obispo — the county seat and the county's largest city — adopted an ordinance regulating the city's future growth by restricting the number of building permits that could be issued. The rationale for these restrictions was the city's limited supply of water. Over the next 15 years, the ordinance did, in fact, limit growth within the city limits — conserving the city's water supply and helping to protect the city's "small-town character."

But the city ordinance did not change the underlying growth dynamics in San Luis Obispo County. The county continued to grow rapidly. And therefore, the city's restrictions simply moved the growth around, pushing it into outlying communities and, in particular, placing more development pressure on the county's farmland. The city had, to a certain extent, saved itself; but it had done so at the county's expense. The result is a much more sprawling and decentralized region than is really necessary.

In California, cities and counties always look out for their own best interests and have little obligation to worry about the other guy. As this book has pointed out, a jurisdiction's "best interest" may mean restricting building permits to limit growth; or it may mean subsidizing auto dealerships in order to generate tax revenue; or it may mean configuring new development so that all the traffic is dumped out onto streets in an adjacent city. In any event, the result is that 450-odd cities and 58 counties all have their own, separate policies on how to handle growth, and those policies are not coordinated.

All these local governments must abide by the slew of state planning laws that this book has described. But they can ignore each other's plans. Generally speaking, they do not have to meet any state planning goals. And, in most cases, there is no regional or state agency with the power to hold these local governments accountable. Regional entities such as SCAG (the Southern California Association of Governments) and ABAG (the Association of Bay Area Governments) do exist, but they are controlled mostly by local government officials who do not want to yield any power to these regional agencies. In effect, these regional agencies have little power and limited influence, and they have no public support to do or be anything more.

The result, especially in the Bay Area and Southern California, is a vast set of imbalances on the metropolitan level. In particular, starter homes and job centers are often located an hour or more apart. Lengthy commuting patterns create traffic congestion and smog. And since metropolitan Los Angeles is expected to grow from 13 million people to 18 million people over the next 20 years, these trends will probably only get worse, especially in Southern California.

Other states have dealt with similar problems in bolder fashion. In 1985, Florida passed a sweeping Growth Management Act, which requires that all local plans be submitted to a powerful state agency for approval. In addition, Florida requires that all local plans within each county be submitted at the same time, so they may be reviewed for consistency with each other. A year later, New Jersey adopted an approach that is similar, though somewhat less harsh on local governments. Each jurisdiction must conform to a statewide plan that specifies the level of growth each region in the state should expect to accommodate. However, the locals may negotiate with the state over the specifics of their respective plans. Also, the New Jersey system has given considerable regional planning power to counties, which previously had little control over land-use matters.

The California planning system already includes many examples of regional planning. The Coastal Commission, a state agency, regulates new development along the coast. The South Coast Air Quality Management District, also a state agency, has approved an air-quality plan that will require local governments in the Los Angeles area to make many changes in its land-use planning processes to minimize air pollution. But these are specialized agencies with a narrow agenda. They do not deal with the broad-based regional planning problems that have arisen in California, nor can they be expected to.

New regional planning efforts have been restricted to a handful of attempts at regional cooperation by local governments. Cities and counties — with their tremendous lobbying power in Sacramento —

have resisted any efforts to follow the lead of Florida and New Jersey into full-blown state planning efforts. And general suspicion about "another layer of government" has probably rendered the creation of more regional planning agencies politically impossible anyway.

But the state can and should take two important steps that would broaden the focus of local planning efforts without creating a new planning bureaucracy.

First, the state itself must lay out a set of clear and simple planning goals, and use the state government's own resources to back them up. As this book has repeatedly pointed out, with the exception of the law on housing elements, virtually all of California's planning apparatus is procedurally driven. This means that California has no statewide policy at all on how the state's astonishing growth is to be accommodated, restricted, or otherwise handled. The state's overall policy is nothing more than the sum total of local growth ordinances. And since, by and large, established communities seek to restrict growth while undeveloped areas usually try to obtain lots of it, California's overall growth policy, by default, encourages sprawl, wasteful competition among local entities, and, often, social exclusivity. But because this situation works to the benefit of local governments, it is tolerated, institutionalized, and even championed by virtue of California's current laws and practices.

By contrast, Florida's growth management system is driven by three clear, overriding state goals determined by the legislature: restrict development in coastal areas, encourage compact urban development, and permit new development only when infrastructure is installed concurrently. As a state, California has never debated what its growth-management goals should address. The governor and the state legislature should engage in this debate, with the goal of arriving at a similar set of clear, strong goals.

Once those goals are in place, the state should use them to shape development patterns — without establishing a politically unpopular bureaucracy — simply by using its financial resources properly. All state agencies should make sure that their own actions — from Caltrans freeway construction to the location of the state's own office buildings — conform with the state's own growth policy. And the state should also allocate state aid — housing subsidies, sewer grants, and so forth — only to those cities and counties whose own general plans conform with the state's goals.

Second, the state should establish some sort of regional structure which would permit local governments to bargain with each other over both "good" and "bad" land uses. The biggest reason that local governments act so aggressively in their own self-interest is that there's no benefit in doing otherwise. A city that lures big tax producers at the expense of low-income housing does so knowing that it will not be penalized for selfish behavior. Similarly, a city that is considering whether to accept a prison or a toxic waste dump knows it will not be rewarded for doing so.

The state, with the assistance of the regional planning agencies that do exist, should take steps to determine the "undesirable" land uses each region must accept — low-income housing, prisons, landfills, and other politically unpopular facilities. Rather than fighting a huge war over siting each individual project, however, the state could establish a "trading pit" for each region, in which local governments would bargain with each other over these facilities.

A city with a lot of redevelopment housing money sitting in the bank, for example, might be able to sell off its low-income housing responsibility to a neighboring city that needs the money and is willing to build the housing. A city luring shopping centers and auto malls should not be able to do so without compensating neighboring jurisdictions that are hit with the resulting traffic. And a locality willing to accept a landfill or a prison would be able to come to the regional bargaining table with a very powerful chip to play. In short, the regional trading pit would force local governments to be accountable to regional needs without creating a large enforcement bureaucracy.

### 4. FISCAL INCENTIVES TO CREATE UNBALANCED COMMUNITIES MUST BE REMOVED.

In most cases, the biggest reason local governments zone certain types of development in or out is money. As this book discussed in Chapters 12 and 14, since Proposition 13 restricted local tax revenue in 1978, cities and counties have engaged shamelessly in economic com-

petition, using redevelopment, turf battles, and other techniques to lure big
tax producers inside their boundaries.
In many parts of the state, fiscal zoning
has led to unbalanced communities,
with cities and counties favoring auto
dealerships, shopping centers, and
other big tax producers at the expense
of housing.

To be fair, local officials cannot really be blamed for engaging in fiscal
zoning. In an environment where needed tax revenue is scarce, they are simply grasping at the tools that are
available to them. For example, as
Chapter 15 explained, cities are able to
use the tool of redevelopment finance
— essentially a property-tax financing
mechanism designed to bring capital
improvements into a depressed area —
to lure big sales-tax producers inside
their boundaries. This method of
manipulation is available to them
because the laws governing both redevelopment and the allocation of sales-
tax revenue were drawn up decades
ago, long before current conditions
came into being.

The state must reduce the incentives
for fiscal zoning. The best solution
would be to permit or require tax-sharing for each metropolitan area, similar
to the model that the Minneapolis-St.
Paul area has used for 20 years. Such a
system would ensure that every city
would benefit from the entire region's

## METROPOLITAN TAX SHARING

All healthy metropolitan
areas generate a great
deal of tax revenue, but
those taxes are not
always equitably distributed among all jurisdictions.
Inner-city areas suffer
from the flight of residents
and businesses to the suburbs and therefore strug-
gle to provide basic
services. Exclusive suburbs
have high property val-
ues and, therefore, gen-
erate far more tax
revenue per capita. And
some clever cities manip-
ulate the game of fiscal
zoning so adroitly that
they have many large tax
producers within their
boundaries even if they
are not especially affluent
communities.

The most logical solu-
tion to this inequity would
seem to be for all jurisdictions within one
metropolitan area to
share their taxes. In
California and elsewhere
in the country, introduc-
ing the idea of metropolitan tax-sharing has
usually been political sui-
cide, since suburban residents shutter at the
thought of subsidizing
inner-city slums. But in one

metropolitan area, tax-sharing has proven surprisingly effective for 20 years.

In 1971, the Minneapolis-St. Paul metropolitan area in Minnesota established a regional "pool" of property tax base. Each jurisdiction in the metropolitan area (195 cities and townships, seven counties, and 50 school districts) was permitted to keep its entire property tax base as of the program's inception in 1971. However, 40 percent of all increases in assessed value had to be committed to the regional pool for redistribution based on need. As of 1987, the pooled portion of the regional tax base had reached $1.5 billion, or about 28 percent of the metropolitan total.

And the program does lead to more equitable tax arrangements. For example, under tax-sharing, the per-capita tax base (commercial and industrial only) in the affluent suburb of Eden Prairie is shaved from about $6,400 to $4,400. In the depressed rural area of Champlin, tax base is boosted from about $400

tax base, reducing the pressure to get big tax producers inside artificial political boundaries.

A broad-based tax-sharing program has always been politically impossible in California and probably will remain so for decades to come. Nevertheless, the state could take several other steps that would reduce fiscal competition among cities.

The single most important step the state could take would be to allocate some sales-tax revenue to cities based on where people live, rather than where they shop. As things stand now, if a resident of Walnut Creek buys a $15,000 Honda in Concord, Concord gets $150 and Walnut Creek gets nothing. This system essentially penalizes cities for having residents and rewards them for having retail sales outlets. Simply changing the formula, so that some sales-tax revenue is distributed on a per-capita basis, would go a long way toward encouraging the creation of more balanced communities throughout California. Short of that, the state could also remove barriers that make it difficult for neighboring cities to share sales- and property-tax revenue. Currently, if neighboring cities wish to enter into such an arrangement — say, for example, because one city is heavily affected by traffic from a shopping center in the other city — the tax revenue cannot be shared unless voters in both cities agree to it. Removal of this requirement would encourage cities to work together in resolving mutual problems.

### 5. THE ELITIST PLANNING AGENDA IN MANY COMMUNITIES MUST BE ABANDONED, ESPECIALLY WITH REGARD TO HOUSING.

On the surface, all the reforms described above would seem to be achievable, even if they are politically difficult in today's context. But in many communities, these reforms would be met with resistance for a darker and mostly unstated reason: elitism. The truth is that in many communities, especially in the suburbs, planning's most important role even today is to keep out undesirable land uses and undesirable people. This hidden agenda is often cloaked in the garb of some other rationale, such as environmental protection, adequate housing, better infrastructure planning, or the need for a sound economic base.

It is compounded all the more by high home prices in California. Most of the wealth of California's middle class is tied up in the value of their houses, and this makes most Californians resistant to any kind of change. In the mind of the average homeowner, a neighboring mental-health clinic, a shopping center — even a tract of houses slightly less expensive than their own — hold

per capita to about $1,200 per capita. Thus, the tax disparity between these two jurisdictions is reduced from 16:1 to 3.6:1.

Local officials in California and elsewhere oppose tax-sharing because they have so much to lose. Having worked hard to bring certain tax producers into their cities, they are not about to share the rewards with other jurisdictions. Yet tax-sharing holds the promise of greatly reducing the fiscal zoning that has afflicted so many of California's metropolitan areas. For example, if the Bay Area and/or Greater Los Angeles — or even smaller sub-regions — formed a pool to share sales-tax revenue, then the crazy competition for retail sales outlets would probably diminish somewhat, and some communities might even decide to permit more housing units, rather than chase auto dealerships.

the potential to decrease property values and, therefore, threaten the financial security of their retirement years. No wonder homeowner groups in California fight so hard against new development.

But planning in California cannot afford to serve as the vehicle for such elitism. If planning is to act as a credible tool for creating healthy and well-balanced communities, then we must find ways to curb its cynical use by exclusionary suburbs.

Planning's greatest sin in furthering an elitist agenda is to exclude low-income housing — and, often, even housing for the middle class — through high building standards, large lot sizes, and other zoning code provisions. Sometimes growth restrictions and a community-wide emphasis on commercial and industrial development, rather than residential, also serves to restrict housing construction.

Because local government is so fragmented, and local control is so jealously guarded, it is difficult for the state or anybody else to overcome an elitist agenda. If the reforms laid out above took hold, however, it would be much more difficult for a suburban community with an elitist agenda to hide behind environmental concerns, fiscal concerns, and other issues. If taxes were more equitably distributed, the rationale for fiscal zoning — which often zones out houses — would be removed. If citizen participation were channeled into more constructive forums, procedural laws could not be perverted so easily by those who simply want to kill new development. If regional planning were reformed, each community would have to face up to its regional responsibilities.

But pressure from above will not be enough to force many communities to abandon their elitist agendas. In many cases, these communities will change their attitudes only when they feel pressure from below — from the grassroots — as well. And in the '90s, they are likely to feel such pressure from private, non-profit organizations that have tried to fill the housing vacuum in California.

Just since the mid-'80s, non-profit housing developers have become a vibrant force, playing an important role in supplying below-market housing in certain areas of the state. In a way, these organizations represent the true maturation of the "citizen participation" movement, because many of them have grown out of neighborhood and citizen groups.

Some have constructed new housing, while others have rehabilitated residential hotels and organized buyouts of mobile-home parks and other existing low-cost housing. Because these organizations are not under pressure to turn a profit, they can sell and rent the housing units at below-market prices.

In many cases, these organizations are based in poor neighborhoods or in more broadly defined "communities" (ethnic, racial, etc.) that are struggling economically. Many of the organizations began as citizen action groups, opposing large development projects and/or pressuring local governments to channel more investment dollars into their communities. As these groups matured, however, they recognized the value of taking a pro-active stance and actually building housing, rather than merely lobbying for more housing funds. The emergence of these organizations is surely one of the most tangible (and heartening) results of the move toward greater citizen involvement in the planning process.

Most of these organizations are financed through a sophisticated statewide network of philanthropic donations from large corporations. (Some money is also received from corporations seeking to take advantage of the federal government's tax credit for low-income housing.) But if local

## BRIDGE HOUSING

Perhaps the biggest success story in the non-profit housing sector is BRIDGE Housing Corp. of San Francisco. Founded with an anonymous donation to the San Francisco Foundation in 1983, BRIDGE now constructs about 1,000 housing units per year, making it one of the biggest homebuilders in the Bay Area. Most of BRIDGE's housing is aimed at households with incomes of $12,000 to $25,000 per year — a group that has been pushed out of the home ownership market in an area where average home price hovers around $250,000.

Impressive as BRIDGE's total output is, the corporation's biggest contribution to planning in California may be its ability to break down elitist barriers in suburban communities.

In the suburbs, all planning issues seem to get narrowed, sooner or later, to a debate over housing density — the number of housing units per acre that will be allowed. BRIDGE's strategy has been to ask suburban communities for increased densities and, in return, promise that the additional units will be made available to people in the $12,000-$25,000 range.

A typical BRIDGE project is the Heritage Park apartments, a senior citizen housing project in Livermore, east of Oakland. BRIDGE bought 10 acres of property zoned for eight units per acre, then persuaded city officials to rezone the property to permit 16 units per acre. With that kind of a bonus, BRIDGE was able to rent 67 units (out of 167 total) at a below-market rent.

How does BRIDGE convince low-density-minded suburban officials to permit more units? The truth is that, even though most suburban debates revolve around the issue, housing density is such an abstraction that few people really understand what it means.

BRIDGE's success in Livermore is a small step, but it reveals an important lesson about how planning can be used to overcome an elitist suburban agenda, rather than reinforce it.

governments feel more pressure to build affordable housing in the '90s, it seems likely that they will forge alliances with these non-profit housing developers to produce more housing.

A few cities have already moved in this direction. For example, most of the money San Francisco receives from its office-housing linkage program is granted to non-profit housing developers who build or rehabilitate affordable housing in the city. And a few redevelopment agencies, especially the Los Angeles Community Redevelopment Agency, use their housing set-aside funds to finance non-profit housing developers. But in the '90s, local governments will probably feel more pressure to take action on the housing front — and, especially, to begin spending the redevelopment housing money they stockpiled in the '80s. If so, the San Francisco and L.A. models are likely to spread to cities all around the state.

By the year 2000, it's possible that a strong network of non-profit housing developers, financed by redevelopment funds, impact fees, and other local government money, will be producing a significant portion of the state's housing. But local governments that currently use planning as a tool of exclusion will not embrace the concept of non-profit housing, unless they also feel pressure to live up to their regional responsibilities.

## MAKING PLANNING WORK IN CALIFORNIA

If the reforms proposed in this chapter were implemented, then California's planning system would, at last, stand a chance of producing the commodity it should have been producing all along: liveable and manageable communities that provide a healthy and equitable balance of jobs, housing, environmental protection, social and cultural institutions, and all the other elements required for daily life.

These reforms will take political courage to pursue, because they demand that all parties — local governments, developers, citizen groups — abandon the sacred cows they have refused to surrender for many years. But the task must be undertaken, because the sacred cows no longer serve us well. The evidence of this failure is all around us — in our traffic jams, our smog, our citizen unrest, and our local politics of rich and poor.

But no set of laws or regulations can, by itself, create a perfect planning process for this large, growing, and often unmanageable state. As imperfect as the "system" is, it also suffers from a lack of vision and integrity on the part of people involved with the process. Structural reforms would make raw manipulation of the planning system more difficult to achieve, but they would not, in and of themselves, eliminate the cynical self-protection that has caused many of our planning problems. Only the people involved in the process themselves can make that kind of change.

In a sense, it doesn't really matter what role these individuals choose to play — politician, staff planner, developer, citizen activist — because all these roles are integral to the planning process. Rather, what matters is the attitude these people bring to their roles. Good planning is the result of the efforts of individual people who have faith that good planning is possible.

Though California is now by far the largest state in the nation, its days as a boom state are far from over. Short-term economic downturns may slow the state's expansion temporarily, but California's growth juggernaut is likely to churn forward for another generation at least. The challenges of this growth simply cannot be met if the status quo is maintained. The planning system must be changed to reflect current conditions, and the attitudes of people involved in planning must be changed so that overarching goals can be agreed upon and achieved.

This will not be an easy task. As the noted urban economist Anthony Downs is fond of saying, inequities occur in the United States because they arise out of social arrangements that benefit most people; not surprisingly, most people are therefore loathe to change those social arrangements. The system pictured in this book may seem bleak, but interest groups are loathe to change it because they believe it works in their short-term interest. To the extent that a problem exists, most people will simply point to their favorite villain — cumbersome CEQA processes, the irresponsible neighboring city, greedy developers, whatever — and insist that if the other guy changes, then the problems will go away.

But this is not so. All of us bear some responsibility for creating the planning mess in California today. All of us must bear some responsibility for cleaning it up. The situation has deteriorated since the 1970s largely because our elected officials from the governor on down have not been willing to lead. Perhaps the next decade will give us better leadership; perhaps not. But one thing is certain. If steps such as these are not taken, then planning in California will continue to "fail" for another generation at least — only the failure will occur on a much more massive and intolerable scale than the state has experienced up to now. If, however, these steps are taken, then planning may actually help California come to grips with its remarkable growth.

# Annotated Bibliography

The research that went into this book came from literally hundreds of different sources. Rather than list them all, however, I thought it would be more useful to provide the dozen or so most important and explain a little about what makes them so good. Here, then, are the books I believe must accompany this one on any California planning bookshelf:

*California Land-Use and Planning Law*, by Daniel J. Curtin, Jr. (Solano Press Books, updated annually). This book has set the standard as a quick, readable overview of all aspects of planning laws in California. In only 200 pages, Curtin covers every topic from the General Plan (on which he is a particular expert) to CEQA, exactions, and initiatives.

*The California Planner's Book of Lists* (Governor's Office of Planning and Research, updated annually). A good compilation of useful information, including a directory of government planning departments and results of OPR's annual survey of local governments. Available from the Publications Section of the Department of General Services, P.O. Box 1015, North Highlands, CA 95660. Telephone (916) 973-3700.

*CEQA Guidelines, General Plan Guidelines,* and *Planning, Zoning, and Development Laws.* (Governor's Office of Planning and Research, updated periodically). An invaluable trio of documents prepared by California's only state planning office. The *CEQA Guidelines* are, in fact, a set of administrative regulations, but they provide valuable insight into how the CEQA process works. The *General Plan Guidelines* are a detailed and valuable set of recommendations about how local governments should go about preparing general plans. *Planning, Zoning, and Development Laws* outlines the basics of California planning law, including requirements for local governments to establish planning agencies and draw up planning documents. Available from the General Services Publications Section, P.O. Box 1015, North Highlands, CA, 95660 (916) 973-3700.

*Guide to the California Environmental Quality Act,* by Michael H. Remy, Tina A. Thomas, and James G. Moose (Solano Press Books, updated annually). Like many environmental documents it describes, this book, written by members of the respected Sacramento environmental law firm of Remy and Thomas, is thick. But it is also good — a detailed compendium of knowledge about this complicated law.

*Land in America: Its Value, Use, and Control,* by Peter Wolf (Pantheon Books, 1981). Written for the general reader, this book is a knowing, if now somewhat dated, overview of the importance of land in both the American economy and the American psyche. Covers a broad range of topics, including zoning and land values, land speculation, federal land, and an excellent discussion of the first (1970s) wave of slow-growth sentiment in California.

*Land Use in a Nutshell,* by Robert R. Wright and Susan Webber Wright (West Publishing Co., 2nd Edition, 1985). This small book provides a valuable national overview on all aspects of land-use law. However, the second edition was published before the landmark U.S. Supreme Court cases were handed down in 1987.

*Land-Use Initiatives and Referenda in California,* by Michael P. Durkee, M. Thomas Jacobson, Thomas C. Wood, and Michael H. Zischke (Solano Press Books, updated annually). A useful overview of the legal aspects of "ballot-box zoning," provided by lawyers who work with Daniel J. Curtin Jr. at McCutchen, Doyle, Brown &

Enersen.

*Longtin's California Land Use* (Local Government Publications, 2nd edition, 1987, with annual supplements). The ultimate legal reference on all aspects of land-use law in California.

*The Practice of Local Government Planning* (Planner's Press). The so-called "green book" is designed as the basic reference book for all American urban planners.

*Public Choices, Private Resources*, by John J. Kirlin and Anne M. Kirlin (California Tax Foundation, 1982). This book, by a public finance expert and a land-use lawyer, was one of the first publications to recognize both (1) the fiscalization of land use in California, and (2) the importance of public-private bargaining on development projects and fiscal matters. It remains an important primer on both subjects.

*Redevelopment in California*, by David F. Beatty, Joseph Coomes, Jr., T. Brent Hawkins, Edward J. Quinn, Jr., and Iris P. Yang (Solano Press Books, updated annually). Like other publications from Solano Press Books, this book is a comprehensive guide, designed to help the reader through the ins and outs of redevelopment in California.

*Successful CEQA Compliance: A Step-By-Step Approach,* by Ronald E. Bass and Albert I. Herson (Solano Press Books, updated annually). Published for the first time in January 1992, this book is the first-ever practical user's guide to explain clearly, yet comprehensively, how to proceed from the beginning to the end of the environmental review process. It summarizes the California Environmental Quality Act and the *CEQA Guidelines,* and focuses on the procedural and substantive requirements of CEQA.

*Subdivision Map Act Manual*, by Daniel J. Curtin, Jr. (Solano Press Books, updated annually). Like Curtin's California Land-Use and Planning Law, this book is a readable quick overview of the legal essentials.

*Windfalls for Wipeouts: Land Value Capture and Compensation*, by Donald Hagman & Dean Misczynski (American Society of Planning Officials, 1978). Dense but vital. This book is a fairly technical discussion of the economic consequences of land-use regulation. But both authors are known for a wry and iconoclastic approach to their work. The innovative ideas about how to harness the power of market economics to solve planning problems are still fresh — and still largely unimplemented. (Out of print.)

*The Zoning Game*, by Richard Babcock. A quarter-century after its publication, *The Zoning Game* remains the most frank and informative explanation of how land-use regulation really works in the United States. Less pathbreaking, though still interesting, is *The Zoning Game Revisited*, by Babcock and Charles F. Siemon, a sequel published in 1985.

# ACKNOWLEDGEMENTS

Although this book was written over a short period of time, it is really the result of a decade of research and writing about planning in California. I can't begin to thank all the people who have helped me, but a few people can't be ignored.

My greatest thanks go to Warren Jones of Solano Press Books, who entrusted me with a project he had originally planned to undertake himself and who now professes, at least, to be pleased with the result. A kinder, gentler, and more perceptive publisher is hard to imagine. I hope I have done his dreams justice. Thanks also go to Warren's partner, Jaimie Levin, whose clear thinking helped guide this book through production and marketing.

I am also extremely grateful to the Department of Urban and Regional Planning at the California State Polytechnic University, Pomona, and especially Chuck Hotchkiss, the department chair, for giving me the chance to teach a class that shaped this book. All my students helped me with the book in their own way, but I am especially grateful to Jeffrey Zill, who provided me with research on the history of general plan consistency requirements, and Pete Kaiser, who filled me in on the Alquist-Priolo Act. The class also gave me a chance to bring in four knowledgeable guest lecturers who will recognize their own contributions in this book: Mark Winogrond on zoning, Adam Relin and Stephen Svete on CEQA, and Keith Breskin on redevelopment.

Over the years, many newspaper and magazine editors gave me the opportunity to dig into various aspects of planning in California, the fruits of which I have continued to reap in writing this book. I am especially grateful to Ken Jost, formerly of the *Los Angeles Daily Journal*; Sylvia Lewis, Ruth Knack, and Dennis McClendon of *Planning* magazine; Ed Mendel of the late *Golden State Report*; and Tom Brom of *California Lawyer* for their support. My thanks also go to the folks at the UCLA Extension Public Policy Program, especially Leroy Graymer and Madelyn Glickfeld, whose programs have provided me with a stimulating post-graduate education in California planning over the last decade.

While the book was being written, a few hardy souls bravely volunteered to read the manuscript. I am grateful to Paul Crawford, Peter Detwiler, and Marci Malaster for their comments. My mother, Fran Fulton, went over the final manuscript with the excellent fine-tooth comb she acquired as a librarian in Old Forge, N.Y.

Despite my thanks to this lengthy cast of characters, all errors remain mine alone.

Many thanks and all my love go to my wife, Victoria Torf Fulton, a gifted graphic designer, for making this book look good in print and also for not squawking too much about all the weekends it took me to write it. And finally, I would be remiss if I didn't also thank my daughter, Sara, for being who she is and also for going to sleep early enough to let me finish the final draft.

**William Fulton**
**Ventura, California**
**May, 1991**

# Index

# ILLUSTRATION CREDITS

Cover Design and Cover Photo: Torf Fulton Associates, Ventura, California

Frontspiece: Tom Toles © 1990 The Buffalo News. Reprinted with permission of Universal Press Syndicate. All rights reserved.

8, 11, 17, 69, 88, 117, 232: Roger K. Lewis. Illustrations on pages 8, 69, 88, 117, and 232 reprinted with permission from *Growth Management Handbook,* MSM Regional Council, Princeton, N.J.

15, 177, 193: Inman & Doty/Inman News Features

49, 55, 234, 252: Torf Fulton Associates

24, 40, 90: Kevin Steadler

153, 160, 185: Richard Hedman

198: William Bogle, Planning & Zoning Center, Inc., Lansing, Michigan. Reprinted with permission from *Planning & Zoning News,* October 1990 issue.

222-223: Terry Allen/*Governing* Magazine

266: Duany Plater-Zyberk Architects, Miami, Florida